Charles V. Riley

**Directions for Collecting and Preserving Insects**

Charles V. Riley

**Directions for Collecting and Preserving Insects**

ISBN/EAN: 9783337825225

Printed in Europe, USA, Canada, Australia, Japan

Cover: Foto ©Andreas Hilbeck / pixelio.de

More available books at **www.hansebooks.com**

# SMITHSONIAN INSTITUTION.
## UNITED STATES NATIONAL MUSEUM.

-------

# DIRECTIONS FOR COLLECTING AND PRESERVING INSECTS.

BY

C. V. RILEY, M. A., PH. D.,

*Honorary Curator of the Department of Insects, U. S. National Museum.*

-------

Part F of Bulletin of the United States National Museum, No. 39
(with one plate).

-------

WASHINGTON:

GOVERNMENT PRINTING OFFICE.

1892

# CONTENTS.

CONTENTS.    [III]

[IV] CONTENTS.

# INTRODUCTORY.

There is a constant demand, especially from correspondents of the Museum and also of the Department of Agriculture, for information as to how to collect, preserve, and mount insects. There is also great need of some simple directions on a great many other points connected with the proper packing of insects for transmission through the mails or otherwise; labeling; methods of rearing; boxes and cabinets; text-books, etc. Interest in the subject of entomology has, in fact, made rapid growth in the last few years, and now that nearly every State has an official entomologist connected with its State Agricultural Experiment Station, the number of persons interested in the subject may be expected to increase largely in the near future. I have hitherto made use of the Smithsonian Miscellaneous Collections, No. 261, which is a pamphlet on collecting and preserving insects prepared by Dr. A. S. Packard. This is out of print, and I have been requested by Prof. Goode to prepare for Bulletin 39, U. S. N. M., something that would cover the whole ground and give the more essential information needed for collectors and students of insect life. I have deemed it unnecessary to go too much into detail, but have studied not to omit anything essential. Customs and methods vary in different countries and with different individuals, but the recommendations contained in the following pages are based upon my own experience and that of my assistants and many acquaintances, and embrace the methods which the large majority of American entomologists have found most satisfactory.

Much of the matter is repeated bodily from the directions for collecting and preserving insects published in my Fifth Report on the Insects of Missouri (1872) and quotations not otherwise credited are from that Report. The illustrations, also, when not otherwise credited or not originally made for this paper, are from my previous writings. Some are taken from Dr. Packard's pamphlet, already mentioned; others, with the permission of Assistant Secretary Willits, from the publications of the Department of Agriculture, while a number have been especially made for the occasion, either from photographs, or from drawings by Miss L. Sullivan or Dr. Geo. Marx or Mr. C. L. Marlatt. When enlarged, the natural size is indicated in hair-line. In the preparation of the pamphlet I have had the assistance of Mr. E. A. Schwarz, and more particularly of Mr. C. L. Marlatt, to both of whom I desire here to express my obligations.

C. V. R.

[3]

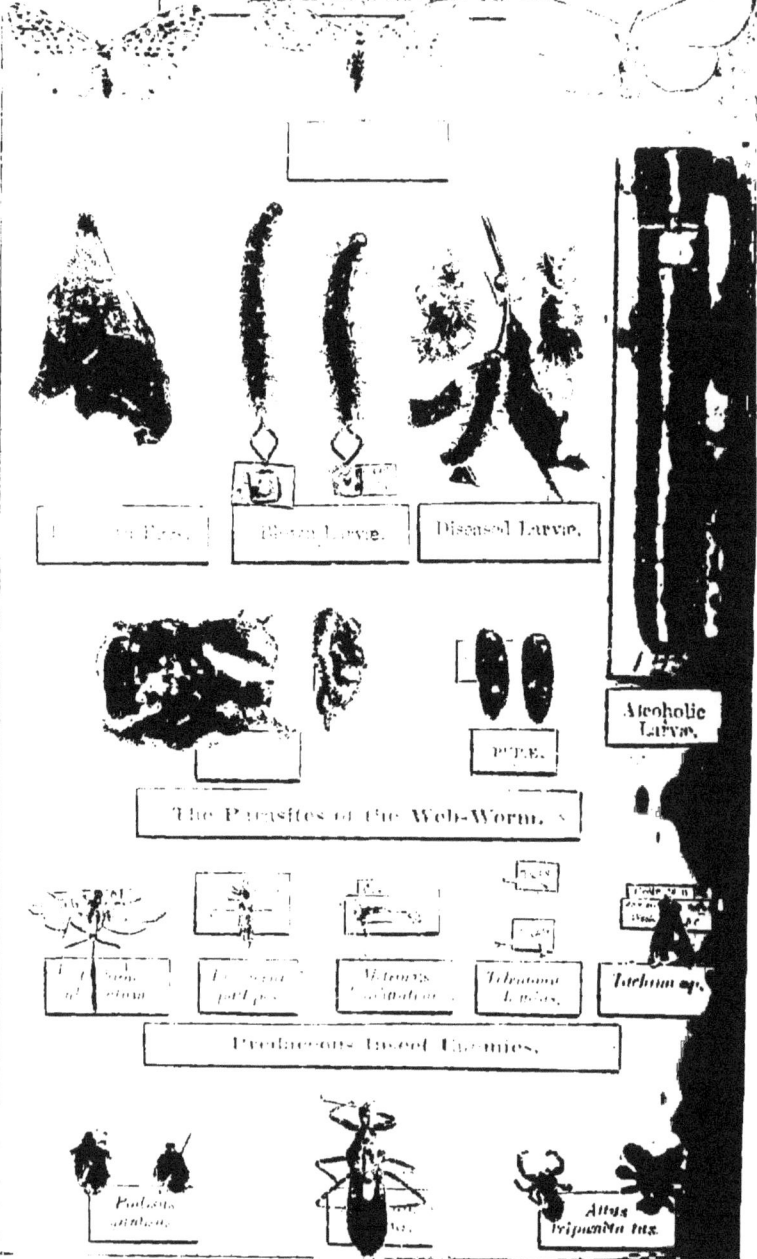

ILLUSTRATION OF BIOLOGIC SERIES.

# MANUAL OF INSTRUCTIONS FOR COLLECTING AND PRE-SERVING INSECTS.

By C. V. RILEY,

*Honorary Curator of the Department of Insects, U. S. National Museum.*

---

## CHARACTERISTICS OF INSECTS.

The term "insect" comes from the Latin *insectum*, and signifies "cut into." It expresses one of the prime characteristics of this class of animals, namely, that of segmentation. This feature of having the body divided into rings or segments by transverse incisions is possessed by other large groups of animals, and was considered of sufficient importance by Cuvier to lead him, in his system of classification, to group with Insects, under the general term Articulata, Worms, Crustacea, Spiders, and Myriopods. Worms differ from the other four groups in having no articulated appendages, and in having a soft body-wall or integument instead of a dense chitinous covering, and are separated as a special class *Vermes*. The other four groups of segmented animals possess in common the feature of jointed appendages and a covering of chitinous plates, and are brought together under the term *Arthropoda*. The division of the body into a series of segments by transverse incisions, characteristic of these animals and these only, justifies the use of Cuvier's old name, Articulates, as this segmented feature represents a definite relationship and a natural division—as much so as the vertebral column in Vertebrates. The Cuvierian name should be retained as a coördinate of Vertebrates, Mollusces, etc., and the terms Vermes and Arthropods may be conveniently used to designate the two natural divisions of the Articulates.

The term "insect" has been employed by authors in two different senses—one to apply to the tracheated animals or those that breathe through a system of air tubes (tracheæ), comprising Spiders, Myriopods, and insects proper or Hexapods,* and the other in its restricted sense as applied to the Hexapods only. To avoid confusion, the latter signification only should be used, and it will be thus used in this article.

---

* From the Greek ἑξάπους, having 6 feet.

We see, then, that insects share, in common with many other animals, the jointed or articulated structure. Wherein, then, do they differ? *Briefly, in having the body divided into thirteen joints and a subjoint,* including the head as a joint, and in the adult having six true, jointed legs, and usually, though not always, wings. The five classes of Articulates differ from each other in the number of legs they possess in the adult form, as follows: Hexapoda, 6 legs; Arachnida, 8 legs; Crustacea, 10–14 legs; Myriapoda, more than 14 legs; Vermes, none. This system holds for the adult form only, because some mites (Arachnida) when young have only 6 legs, and many true insects in the larva state either have no legs at all, or have additional abdominal legs which are not jointed, but membranous, and are lost in the perfect or adult state. These are called false or prolegs.

It will serve to make these instructions clear if I at once explain that the life of an insect is marked by four distinct states, viz, the egg, the larva, the pupa, and the imago, and that the last three words will constantly recur. We have no English equivalent for the words larva and pupa, for while some authors have written them with the terminal *e*, so as to get the English plural, yet "larves" and "pupes" so shock the ear that the terms have not been (and deserve not to be) generally adopted.

We have seen that an insect in the final state has six true legs. Yet even here many species depart from the rule, as there are many in which the perfect insect, especially in the female sex, is apodous or without legs, just as there are also other cases where they are without wings. Sometimes the legs seem to be reduced in number by the partial or total atrophy of one or the other pair, but in all these exceptional cases there is no difficulty in realizing that we have to deal with a true insect, because of the other characters pertaining to the class, some of which it will be well to allude to.

Insects are further characterized by having usually three distinct divisions of the body, viz.: head, thorax, and abdomen, and by undergoing certain metamorphoses or transformations. Now, while a number of other animals outside of the insect world go through similar transformations, those in the Crustacea being equally remarkable, yet, from the ease with which they are observed and the completeness of the transformations in most insects, the metamorphoses of this class have, from time immemorial, excited the greatest curiosity.

## SCOPE AND IMPORTANCE OF ENTOMOLOGY.

But few words are necessary to indicate the importance of entomology, especially to the farming community; for while insects play a most important part in the economy of nature and furnish us some valuable products and otherwise do us a great deal of indirect good, yet they are chiefly known by the annoyances they cause and by the great injury they do to our crops and domestic animals. Hence some knowledge of insects and how to study them becomes important, almost necessary, to every farmer.

The scope of the science may best be indicated by a statement of the number of species existing, as compared with other animals. The omnipresence of insects is known and felt by all; yet few have any accurate idea of the actual numbers existing, so that some figures will not prove uninteresting in this connection. Taking the lists of described species, and the estimates of specialists in the different orders, it is safe to say that about thirty thousand species have already been described from North America, while the number of species already described or to be described in the Biologia Centrali-Americana, i. e., for Central America, foot up just about the same number, Lord Walsingham having estimated them at 30,114 in his address as president of the London Entomological Society two years ago, neither the Orthoptera nor the Neuroptera being included in this estimate. By way of contrast the number of mammals, birds, and reptiles to be described from the same region, is interesting. It foots up 1,937, as follows:

Mammals, 180; birds, 1,600; reptiles, 157.

If we endevor to get some estimate of the number of insects that occur in the whole world, the most satisfactory estimates will be found in the address just alluded to, and in that of Dr. David Sharp before the same society. Linnaeus knew nearly 3,000 species, of which more than 2,000 were European and over 800 exotic. The estimate of Dr. John Day, in 1853, of the number of species on the globe, was 250,000. Dr. Sharp's estimate thirty years later was between 500,000 and 1,000,000. Sharp's and Walsingham's estimates in 1889 reached nearly 2,000,000, and the average number of insects annually described since the publication of the Zoölogical Record, deducting 8 per cent for synonyms, is 6,500 species. I think the estimate of 2,000,000 species in the world is extremely low, and if we take into consideration the fact that species have been best worked up in the more temperate portions of the globe, and that in the more tropical portions a vast number of species still remain to be characterized and named, and if we take further into consideration the fact that many portions of the globe are yet unexplored, entomologically, that even in the best worked up regions by far the larger portion of the Micro-Hymenoptera and Micro-Diptera remain absolutely undescribed in our collections, and have been but very partially collected, it will be safe to estimate that not one-fifth of the species extant have yet been characterized or enumerated. In this view of the case the species in our collections, whether described or undescribed, do not represent perhaps more than one-fifth of the whole. In other words, to say that there are 10,000,000 species of insects in the world, would be, in my judgment, a moderate estimate.

## CLASSIFICATION OF HEXAPODS.

Seven orders of insects were originally recognized by Linnæus, namely, Neuroptera, Diptera, Hemiptera, Lepidoptera, Coleoptera, Hymenoptera, and Aptera. This classification was based on the organs of flight only, and while in the main resulting in natural divisions which still furnish the basis of more modern classifications, was faulty in several particulars. For instance, the Aptera, which included all wingless insects, was soon found to be a very unnatural assemblage and its components were distributed among the other orders. The establishment of the order Orthoptera by Olivier to include a large and well-defined group of insects associated with the Hemiptera by Linnæus, restored the original seven orders, and this classification has, in the main, been followed by entomologists up to the present time.

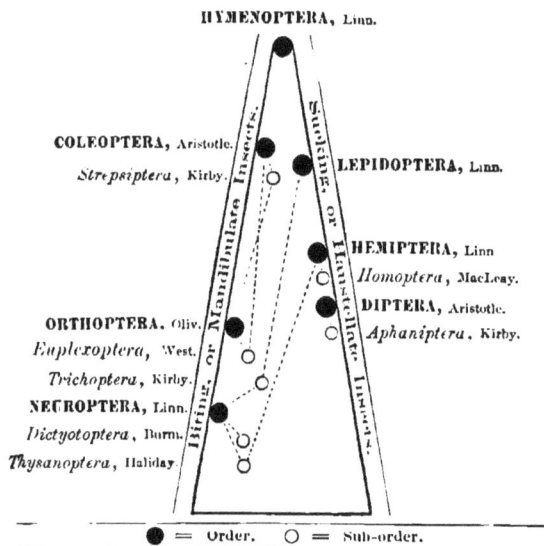

FIG. 1.—Pyramid showing the nature of the mouth, and relative rank of the Orders, and the affinities of the Sub-orders of Insects.

All insects are, in a broad way, referable to one or the other of these seven primary orders by the structure of the wings and the character of the mouth-parts in the imago, and by the nature of their transformations.

Some of these orders are connected by aberrant and osculant families or groups, which have by other authors been variously ranked as independent orders, but which, following Westwood substantially, I have considered, for convenience, as suborders. (*See* Fifth Report, Insects of Missouri, etc., 1872.)

In the article just cited, I made use of the accompanying diagram in the form of a pyramid (Fig. 1), which gives a graphic representation of the distinguishing characters and the relative rank as usually accepted, of the orders and suborders.

Full discussion of the different classifications is unnecessary in this connection. Authors have differed in the past and will differ in the future as to what constitutes a natural system, and it would require many pages to give even a brief survey of the various schemes that have been proposed. As I have elsewhere said, " We must remember that classifications are but a means to an end—appliances to facilitate our thought and study—and that, to use Spencer's words, 'we cannot, by any logical dichotomies, actually express relations which in nature graduate into each other insensibly.'"

The most philosophical, perhaps, of the more modern systems of classification is that of Friedrich Brauer, who has carefully studied the subject, and has given us an arrangement consisting of sixteen orders. This has many merits and has been adopted, with slight modifications, by Packard in his "Entomology for Beginners," and by Hyatt and Arms in their recent and valuable text-book "Insecta." Comstock, in his "Introduction to Entomology" strongly recommends Brauer's classification, but for reasons of simplicity and convenience adheres to a modification of the old classification of Westwood.

For purposes of comparison the classification by Hyatt and Arms, which is substantially that of Brauer, may be introduced.

In linear arrangement it is as follows:

 I. Thysanura (*Springtails*, etc.).
 II. Ephemeroptera (*Ephemeridæ;* May-flies). (=*Plectoptera* Pack.)
 III. Odonata (*Libellulidæ;* Dragon-flies).
 IV. Plecoptera (*Perlidæ;* Stone-flies).
 V. Platyptera (*Termites, Mallophaga,* etc.).
 VI. Dermaptera (*Forficulidæ;* Earwigs).
 VII. Orthoptera (Locusts, Grasshoppers, etc.).
 VIII. Thysanoptera (*Thripidæ;* Fringe-wings).
 IX. Hemiptera (Bugs).
 X. Coleoptera (Beetles).
 XI. Neuroptera (*Sialidæ, Hemerobiidæ;* Lace-wings, etc.).
 XII. Mecoptera (*Panorpidæ;* Scorpion-flies).
 XIII. Trichoptera (*Phryganeidæ;* Caddis-flies).
 XIV. Lepidoptera (Butterflies and Moths).
 XV. Hymenoptera (Bees, Wasps, etc.).
 XVI. Diptera (Two-winged flies).

The relationship of these orders cannot be indicated in a linear arrangement, and is admirably shown by Hyatt and Arms by means of diagrams which I reproduce (Figs. 2, 3.)

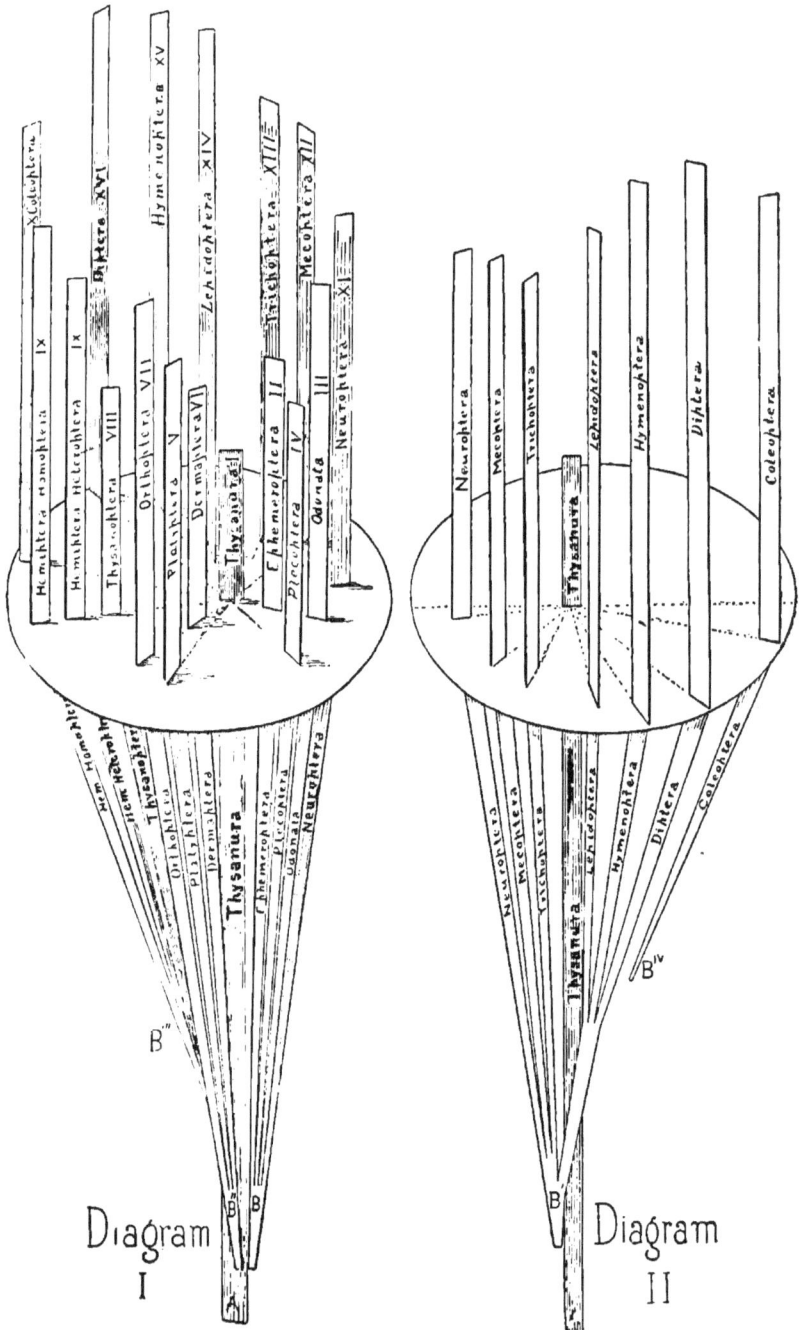

FIG. 2.—Scheme illustrating origin and relationship of Orders. (After Hyatt.)

The relation of these sixteen orders to the older, septenary scheme is shown by the following arrangement:

1. Hymenoptera .. Hymenoptera XV.
2. Coleoptera ..... Coleoptera X.
3. Lepidoptera .... Lepidoptera XIV.

4. Hemiptera ..... { Hemiptera IX....... } Homoptera.
                   { Thysanoptera VIII.   } Heteroptera.

5. Diptera ........ { Diptera XVI. } Including Aphaniptera or Si-
                                       phonaptera of some authors.

6. Orthoptera ..... { Orthoptera VII.
                    { Dermaptera VI.

7. Neuroptera..... { Trichoptera XIII }
                   { Mecoptera XII    } Neuroptera.
                   { Neuroptera XI    }
                   { Platyptera V     }
                   { Plecoptera IV    }
                   { Odonata III      } Pseudo-neuroptera.
                   { Ephemeroptera II }
                   { Thysanura I      }

It will be seen that the changes are not so great as would at first appear. The three more important orders, namely, the Hymenoptera, Coleoptera, and Lepidoptera, remain substantially the same in all classifications, and so with the three orders next in importance—the Hemiptera, Diptera, and Orthoptera. All that has been done with these

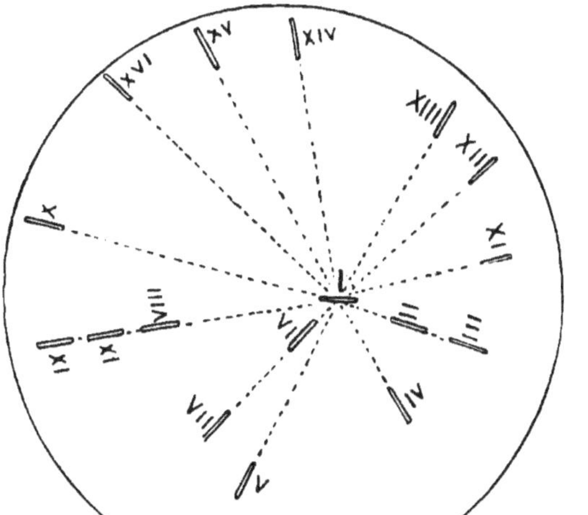

Diagram III
FIG. 3.--Cross section of Fig. 2.

three has been to rank as separate orders what by former authors were preferably considered as either families or suborders. The principal change is in the Neuroptera, of which no less than eight orders have been made. This is not to be wondered at, because the order, as formerly construed, was conceded to be that which represents the lowest forms and more synthetic types of insects, and as such necessarily contained forms which it is difficult to classify definitely.

In the discussion of the characteristics, habits, number of species, and importance of the several groups, I follow, with such changes as the advances in the science of entomology have made necessary, the arrangement shown in Fig. 1.

"Order HYMENOPTERA (ὑμήν, a membrane; πτερόν, wing).  Clear or Membrane-winged Flies: Bees, Wasps, Ants, Saw-flies, etc.  Characterized by having four membranous wings with comparatively few veins, the hind part smallest.  The transformations are complete: i. e., the larva bears no resemblance to the perfect insect.

"Some of the insects of this order are highly specialized, and their mouth-parts are fitted both for biting and sucking, and in this respect they connect the mandibulate and haustellate insects.  The common Honey-bee has this complex structure of the mouth, and if the editors of our agricultural papers would bear the fact in mind, we should have less of the never-ending discussion as to whether bees are capable of injuring fruit at first hand.  The lower lip (labium) is modified into a long tongue, sheathed by the lower jaws (maxillæ), and they can sip, or, more properly speaking, lap up nectar; while the upper jaws (mandibulæ), though not generally used for purposes of manducation, are fitted for biting and cutting.  The Hymenoptera are terrestrial, there existing only a very few degraded, swimming forms.

Fig. 4.—Bald-faced Hornet, Vespa maculata. (After Sanborn).

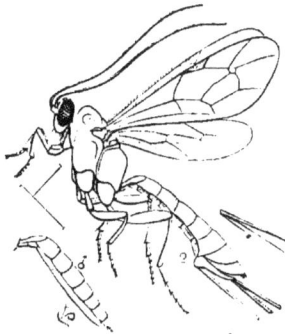

"This order is very naturally divided into two sections—the ACULEATA and TEREBRANTIA.  The aculeate Hymenoptera, or Stingers, comprise

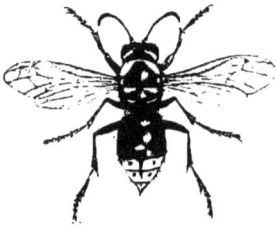

Fig. 5.—An Ichneumon Parasite, Pimpla annulipes, showing male and female abdomen.

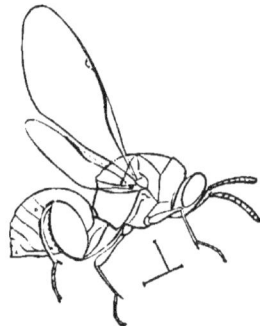

Fig. 6.—A Chalcid Parasite, Chalcis flavipes.

all the families in which the abdomen in the female is armed with a sting connected with a poison reservoir, and may be considered the typical form of the order, including all the social and fossorial species. The insects of this section must be considered essentially beneficial to man,

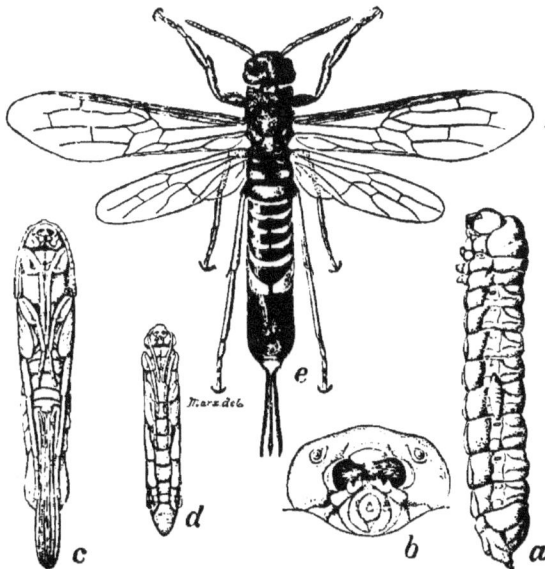

FIG. 7.—A Horn-tail, *Tremex columba.*  *a,* larva, showing Thalessa larva attached to its side; *b,* head of larva, front view, enlarged; *c,* female pupa, ventral view; *d,* male pupa, ventral view; *e,* adult female—all slightly enlarged.

notwithstanding the occasional sting of a bee or wasp, the boring of a carpenter bee, or the importunities of the omnipresent ant. Not only do they furnish us with honey and wax, but they play so important a part in the destruction of insects injurious to vegetation that they may be looked upon as God-appointed guards over the vegetal kingdom—carrying the pollen from plant to plant, and insuring the fertilization of diœcious species, and the cross-fertilization of others; and being ever ready to clear them of herbivorous worms which gnaw and destroy. The whole section is well characterized by the uniformly maggot-like nature of the larva. The transformations are complete, but the chitinous larval covering is often so very thin and delicate that the budding of the members, or gradual growth of the pupa underneath, is quite plainly visible, and the skin often peels off in delicate flakes, so that the transition from larva to pupa is not so marked and sudden as in those insects which have thicker skins.

"The terebrantine Hymenoptera, or Piercers, are again divisible into two subsections: first, the ENTOMOPHAGA, which are, likewise, with the exception of a few gall-makers, beneficial to man, and include the parasitic families, and the gall-flies; second, the PHYTOPHAGA, comprising the Horn-tails (*Uroceridæ*), and the Saw-flies (*Tenthredinidæ*), all of which are vegetable feeders in the larval state, those of the first family boring into trees, and those of the second either feeding externally on leaves or inclosed in galls. They are at once distinguished from the other Hymenoptera by the larvæ having true legs, which, however, in the case of the Horntails, are very small and exarticulate. The larvæ of many Saw-flies have, besides, prolegs, which are, however, always distinguishable from those of Lepidopterous larvæ by being more numerous and by having no hooks.

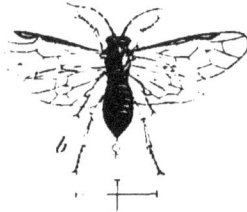

FIG. 8.—Sawfly and Larva. *Pristiphora grossulariæ*; *a*, larva; *b*, imago. Walsh.

"Order COLEOPTERA (κολεός, a sheath: πτερόν, wing). Beetles or or Shield-winged Insects. Characterized by having four wings, the front pair (called *elytra*) horny or leathery, and usually united down the back with a straight suture when at rest, the hind ones membranous and folded up under the elytra when at rest. Transformations complete.

"This is an order of great importance, and in the vast number and diversity of the species comprised in it outranks any of the others. The ease with which the insects of this order are obtained and preserved make it one of the most attractive to the amateur, and beetles are, perhaps, of all insects, the best known and understood in the popular mind. For the same reason they have, in the perfect state, received most attention from the entomologists, but their transformations and preparatory forms yet offer a wide and inviting

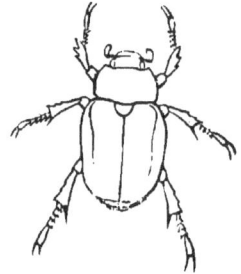

FIG. 9.—A Chafer, *Catalpa lanigera*. (After Packard.)

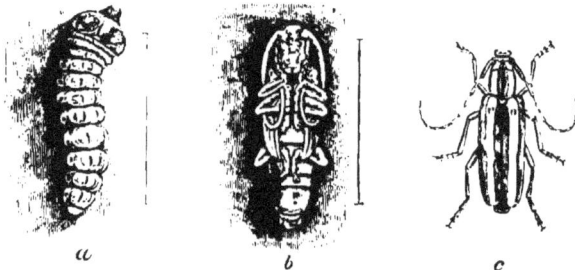

FIG. 10.—A Longicorn. *Saperda candida*. *a*, larva; *b*, pupa; *c*, beetle.

field for the student. The simplest and best-known classification of the beetles is the tarsal system, founded on the number of joints to the tarsi, by which we get four great sections: (1) PENTAMERA, in which

all the tarsi are 5-jointed; (2) HETEROMERA, with the four anterior 5-jointed and the two posterior 4-jointed; (3) PSEUDO-TETRA
MERA, with apparently only four joints
to all the tarsi, though, in reality, there
is a fifth penultimate joint, diminutive
and concealed; (4) PSEUDO-TRIMERA,
with apparently only three joints to all
the tarsi. This system, like most others,
is not perfect, as there are numerous species not possessing five joints to the tarsi
belonging to the first section; and for
practical purposes beetles may be very
well arranged according to habit. We
thus get, first, the ADEPHAGA, or carnivorous species, including all those which

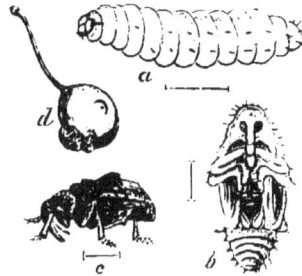

FIG. 11.  The Plum Curculio. *Conotrache-
lus nenuphar.*  a. larva; b. pupa; c,
beetle; d. plum showing egg-puncture
and crescent.

prey on other living insects, and to which, following Mr. Walsh, I have,
for obvious reasons, applied the suggestive term "Cannibal"; second,
the NECROPHAGA, comprising those
which feed on carrion, dung, fungi,
and decaying vegetation; third, the
PHYTOPHAGA, embracing all those
feeding on living vegetation. This
arrangement is by no means perfect,
for there are beetles which are carnivorous in the larva and herbivorous in the imago state; while some of
the NECROPHAGA are actually para-

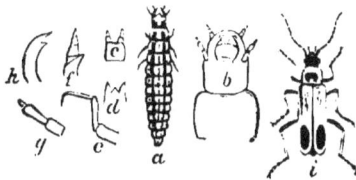

FIG. 12.—A Soldier-beetle. *Chauliognathus
pennsylvanicus.*  a, larva; b-h, parts of
larva enlarged; i, beetle.

sitic. Yet, it is not more artificial than others which have been proposed.
The carnivorous species, broadly speaking, are *Pentamerous*, the only
striking exception being the Coccinellidæ (Lady-birds), which are
*Pseudo-trimerous.* The carrion-feeders are also *Pentamerous;* but veg-

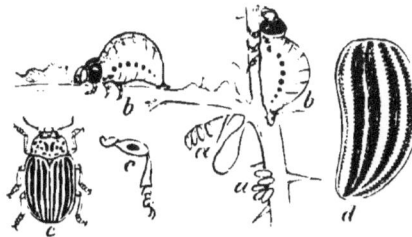

FIG. 13. - The Bogus Potato-beetle, *Doryphora juncta.*  a.
eggs; b. larvæ; c, beetle; d and e, parts of beetle enlarged.

etable-feeders are found in all the tarsal divisions, though the *Pseudo-
tetramera* are the more essentially herbivorous, and consequently the
most injurious."

"Order LEPIDOPTERA (λεπίς, a scale; πτερόν, wing). Butterflies and Moths, or scaly-winged insects. Characterized by having four branching-veined membranous wings, each more or less densely covered on both sides with minute imbricated scales which are attached by a stalk, but which easily rub off, and appear to the unaided eye like minute particles of glistening dust or powder. Transformations complete.

Fig. 14.—A Butterfly. *Pieris oleracea.*

"Next to the Lepidoptera, the Coleoptera are, perhaps, most familiar to the popular mind. Every one admires the beauty of these frail creatures, dressed in every conceivable pattern, and adorned with every conceivable color, so as to rival the delicate hues of the rainbow, and eclipse the most fantastic and elaborate designs of man. When magnified, the scales, to which this beauty of pattern and color is entirely due, present all manner of shapes, according to the particular species or the particular part of the individual from which they are taken. According to Lewenhoeck, there are 400,000 of these scales on the wing of the common silk-worm.

"The transformations of these insects are complete,

Fig. 15.—A Sphingid. *Ampelophaga myron.*

and the changes are usually so sudden and striking as to have excited the wonder and admiration of observers from earliest times.

"The more common form of the larva is exampled in the ordinary caterpillar—a cylindrical worm with a head, twelve joints and a sub-joint; six thoracic or true legs, four abdominal and two anal prolegs. But there is a great variety of these larvae, some having no legs whatever, some having only the jointed legs, and others having either four, six, eight, or ten, but never more than ten prolegs. With few exceptions they are all vegetable-feeders, and with

Fig. 16.—A Moth, *Utetheisa bella.*

still fewer exceptions, terrestrial. The perfect insects make free use of their ample wings, but walk little; and their legs are weak, and not modified in the various ways so noticeable in other orders, while the front pair in some butterflies are impotent.

"As an order this must be considered the most injurious of the seven.

"A convenient system of classification for the Lepidoptera is based on the structure of the antennae. By it we get two great sections: 1st, Butterflies (RHOPALOCE-
RA); 2d, Moths (HET-
EROCERA), which lat-
ter may again be di-
vided into Crepuscu-
lar and Nocturnal
Moths. Butterflies
are at once distin-
guished from moths
by their antennae be-
ing straight, stiff and
*knobbed*, and by being
day-fliers or diurnal;

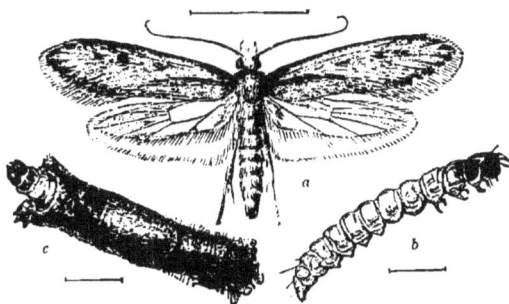

FIG. 17.—A Clothes-moth (*Tinea pellionella*)—enlarged. *a*, adult; *b*, larva; *c*, larva in case.

while moths have the antennae tapering to a point, and are, for the most part, night-flyers or nocturnal. The crepuscular moths, composed mostly of the Sphinges or Hawk-moths, hover over flowers at eve, and connect the two sections not only in habit, but in the character of the antennae which first thicken toward the end, and then suddenly termi-
nate in a point or hook.

"Order HEMIPTERA (ἥμι, half; πτερόν, wing), Bugs. The insects of
this order are naturally separated into two great sections; 1st, Half-winged Bugs, or HETEROPTERA (ἕτερος,
different; πτερόν, wing) having the basal half of the
front wings (called *hemelytra*) coriaceous or leathery,
while the apical part is membranous. The wings
cross flatly over the back when at rest; 2d, Whole-
winged Bugs, or HOMOPTERA (ὅμός, equal; πτερόν,
wing), having all four wings of a uniform membranous nature and folding straight down the back

FIG. 18.—A Plant-
bug (*Euschistes
punctipes*).

when at rest. The latter, if separated, may be looked upon as a Suborder.

"Transformations incomplete; *i. e.*, the larvæ and pupæ have more or
less the image of the perfect insect, and differ
little from it except in lacking wings.

"The genuine or half-winged Bugs (Figs.
18 and 19) are usually flattened in form,
when mature; though more rounded in the
adolescent stages. They may be divided
into Land Bugs (*Aurocorisa*) and Water
Bugs (*Hydrocorisa*). The species of the first
division very generally possess the power
of emitting, when disturbed or alarmed,
a nauseous, bed-buggy odor, which comes from a fluid secreted

FIG. 19.—A Soldier-bug (*Milyas
cinctus*). *b*, beak enlarged.

2564——2

from two pores, situated on the under side of the metathorax. Such well-known insects as the Bed-bug and Chinch-bug belong here. The habits of the species are varied. and while some are beneficial, others are quite injurious to man.

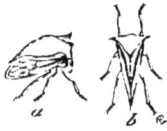

Fig. 20.—A Tree-hopper (*Ceresa bubalus*). *a*, side; *b*, top view.

"The Whole-winged Bugs (Figs. 20 and 21), on the contrary, are all plant-feeders, and with the exception of a few, such as the Cochineal and Lac insects, are injurious. The secretion of a white, or bluish, waxy, or farinose substance from the surface of the body is as characteristic of this section as the nauseous odor is of the first. It forms three natural divisions, arranged according to the number of joints to the tarsi—namely TRIMERA, with three joints; DIMERA, with two joints, and MONOMERA, with one joint to the tarsi."

Suborder THYSANOPTERA (θύσανος, a fringe; πτερόν, wing): This suborder contains the single family *Thripidæ*, which comprises minute insects commonly known as

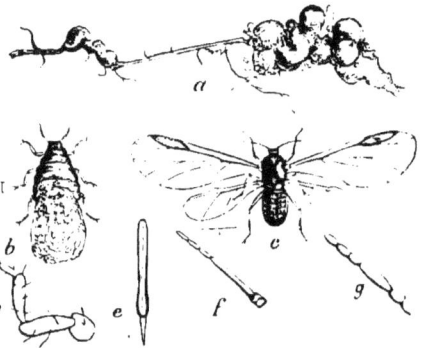

Fig. 21.—A Plant-louse (*Schizoneura lanigera*). *a*, infested root; *b*, larva; *c*, winged insect; *d–g*, parts of perfect insect enlarged.

Thrips, and of which a common species, *Thrips striatus*, is shown in the accompanying figure. (See Fig. 22.) They bear strong relations to both the Pseudoneuroptera and the Hemiptera and by later writers are generally associated with the latter order. They feed on plants, puncturing and killing the leaves, or on other plant-feeding species of their own class, and are characterized by having narrow wings crossed on the back when at rest, and beautifully fringed, from which latter feature the name of the suborder is derived.

The mouth parts are peculiar in that they are intermediate in form between the sucking beak of Hemiptera and the biting mouth parts of other insects.

Their eggs resemble those of Hemiptera; the larvæ and pupæ are active, and in form resemble

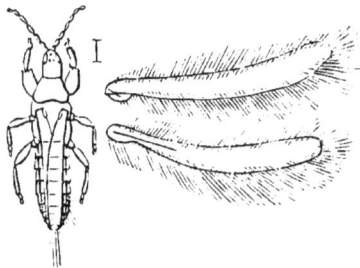

Fig. 22.—*Thrips striatus*, with wings enlarged at side.

the adult, except in the absence of wings. Some species, also, are wingless in the adult stage.

The pupæ are somewhat sluggish and the limbs and wings are enclosed in a thin membrane which is expanded about the feet into bulbous enlargements, giving rise to the name "bladder-footed" (Physopoda) applied to these insects by Burmeister.

"Order DIPTERA (δίς, twice; πτερόν, wing) or Two-winged Flies. The only order having but two wings, the hind pair replaced by a pair of small, slender filaments clubbed at tip, and called halteres, poisers, or balancers.

"No order surpasses this in the number of species or in the immense swarms of individuals belonging to the same species which are frequently met with. The wings, which are variously veined, though appearing naked to the unaided eye, are often thickly covered with very minute hairs or hooks. As an order the Diptera are decidedly injurious to man, whether we consider the annoyances to ourselves or our animals of the Mosquito, Buffalo-gnat, Gad-fly, Breeze-fly,

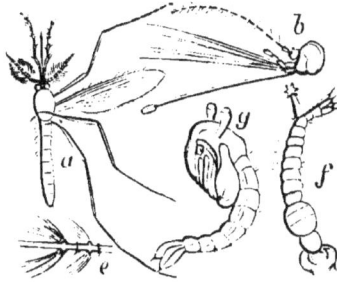

Fig. 23. A Mosquito (Culex pipiens). a, adult; b, head of same enlarged; c, portion of antenna of same; f, larva; g, pupa. (After Westwood.)

Zimb or Stomoxys, or the injury to our crops of the Hessian-fly, Wheat-midge, Cabbage-maggot, Onion-maggot, etc. There are, in fact, but two families, Syrphidæ and Tachinidæ, which can be looked upon as beneficial to the cultivator, though many act the part of scavengers. No insects, not even the Lepidoptera, furnish such a variety of curious larval characters, and none, perhaps, offer a wider or more interesting field of investigation to the biologist. It is difficult to give any very satisfactory arrangement of these Two-winged flies, though they easily fall into two rather artificial sections. These are: 1st, NEMOCERA, or

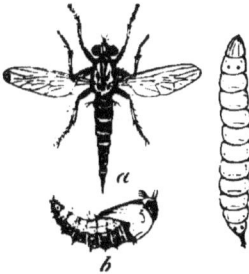

Fig. 24.—A Hawk-fly (Erax bastardi). a, perfect insect; b, pupa; larva shown at side.

those with long antennæ, having more than six joints, and palpi having four or five joints. The pupa is naked, as in the Lepidoptera, with the limbs exposed. This kind of pupa is called obtected. 2d, BRACHOCERA, or those with short antennæ, not having more than three distinct joints, and palpi with one or two joints. The pupa is mostly coarctate, i. e., is formed within, and more

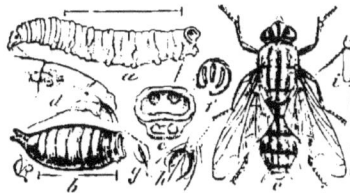

Fig. 25.—A Flesh-fly (Sarcophaga carnaria, var. saracenæ). a, larva; b, puparium; c, adult insect with enlarged parts.

or less completely connected with the hardened and shrunken skin of the larva.

"The most anomalous of the Diptera are the Forest-flies and Sheepticks (*Hippoboscidæ*). They have a horny and flattened body, and resemble lice in their parasitic habits, living beneath the hair of bats and birds. Their mode of development has always attracted the attention of entomologists. The larvæ are hatched in the abdomen of the female, which is capable of distention. There it remains and, after assuming the pupa state, is deposited in the form of a short, white, egg-like object, without trace of articulation, and nearly as large as the abdomen of the female fly. Closely allied to these are the Batticks (*Nycteribidæ*), which possess neither wings nor balancers, and remind one strongly of spiders.

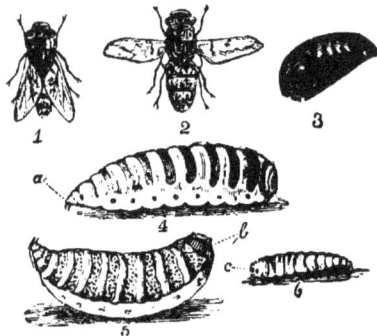

FIG. 26.— The Sheep Bot (*Œstrus ovis*). 1, 2, flies; 3. puparium; 4, 5, and 6. larvæ or bots.

"In this order we may also place certain wingless lice (such as *Braula cæca*, Nitzsch), which infests the Honey-bee in Europe, northern Africa, and western Asia, but which has not yet been detected in this country.

"Suborder APHANIPTERA (ἀφανής, inconspicuous; πτερόν, wing) or Fleas, comprising the single family Pulicidæ, now placed with the Diptera. Everybody is supposed to be familiar with the appearance of the Flea—its bloodthirsty propensities and amazing muscular power; and while everyone may not have the leisure and means to experience the exhilarating

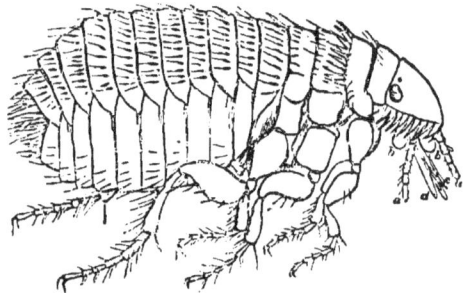

FIG. 27.—A Flea (*Pulex*). (From Packard.)

influence of the chase after larger animals, there is no one—be he never so humble—who may not indulge in the hunt after this smaller game! In place of wings the flea has four small, scaly plates. The minute eggs—about a dozen to each female—are laid in obscure places, such as the cracks of a floor, the hair of rugs, etc., and the larva is wormlike and feeds upon whatever animal matter—as grease and blood—or decaying vegetable matter it can find.

"Order ORTHOPTERA (ὀρθός, straight; πτερόν, wing), or Straight-winged Insects. Characterized by having the front wings (called

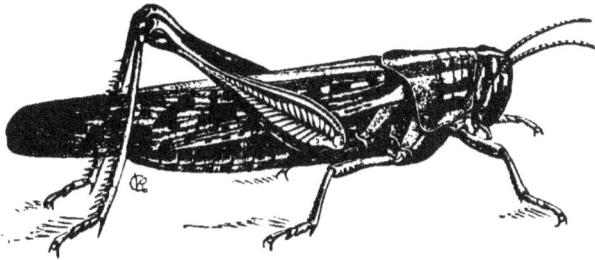

FIG. 28.—A Locust (*Acridium americanum*).

*tegmina*) straight and usually narrow, pergameneous or parchment-like, thickly veined, and overlapping at tips when closed; the hind wings large and folding longitudinally like a fan. Transformations incomplete.

"The insects of this order have a lengthened body and very robust jaws, with a correspondingly large head. The legs are strong, and fashioned either for grasping, running, climbing, jumping, or burrowing. As in the other orders, where the transformations are

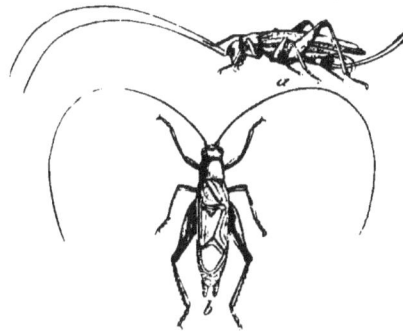

FIG. 29.—A Tree-cricket (*Oecharis saltator*). *a*, female; *b*, male.

incomplete, the young differ little from the parent, except in the want of wings: and in many instances even this difference does not exist, as

FIG. 30.—The Croton Bug or German Cockroach (*Phyllodromia germanica*.) *a*, first stage; *b*, second stage; *c*, third stage; *d*, fourth stage; *e*, adult; *f*, adult female with egg-case; *g*, egg-case—enlarged; *h*, adult with wings spread—all natural size except *g*.

there are numerous species which never acquire wings. There are no aquatic Orthoptera. Some are omnivorous, others carnivorous, but most of them herbivorous. They form four distinct sections: 1st, CURSORIA, Cockroaches; 2d, RAPTATORIA, Mantes; 3d, AMBULATORIA, Walking-sticks; 4th, SALTATORIA, Crickets, Grasshoppers, and Locusts.

"Suborder DERMAPTERA* (δέρμα, skin; πτερόν, wing), or "Earwigs, consisting of the single family Forficulidae, which may be placed with the Orthoptera. They are rare insects with us, but very common in Europe, where there prevails a superstition that they get into the ear and cause all sorts of trouble. The front wings are small and leathery; the hind ones have the form of a quadrant, and look like a fan when opened:

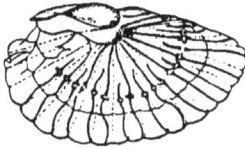

Fig. 31.—Hind wing of Earwig. (From Comstock.)

and the characteristic feature is a pair of forceps-like appendages at the end of the body, best developed in the males. They are nocturnal in habit, hiding during the day in any available recess. The female lays her eggs in the ground, and singularly enough, broods over them and over her young, the latter crowding under her like chicks under a hen."

Fig. 32.—An Earwig. (From Packard.)

"Order NEUROPTERA (νεῦρον, nerve; πτερόν, wing), or Nerve-winged insects. Characterized by having the wings reticulate with numerous veins so as to look like net-work. The order forms two natural divisions, the first including all those which undergo a complete, and the second, called Pseudo-neuroptera (Dictyotoptera, Burmeister), those which undergo an incomplete metamorphosis. * * * The insects of this order are, as a whole, more lowly

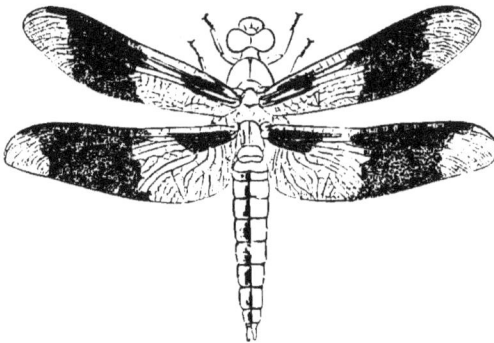

Fig. 33.—A Dragon-fly (Libellula trimaculata). (From Packard.)

organized, and more generally aquatic, than either of the others. A natural arrangement of them is difficult on account of their degradational character. They present forms which are synthetic and closely approach the other orders, and the evolutionist naturally looks upon them as furnishing an idea of what the archetypal forms of our present insects may have been. They are, as a rule, large and sluggish, with

Euplexoptera of some authors from εὖ, well; πλέκω, folded, referring to the folded wings.

the body parts soft and little specialized, and the muscles weak. Their remains are found in the Devonian and Carboniferous deposits.

"They are mostly carnivorous, and with the exception of the White-ants and certain Book-lice they none of them affect man injuriously, while some are quite beneficial."

The first division of this order, or the Neuroptera proper, characterized by having incomplete metamorphoses, may be considered under the three following suborders:

"Suborder TRICHOPTERA (θρίξ. hair; πτερόν. wing), or Caddis-flies, containing the single family Phryganeidae, and placed with the Neurop-tera, though bearing great affinities with the Lepidop-tera. Every good disciple of Walton and lover of the "gentle art" knows the value of the Caddis-fly, or Water-moth, as bait. These flies very much resemble certain small moths, the scales on the wings of the latter being replaced in the former with simple hairs. The larvæ live in the water and inhabit silken cases, which are usually cylindrical and covered with various substances, according to the species, or the material most conveniently obtained by the individual."

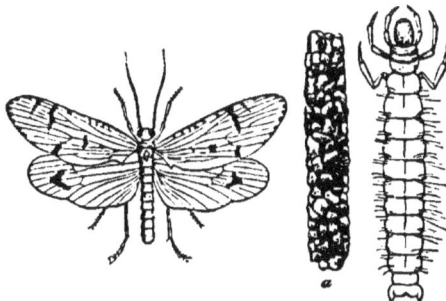

Suborder MECOPTERA (μῆκος, length; πτερόν. wing). This suborder includes a peculiar group of insects, the most striking characteristics of which are the mouth-parts, which are pro-longed into a rostrum or beak. The wings are long and narrow, and ot nearly equal size. The abdomen of the male is constricted near its posterior end and terminates in long clasp-ing organs from which these insects obtain the common name of Scorpion-flies.

The larvæ of one genus (*Panorpa*) are re-markable for their great resemblance to the larvæ of Lepidoptera. They have, however, eight pairs of abdominal legs. The habits of these insects are not well known, but they are sup-posed to be generally predaceous.

Suborder NEUROPTERA. This group as restricted by modern au-thors is a small one, including the largest species, as in the Hellgram-mite, the Lace-wing Flies, the Ant-lions, and the Mantispas represent-ing the families. Sialidae and Hemerobiidae, with their subfamilies. The first includes the so-called Hellgrammite Fly (*Corydalus cornutus*), one

Fig. 34.— Caddis-fly, larva and its case. (From Packard.)

Fig. 35.— Panorpa or Scorpion-fly. (From Packard.)

of our largest and most striking insects, the larvæ of which is known as
Dobsons by anglers, and is aquatic and carnivorous in habit. The Hemerobiidæ is a large family, com-
prising, as a rule, delicate
insects with rather ample
gauzy wings. The larvæ are
predaceous. The common
Lace-wing flies are among our
most beneficial insects, destroying plant-lice and other
soft-bodied species. To the
same family belongs the Ant-lion (*Myrmeleon*), the larvæ of which have
the curious habit of constructing
a funnel-shaped burrow in the
sand, in the bottom of which they
conceal themselves and wait for
any soft-bodied insects which
may fall into the trap. This family also includes the
peculiar Mantis-like in-
sects belonging to the
genus *Mantispa*. As in the true Mantis, the prothorax of
these insects is greatly elongated and the first pair of legs
are fitted for grasping. The larvæ
are parasitic in the egg-sacs of certain large spiders (genera *Licosa*,
*Dolomedes*, etc.), and undergo a remarkable
change in form after the first molt. In the
first stage the larvæ are very agile, with slender bodies and long legs. After molting the
body becomes much swollen and the legs are
much shortened, as are also the antennæ, the
head becoming small and the general appearance reminding one of the
larva of a bee.

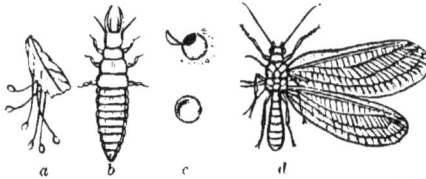

FIG. 36.—Lace-wing fly. *a*, eggs, *b*, larva, *c*, cocoons, *d*, fly with left wings removed.

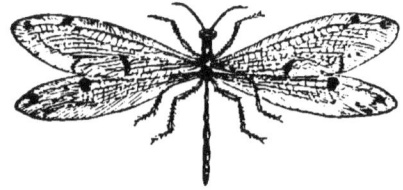

FIG. 37.—An Ant-lion (*Myrmeleon*). (From Packard.)

FIG. 38.—Myrmeleon larva.

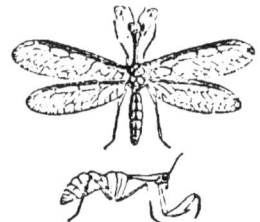

FIG. 39.—*Mantispa* with side view beneath. (From Packard.)

The second section of the Neuroptera, characterized by complete
metamorphosis, comprises the following suborders:

Suborder PLATYPTERA (πλατύς, flat; πτερόν, wing). Under this head
are grouped the White-ants (*Termitidæ*), the Bird-lice (*Mallophaga*),
and the Book-mites (*Psocidæ*). The suborder receives its name from
the fact that in the case of the winged forms the wings, when at rest,
are usually laid flat upon the back of the insect. The Mallophaga, or
Bird-lice, are degraded wingless insects, and are parasitic chiefly on
birds, but also on mammals. In shape of body and character of the
mouth parts they are most nearly allied to the Psocidæ. The latter
family includes both winged and wingless forms, the Book-mites belonging to the latter category. The winged forms may be illustrated

by the common species, *Psocus venosus* (see Fig. 40). The legs and antennæ are long and slender and the wings are folded roof-like over the body when the insect is at rest. They feed on lichens and dry vegetation.

The Termitidæ are represented in this country by the White-ant (*Termes flavipes*), which is frequently so destructive to woodwork, books, etc. The term White-ant applied to these insects is unfortunate, as in structure they are widely separated from ants and resemble them only in general appearance and also in their social habits. Like the ants they live in colonies and have

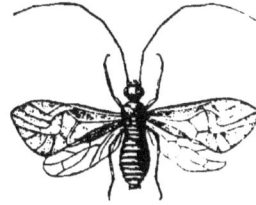

Fig. 40.—*Psocus venosus.* (From Comstock.)

a number of distinct forms, as winged and wingless, males and females, and workers and soldiers.

Suborder PLECOPTERA (πλεκτός, plaited; πτερόν, wing). Closely allied to the latter suborder is the suborder Plecoptera, which includes the single family Perlidæ or Stoneflies. The larvæ and pupæ of these insects are aquatic, being often found under stones in water, whence the name. The adults are long, flattened insects, with long antennæ. The wings are ample and are somewhat folded or plaited, from which character the suborder takes its name.

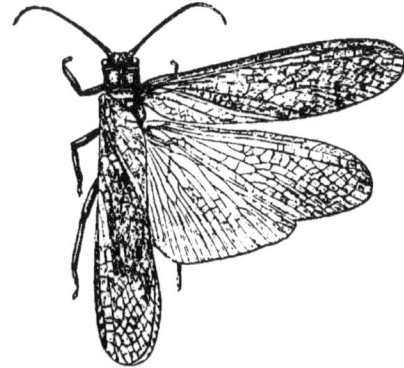

Fig. 41.—A Stone-fly (*Pteronarcys regalis*). (From Comstock.)

Suborder ODONATA (ὀδούς, tooth). This includes the Dragon-flies or Libellulidæ, the most common and the best known of the Neuroptera. The larva and the active pupa or nymph are aquatic and are predaceous, as is also the adult. A common species is represented at Fig. 33.

The Suborder EPHEMEROPTERA (ἐφήμερον, a day-fly; πτερόν, wing) comprises the May-flies, or Ephemeridæ (see Fig. 42). These insects are very fragile and are often attracted in enormous numbers to electric lights. They have large front wings, while the hind wings are small, rudimentary, or wanting. They are furnished with two or three very long, jointed, threadlike caudal appendages. The larval and nymphal stages are passed in the water and aquatic vegetation furnishes the food, although some species may be predaceous. The adults have very rudimentary

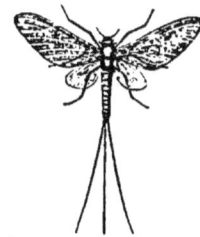

Fig. 42. A May-fly (*Prota manthus marginatus*). (From Packard.)

mouths and eat nothing; their term of life is also very limited, not exceeding 2–4 days.

Suborder THYSANURA (θύσανος, tassel; οὐρά, tail).   This suborder comprises minute, degraded insects commonly known as Spring-tails, Bristle-tails, Fish-moths, Snow-fleas, etc.   They occur in damp situations and also infest books, wall-paper, etc., eating the starch paste in the book-bindings, or beneath the wall paper.   They comprise very primitive forms and are interesting because they are supposed to represent the original stock from which the higher orders of insects have sprung.   They are wingless, usually with simple eyes, and clothed with scales, and undergo no metamorphosis.   Some of them, as the Fish-moth (*Lepisma* sp.), run very rapidly and are furnished at the end of the body with a number of long bristles.   In other forms these anal bristles or stylets are

Fig. 43.—(*Lepisma 4-seriata*).
(After Packard.)

united at the base and bent under the body and become a powerful jumping organ, giving them the very appropriate name of Spring-tails.

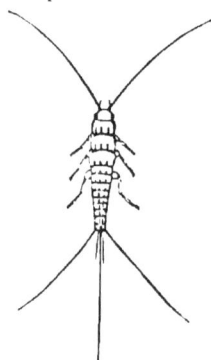

## COLLECTING.

GENERAL CONSIDERATIONS.—" Few departments of natural history offer greater inducements or facilities to the student than Entomology. He need not pass his threshold for material, for it may be found on every hand and at all seasons.   The directions for collecting, preserving, and studying insects might be extended indefinitely in detail, as volumes have already been written on the subject; but the more general and important instructions are soon given.

" Beginners are very apt to supply themselves with all sorts of appliances advertised by natural history furnishing stores.   Many of these appliances, when it comes to real, practical field-work, are soon abandoned as useless incumbrances; and the greater the experience, the simpler will be the paraphernalia.   My own equipment, on a collecting trip, consists chiefly of a cotton umbrella, a strong and narrow steel trowel or digger, a haversack slung across the shoulders, a cigar box lined with sheet cork, and a small knapsack attached to a waistbelt which girts a coat, not of many colors, but of many pockets, so made that in stooping nothing falls out of them.   The umbrella is one of the indispensables.   It shields, when necessary, from old Sol's scorching rays and from the pelting, drenching storm; brings within reach, by its hooked handle, many a larva-freighted bough which would otherwise remain undisturbed; and forms an excellent receptacle for all insects that may be dislodged from bush or branch.   Opened and held inverted under a bough with the left hand, while the right manipulates a beating-stick, cut for the occasion, it will be the recipient of many a choice specimen that would never have been espied amid its protective surroundings. Some collectors use an umbrella painted or lined on the inside with white, to facilitate the detection of any object that drops into it; but as there are fully as many, if not more, pale and white insects as there are dark or black ones, the common dark umbrella is good enough for all ordinary purposes; and if any improvement on the ordinary cotton umbrella is desired, it should be in the way of a joint or knuckle about the middle of the handle, which will facilitate its packing and using. The trowel is valuable for prying off the loosened bark from old trees, whether felled or standing, and for digging into the ground or into decaying stumps and logs. The haversack is for the carriage of different kinds of boxes (those made of tin being best) intended for larval and other forms which it is necessary to bring home alive for breeding purposes; and if made with a partition so that the filled and empty boxes may be separated, all the better; it may also be used for nets and other apparatus to be mentioned, and for such provender as is necessary on the trip. The knapsack may be made on the plan of a cartridge box, of stout canvas or leather, and should be of moderate size and slung onto the belt so as to be slipped to any part of the waist and not hinder free bodily motion. It may be used to carry bottles, phials, and other small appliances, and should be accordingly partitioned and furnished with loops or pockets on the inside. The cigar-box is for the reception of pinned specimens, and may be slipped onto the belt, or buttoned to the trousers by means of leather.

"The greatest requisites in collecting are a pair of sharp eyes and ready hands, with coolness and self-possession; but a few traps will materially aid. One of the most important is the hand-net, which may be made so as to subserve the two purposes of a sweeping and an air-net."

"The frame of the net which I use is illustrated herewith (Fig. 44), and will be found strong and serviceable and conveniently portable. It is constructed as follows: Take two pieces of stout brass wire, each about 20 inches long; bend them half-circularly and at one end by a folding hinge having a check on one side, b.

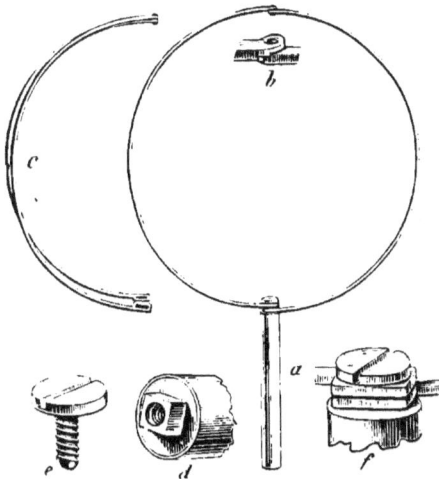

FIG. 44. —The Butterfly net-frame.

The other ends are bent and beaten into two square sockets, f, which fit to a nut sunk and soldered into one end of a brass tube, d. When so fitted, they are secured by a large-headed screw, *e*, threaded to fit into the nut-socket, and with a groove wide enough to receive the back of a common pocket-knife blade. The wire hoop is easily detached and folded, as at *e*, for convenient carriage; and the handle may be made of any desired length by cutting a stick and fitting it into the hollow tube *a*, which should be about 6 inches long. It is well to have two separate hoops, one of lighter wire, furnished with silk gauze or some other light material, for catching flying insects, and one which is stouter and furnished with a net of stronger material for sweeping non-flying specimens.

"Another still more simple, but less convenient frame, is thus described by my friend F. G. Sanborn, of Boston, Mass.:

'Make a loop of strong iron or brass wire, of about 3-16ths of an inch in thickness, so that the diameter of the loop or circle will not exceed 12 inches, leaving an inch to an inch and a half of wire at each end bent at nearly right angles. Bind the two extremities of the wire together with smaller wire (Fig. 45, *a*), and tin them by applying a drop of muriate of zinc, then holding it in the fire or over a gas flame until nearly red hot, when a few grains of block tin or soft solder placed upon them will flow evenly over the whole surface and join them firmly together. Take a Maynard rifle cartridge tube, or other brass tube of similar dimensions: if the former, file off the closed end or perforate it for the admission of the wire, and having tinned it in the same manner on the inside, push a tight-fitting cork half way through (Fig. *c*) and pour into it melted tin or soft solder, and insert the wires; if carefully done, you will have a firmly constructed and very durable foundation for a collecting net. The cork being extracted will leave a convenient socket for inserting a stick or walking cane to serve as a handle.'

"My friend, J. A. Lintner, of Albany, N. Y., makes very good use, in his ordinary promenades, of a telescopic fish-rod, with a head (Fig. 46) screwed on to one end, in which to fasten an elastic brass coil on which the net is drawn, but which when not in use sits snugly inside his silk hat.

"The bag should taper to the bottom, and in any case its length should be fully twice the diameter of the hoop, so that by giving the net a twist, the mouth may be closed and the contents thus secured. The sweeping-net may be protected around the hoop with leather, and in use should be kept in a steady and continued back-and-forth motion, over and touching the plants, until the contents are to be examined; when, by placing the head at the opening and quietly surveying the restless inmates, the desiderata may be secured and the rest turned out. A sudden dash of the air-net will usually lay any flying object at the bottom. A net for aquatic insects may be made on the same principle, but should be stout, with the meshes open enough to allow free passage of water, and the bag not quite

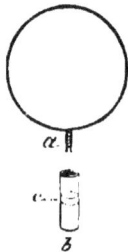

Fig. 45.—The Sanborn net-frame.

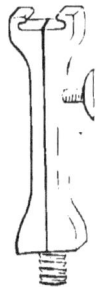

Fig. 46.—Clamp of the Lintner net.

as deep as the diameter of the hoop. A forceps net, which consists of two gauze or bobbinet covered frames, having riveted handles, so as to close like a pair of scissors, is employed for small insects; but I find little use for it. A coarse sieve, together with a white towel or sheet, will be found of great service for special occasions, particularly in the spring, when the search for minute insects found under old leaves, or for pupæ around the butts of trees, is contemplated. With the sheet spread on the ground, and a few handfuls of leaves and leafy mold sifted over it, many a minute specimen will be separated from the coarser particles and drop to the sheet, where the eye may readily detect it. Conversely, the earth taken from around trees may be sifted so as to leave in the sieve such larger objects as pupæ, etc. Another favorite plan, with some collectors, of obtaining specimens, especially night-flying moths, is by ·sugaring.' This consists of applying to the trunks of trees or to strips of cloth attached to the trees some sweet, attractive, and stupefying preparation. Diluted molasses or dissolved brown sugar, mixed with rum or beer, is most frequently employed. I have found sugaring of little use till after the blossoming season, and it is almost impossible to so stupefy or intoxicate an insect that it will remain upon the sugared tree till the next morning. I generally sugar at eve, and visit the tree several times between sundown and midnight, armed with wide-mouthed killing-bottles and accompanied by a second person, who carries a dark-lantern. Isolated trees, on the edges of woods, give the best results. Everybody knows how some poor moths will persist in flitting around a light until they singe their wings; and, as many insects are strongly attracted to bright artificial light, it may be employed with good results, especially during warm and damp evenings. The collector should never go unprovided with a small box or tube full of different sized pins (a corked cartridge-tube makes a good box,) a pair or two of forceps, a pair of scissors, a little mucilage, and the killing apparatus to be described."

With these general remarks, it will be well to consider some of the important paraphernalia more in detail.

### COLLECTING APPARATUS.

*The Sweeping Net.*—A multitude of insects of all orders feed or rest on grasses and other low plants. Upon close inspection of these plants a careful observer will be able to secure, without any instruments, not only many mature insects, but also many larvæ in connection with their food-plants. This is laborious and slow work, only necessary on special occasions. The beating net, which is constructed on the same general plan as the butterfly net, is valuable here as a time saver. By holding the handle of the net firmly in one hand and quickly sweeping over the plants first from right to left, and then, after quickly turning the net again, sweeping from left to right, most insects coming within reach of the sweep will fall into the bag and may be easily taken

out and put into the collecting-vials. From this mode of operation it
is evident that the sweeping net must be stronger in all its parts than
the butterfly net. but otherwise it may be made on the same plan.

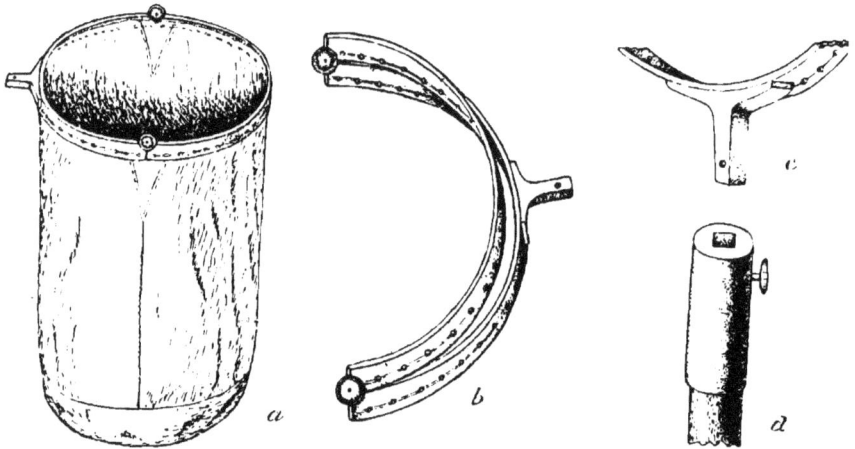

FIG. 47.—The Deyrolle Sweeping Net. *a*, net entire; *b*, frame; *c* and *d*, attachment of frame and
handle (original).

The ring should be rigid, made of brass or iron, either of one piece
or of two pieces, and fastened to the handle or stick in the same way
as the butterfly net. The bag need not be as long as in the butterfly net,
about 18 inches being sufficient, but it should be of stout cotton or linen
and the bottom should preferably be sewed in as a round piece, so as to
avoid corners. Care needs to be bestowed on the fastening of the bag
on the ring, for by the use of the net the part of the bag sewed around
the ring is soon chafed through. To prevent this a strip of leather is
sewed over the cotton along the rim, but since even this must be frequently renewed some other devices are used to give greater durability
to the net. In the pattern of a beating-net originally sold by Deyrolle
in Paris, the metal ring was flattened, with the narrow edge pointing
upwards and the broad side pierced with holes at suitable intervals and
grooved on the outer surface between the holes. The bag is sewed on
to the inner side of the ring by stout twine, which passes from one
hole to the next and is thus prevented from coming in contact with ob-
structive objects, and only the bottom of the bag wears and will need to
be occasionally mended or renewed.

Another method of preventing the tearing of the upper rim of the
bag is described and illustrated in Kiesenwetter's useful volume " Der
Naturaliensammler" from which I shall frequently have occasion to
quote. In this net the main ring is of rounded iron wire on which a
number of brass rings are slipped. These must be but little larger

than the diameter of the wire. These little brass rings should not be more than 30 mm. or at most 40 mm., distant from each other, and to them the upper rim of the bag is sewed with very strong twine and is thus protected from wear and tear. The handle or stick of the net should be firmly and solidly attached to the ring and should be stout and not liable to break. I prefer a rather short stick, say not longer than two feet.

I figure herewith the ring of a very convenient net for sweeping or beating purposes. It has the advantage of being for sale on the market, and

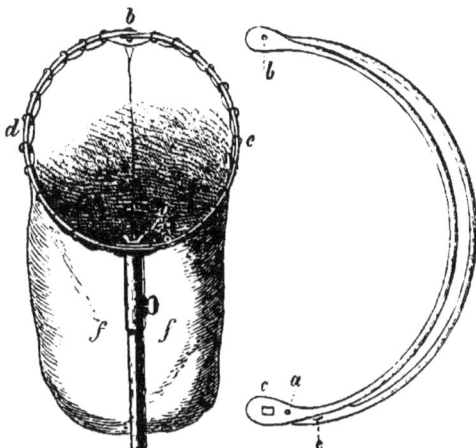

FIG. 48.—Beating net, opened and attached to handle, with frame of same folded. (After Kiesenwetter.)

in fact is an ordinary fishing dip net of small size. It is hinged in three places, as shown in the figure, and folds into very small compass. When unfolded and brought together, it screws into a ferrule which may be attached to a cane or a special handle.

The beating net can be successfully used at almost every season of the year. Even on warm days in winter time many specimens can be swept from the dead grass. So long as the dew is on the plants or in rainy weather no beating should be attempted, as the more delicate species are more or less spoiled by the moisture. After one or two minutes' sweeping the contents should be examined. Those insects which are quick to take wing or which are good runners should first receive attention; the less active can then be examined more at leisure.

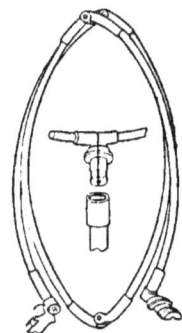

FIG. 49.—Folding ring for beating net (original).

The desiderata are then disposed of, the rest thrown away, and the beating renewed.

The beating net is an important instrument for collecting all insects excepting mature Lepidoptera, which are apt to get rubbed. Many larvæ, especially of Lepidoptera, are caught by beating and are mostly in good condition, but it is usually difficult to ascertain the food plant.

*The Water Net.*—The numerous insects or insect larvæ which live in the water can not be conveniently collected without the use of a net, except where they live in small shallow streams or creeks with gravelly or stony bottoms. A suitable water net can readily be made by using the frame of the beating net and attaching to it a rather short bag of some coarse material, e. g., "grass cloth," coarse millinet. The mode of operation with this net is very simple: if some insect is seen swimming in the water, the net is carefully brought beneath the specimen, which is thus lifted out of the water. Most water insects are, however, not seen swimming about freely, but hide amid the various plants, mosses, etc., or in the mud at the base of the plants, and they can best be captured by dragging the net through these plants. When taken from the water the net is more or less filled with mud and parts of plants, and the water must be allowed to run out and the contents of the net spread out on a cloth or on a flat stone, if such be at hand. The insects are at first not readily seen, but after a short while they begin to emerge from the mud and crawl about, and can readily be taken up with a forceps.

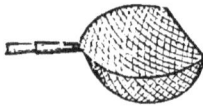

Fig. 50.—The Water Net. (After Packard.)

*Water Dip Net.*—The small water sieve, shown in the accompanying illustration (Fig. 51), and somewhat resembling in appearance a jockey cap, is frequently of service in collecting the larvæ of aquatic insects, especially where it is necessary to scrape submerged stones or timbers. In use it is fastened on the end of a cane or stick, and can be easily made by any tinsmith.

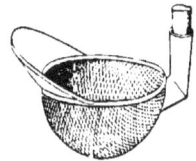

Fig. 51.—Small Water Dip Net (original).

*The Umbrella.*—The umbrella, as already stated, is one of the most useful instruments of the collector, since it enables him to obtain all those numerous insects which live on the branches of trees, on shrubs, and on other large plants. A common stout cotton umbrella is sufficiently large, but is liable to get out of joint, and moreover the specimens hide themselves under the ribs. It is well, therefore, to have the inside of such umbrella lined along the ribs with muslin, or some other material, preferably of a light color. An umbrella specially constructed for entomological purposes is offered for sale by E. Deyrolle, in Paris. It resembles a stoutly built common umbrella, but has the inside lined with white linen and the handle has a joint near the middle, so that the umbrella can be more conveniently held and more readily packed away. The opened and inverted umbrella is held with the left hand under the branch which the collector intends to relieve of its entomological inhabitants, while the right hand, armed with a heavy stick, is free to properly jar the branch. Care must be taken in the jarring, lest the insects are knocked beyond the circumference of the umbrella. The larger the umbrella the greater are the chances of making rich captures, but the more difficult it becomes to manipulate, especially where the woods are dense or where there are many vines, etc. In the absence of an umbrella the butterfly net or the beating net can be used.

A drawback to collecting with the umbrella is that many insects take wing and escape before being secured. This can hardly be avoided,

FIG. 52.—The Umbrella and its mode of use. (After Kiesenwetter.)

and experienced collectors, in southern countries more particularly, have found it advisable to discard the umbrella and to use in its stead a very large butterfly net, 2 feet or more in diameter.

*The Beating Cloth.*—A very simple substitute for the umbrella, and one which can always be carried without inconvenience, may here be described. It consists of a piece of common unbleached cotton cloth (1 yard square), to each corner of which a loop of stout twine is sewed. Upon reaching the woods, two straight sticks, each about 5 feet in length and not too heavy, but also not so small as to be liable to break or to bend too easily, are cut from a convenient bush. The sticks are placed crosswise over the cloth and fastened to the loops at the four ends. This is easily and quickly done by making sliding loops of the simple loops. The cloth is thus kept spread out between the sticks, and forms a very good substitute for an umbrella. In beating, the sticks are held at their intersecting points. When not in use one of the loops is detached from the stick and the instrument can be rolled up and carried under one arm without seriously interfering with other operations of the collector. When laid on the ground, with the sticks on the underside, this simple instrument may be advantageously used

2564——3

as a cloth on which to sift or examine fungi, moss, pieces of bark, etc., and since the cloth is always tightly expanded, it offers a smooth and level surface, where examination of various objects can be made with ease and accuracy.

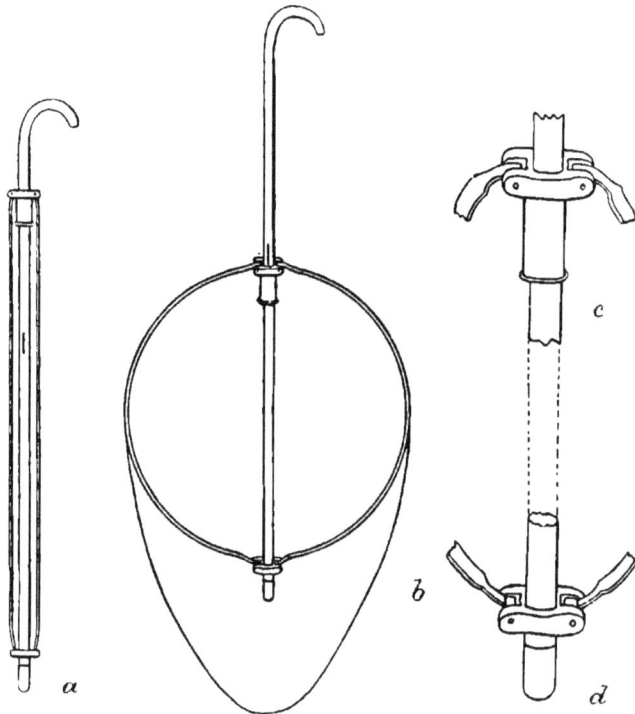

FIG. 53.—The umbrella beating and sweeping net (original).

*The Umbrella Net.*—A very convenient form of net for both sweeping and for use in place of an umbrella for beating has been devised by Dr. George Marx. (See Fig. 53.) It is constructed from an old umbrella, as follows: To the handle of the umbrella are attached two steel rods working on hinges at the apex of the umbrella, as do the ordinary umbrella ribs, and attached to the sliding piece of the umbrella in the same manner, as shown at *a*. These rods should be about 2½ feet long. When the sliding piece is pushed up and caught behind the spring clip, as shown at *b*, a circular loop is formed giving the framework for the net. The latter, which should be comparatively shallow, is made of stout muslin and sewed to the frame, as in the ordinary sweeping net. The enlarged drawings *c* and *d* illustrate clearly the manner of constructing the frame. The advantage of this net is its convenience in carrying and its general usefulness, taking the place of both the umbrella and the sweeping net. When not in use the frame is allowed to assume the position shown at A, and the net may be wrapped about the frame and the whole inserted in an ordinary umbrella cover.

*The Sieve.*—This useful aid to good collecting has not been generally employed by American entomologists. It facilitates the finding of small insects living under old leaves, in moss, in decayed trees, in fungi, in ants' nests, or in the ground. Any ordinary sieve about a foot in diameter and with meshes of about one-fifth of an inch will answer, though for durability and convenience of carriage one made of two wire or brass rings and muslin (Fig. 54), as follows, is the best. The ends of the wire netting should be bent around the ring so as not to project. A piece of common muslin about 1 foot wide and long enough to go around the circumference of one of the rings is then sewed together so as to form a kind of cylinder or bag without bottom, and the upper and lower rims of this bag are then sewed on around the two rings. The whole instrument thus forms a bag, the top of which is kept open by the simple wire ring, and the bottom is closed by the second ring covered with the wire netting. After choosing a suitable locality a white cloth is spread as evenly as possible on the ground:

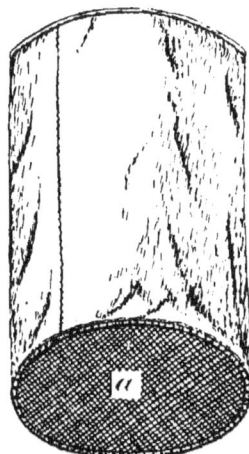

FIG. 54.—The sieve. *a*, wire netting (original).

the collector then takes the sieve, places therein two or three handfuls of the material to be sifted, returns to his cloth, and, holding with his right hand the lower ring and with the left hand the upper ring, shakes the sieve over the cloth. The larger particles and specimens are retained in the sieve while the smaller fall through the meshes on to the cloth. Care must be taken that the siftings form an even and thin layer on the surface of the cloth, so as to be easily examined from time to time. If the locality is favorable many insects will be seen at the first glance crawling or running about, and these can easily be picked up by means of a moistened brush, or with the forceps. Many other insects, however, either feign death or, at any rate, do not move until after the lapse of several minutes, and the proper investigation of a single sifting often requires much time, and patience will be more fully rewarded here than in any other mode of collecting.

The size of the wire meshes given above is best adapted for sifting the fragments of old decayed trees, which furnish the most frequent material for the use of the sieve, but for sifting ants' nests, soil, etc., a sieve with smaller meshes is desirable.

The sieve is indispensable to the Coleopterist, the Arachnologist, and to the specialist in the smaller Hemiptera and Hymenoptera, but it is also useful for most other orders, many interesting species existing which can be secured in numbers only by this mode of collecting. Many

Tineidæ and even Noctuidæ hide under old leaves, but the specimens are usually rubbed and rendered useless in the process of sifting. Many larvæ and pupæ can, however, thus be obtained.

If the locality chosen for sifting prove to be a good one, it pays to put the sifted material in a small sack and to carry it home where it can be investigated at leisure, and with a greater thoroughness than is usually possible outdoors. This sack can be easily arranged to be attached to or drawn over the lower ring of the sieve, so that the sifting can be done directly into the sack.

As a rule it may be said that very dry places are least productive, while more or less moist places are apt to furnish a rich harvest. Old wet leaves lying immediately along the edges of swamps, or wet moss, harbor many interesting insects, but such wet material is sifted with difficulty.

The sieve can be used with great advantage at all seasons of the year, but more especially late in fall or early in spring, when so many species are still hibernating.

*The Chisel.*—For securing the many insects living or hiding under bark of dying or dead trees an instrument of some sort is indispensable, as, in most cases, the bark so firmly adheres to the wood that it cannot be torn off with the hand. A stout pocket-knife will do good service, but far better is a common chisel of medium size and with a short handle. This chisel is also useful as an instrument for digging in the ground or for investigating the interior of partly decayed logs.

*The Trowel.*—Aside from the fact that many insects enter the ground for the purpose of hibernation in various stages, there is a rich subterranean life to be found during the summer. There are many burrowing Coleoptera; many, if not most, ants construct subterranean nests; the number of other fossorial Hymenoptera is very large, and there are also various burrowing Orthoptera and many Lepidopterous larvæ which hide in the ground during the day. Some instrument for digging in the ground is therefore of great importance, and while, as stated above, the chisel will answer this purpose if nothing else be at hand, yet there are other instruments which perform the work much quicker and more thoroughly. The most available instrument is a rather small steel trowel, such as can be had at the hardware stores in a great variety of patterns, and which can be carried on excursions without much inconvenience. One with a long and narrow blade, made very stout, I have found very useful, though somewhat awkward to carry.

FIG. 55.—The collecting tweezers.

*The collecting Tweezers.*—In the picking up of specimens and transferring them into the various bottles, vials, or boxes, the trained collector will gather by hand the most delicate specimens without injuring them. Yet this labor will be greatly facilitated by the use of the

FIG. 56.— Pinning forceps.

tweezers or the brush. The former is a small, light pair of forceps, made of steel or brass. It should be as pliable as possible, and the tip should be narrow and rounded off and not pointed. It may be either straight or curved at tip, according to individual preference.

Suitable tweezers may be obtained at the larger hardware stores or of watchmakers. Excellent tweezers made of steel (see Fig. 55) are

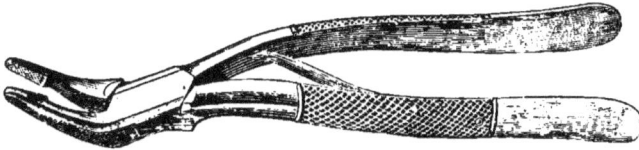

FIG. 57.—Pinning forceps.

sold for about 40 cents a pair by Codman, Shurtleff & Co., Tremont street, Boston, Mass. Aside from their utility in picking up specimens from the collecting cloth or the umbrella, the tweezers are indispensable for extracting insects from cracks, or holes in timber, or from their burrows in branches and stems of plants, or from places whence it is impossible to dislodge them by hand. The

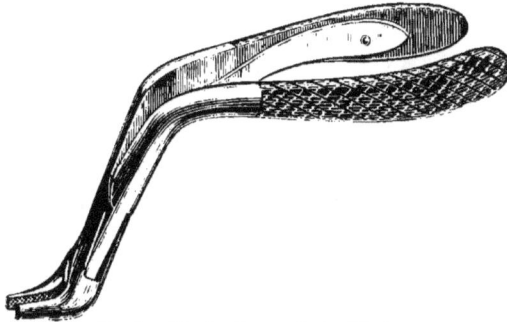

FIG. 58.—Pinning forceps for Lepidoptera.

larger " collecting forceps," sold by various dealers, do good service in certain emergencies, as when large scorpions or other very large and ferocious insects are to be secured.

For the handling of mounted insects various special forceps are employed, a number of styles of which are shown at Figs. 56–8.

*The Brush.*—A common camel's hair brush, of smaller or larger size according to individual preference, is useful for picking up very small or soft-bodied insects. For this purpose the brush is slightly moistened with saliva, and the tip brought in contact with the specimen, which then adheres to the brush, so that it can readily and without injury be transferred to the collecting bottle or box. The brush is indispensable also for preparing small specimens for the cabinet. If taken into the field the handle of the brush should be of a bright color, otherwise the brush is often lost.

*The Fumigator.*—This is not used by American collectors, but there are several patterns sold by European dealers. It is intended to smoke out specimens that hide in otherwise inaccessible places, *e. g.,* cracks in the ground, holes in hard wood, etc. The accompanying figure and the following description of a fumigator are taken from Kiesenwetter. A common smoking-pipe mouthpiece (Fig. 59, *a*) with flexible rubber joint (*b*) is attached to the cover (*c*) of a very large smoking-pipe head (*d*). To the mouth (*e*) of the latter a rubber hose (*f*) is attached, which has a convenient discharge at its end (*g*). The pipe is then filled with tobacco, and the latter ignited by means of a piece of burning tinder placed on top; the cover is then screwed on, and the smoke can be directed to any desired point by blowing air through the mouthpiece. The smoke from a common pipe or cigar is often useful. In sifting in cold weather a puff of tobacco smoke gently blown over the débris on the collecting cloth will in-

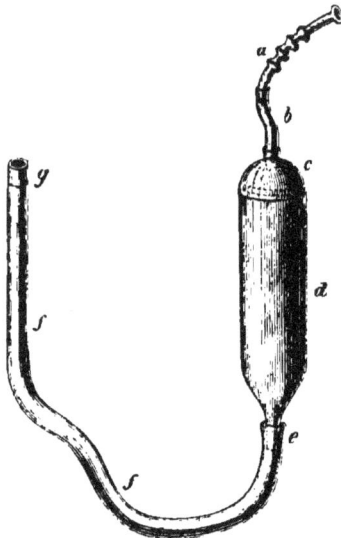

Fig. 59. The Fumigator. (After Kiesenwetter).

duce many specimens to move, which otherwise " play possum " and could not be observed; and, further, tobacco smoke blown into holes and cracks in timber by means of an improvised funnel made of a piece of paper will be the means of securing many rare specimens.

*The Haversack.*—In order that the above-mentioned instruments and the various bottles, vials, and boxes which are needed for the preservation of specimens may most conveniently and with the least impediment to the collector be carried along on excursions, a haversack is indispensable. This is made either of leather or, still better, of some waterproof cloth, and should contain various compartments of different sizes: one for stowing away the nets, the sieve, and the larger instruments, and several smaller ones for boxes and vials—the whole so arranged that each desired object can readily be taken out and that nothing will drop out and get lost. The haversack is slung across the shoulders by means of a leather strap, and a full field outfit need not be very heavy nor seriously interfere with free bodily movements.

Many of the smaller objects are most conveniently carried in the pockets of the coat, which acquires, therefore, some importance to the collector. The coat should be of some durable stuff and provided with many pockets, so arranged that in stooping nothing falls out of them.

*The Lens and Microscope.*—In the examination of the minuter forms of insect life the naked eye is not sufficient, and a hand-lens, or, for more delicate work, the compound microscope will be found neces sary. I had, in my early experience, some difficulty in getting a satisfactory hand-lens, and the use of a poor hand-lens in time injures the eyesight, as I know by a year's rather disagreeable experience. For a hand-lens the achromatic lenses formerly manufactured by A. K. Eaton, of Brooklyn, N. Y., and now made by John Green, 35 Liverpool street, East Boston, Mass., are most excellent in workmanship and are satisfactory in every respect. A very good lens can also be purchased of any of the leading manufacturers of microscopical apparatus in this country. The kind of compound microscope to be purchased will depend upon the nature of the work of the investigator. Very serviceable instruments are made by J. W. Queen & Co., Philadelphia, Pa., and by the Bausch & Lomb Optical Company, of Rochester, N. Y., and others. The German microscopes are in many respects superior to those of American make, and if one has sufficient means, I would recommend the purchase of one of the better instruments of Zeiss's manufacture, which may be obtained either direct from the manufacturers or through Queen & Co., or from the Boston Educational Supply Company. Microscopic material, including slides, cover glasses, instruments for mounting, mounting media, staining fluids, etc., may be obtained of either of the firms named above.

Having thus indicated somewhat fully the general methods of collecting, and the paraphernalia most desirable in collecting, it will be well to go still further into detail, and in connection with the different orders give some more specific information that will be valuable as a guide not only to the general collector, but to the specialist.

### COLLECTING HYMENOPTERA.

The insects of this order, including Bees, Wasps, Ants, Ichneumon-flies, Gall-flies, Saw-flies, and allied insects have always been of unusual interest both to entomologists and non-entomologists on account of their diversified and peculiar habits. In abundance of species they exceed perhaps even the Coleoptera. In general they are day fliers and always to be found in abundance on bright days about flowers. The best season for collecting is in early spring, on the bloom of the Willow, Alder, and other trees. They may also be found at any season of the year, but the males of many species are only to be taken in fall. In this order, species of many groups can be most easily obtained by breeding. This includes the gall-making family, Cynipidae, and the parasitic families Chalcididae, Proctotrypidae, Ichneumonidae and Braconidæ. The Chrysididæ and certain other less important families are also parasitic, but are more easily obtained by general collecting. The implements necessary for collecting Hymenoptera are the sweeping-net and the beating-net. Many rare forms of the smaller parasitic families may be obtained by sweeping the grass and foliage of all sorts. The

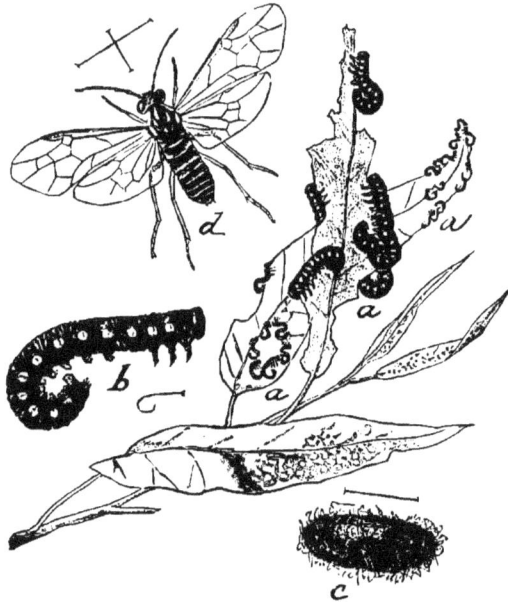

FIG. 60.—A Saw-fly (*Nematus ventralis*). *a, a, a,* young larvæ; *b,* full-grown larva; *c,* cocoon; *d,* adult; all slightly enlarged.

Proctotrypidæ may be collected in quantity by sifting leaves and rubbish collected in the woods. Mr. William H. Ashmead, who has made an especial study of this group, finds winter sifting profitable. Dried leaves and rubbish are sifted, the finer portion being retained and transferred to a bag. When a sufficient quantity is collected it is removed to a warm room. Many hibernating species are taken in this way, and, revived by the warmth, are easily noticed when the material is spread on white paper.

On account of the interest attaching to a knowledge of the various hosts of parasitic insects the collector should always aim to obtain the latter by breeding as much as possible. This can easily be done by keeping a lookout for larvæ of all sorts which give evidence of being parasitized. The larvæ of Lepidoptera found late in the fall are very apt to be parasitized, and should be collected and kept over the winter. The parasites will emerge throughout the winter season and in the early spring. Such larvæ will be found on the trunks of trees, in the crevices of the bark, and the cocoons of parasites will also be found in similar situations.

The Tenthredinidæ (Saw-flies) are not so often found about flowers but usually remain in the vicinity of the food-plant of the larva, and may many of them be collected by sweeping. The larvæ of this family are in many cases difficult to breed, as most of them are single-brooded, and it becomes necessary to carry the larvæ over the winter.

The Gall-flies, Cynipidæ, are the easiest of the families to collect, because of their abundance and because of the ease with which they may be reared. Their galls occur in enormous variety on oaks of various species and also upon brambles and certain common weeds. These should be collected when mature and be kept in glass jars. The Gall-flies and inquilinous and parasitic species may thus be easily obtained, the former appearing at particular seasons and the latter emerging from the galls at all seasons of the year, and sometimes continuing to escape for a period exceeding two years.

One of the most interesting families in this order is the Formicidæ, which comprises the true ants. In the case of these insects isolated specimens should not ordinarily be collected, and it is especially desirable to collect the species from colonies so that the three forms (males, females, and workers) may be obtained together. This holds also in the case of the social wasps and bees, but the different sexes of the latter may be collected in a season's collecting about flowers, the females and workers in early spring and the males in the fall.

The Uroceridæ or woodborers are to be found only about trees in which the larvæ breed. They may frequently be taken about tree trunks, or burrowing with their long gimlet-like ovipositors into the trunks of trees to oviposit.

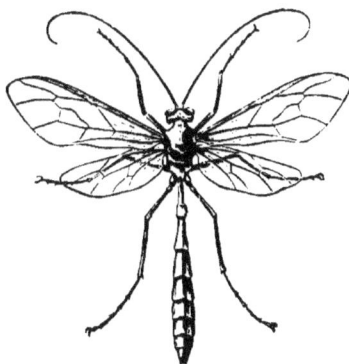

Fig. 61.—An Ichneumon (Ophion).

Breeding is also a satisfactory method of obtaining these insects.

Some special methods of collecting Hymenoptera may be briefly outlined. In the case of the social bees, particularly bumble-bees, and also the smaller wasps and yellow-jackets, a very satisfactory method of collecting consists in first stupefying the insects in the nest by introducing a small amount of chloroform, benzine, or bisulphide of carbon. This should preferably be done in the late evening, after all the insects have come in for the night. The nest may then be opened and examined without any danger of being stung, and the different forms may thus easily be obtained, together with any rare parasitic or inquilinous insects. In the case of the nests of Bombi this is the best method of obtaining the inquilinous Apathus species.

On account of the danger of being stung, and also on account of the extremely quick flight of these insects, the removing of Hymenoptera from the net is not always an easy task, and in many cases rare specimens escape. One method of avoiding the danger of being stung is to have the collecting net constructed with an opening at the bottom which, during the sweeping, is tied with a string. When a sufficient quantity of insects is obtained they are, by a few quick motions, driven to the bottom of the net, and the net is then seized just above the insects with the hand, the folds of cloth preventing the insects from getting to the hand, so that there is little danger of being stung. The lower end is then carefully untied and inserted into a wide-mouthed bottle, and the contents of the net shaken out into the bottle. After the catch is stupefied the vial may be turned out and the undesirable material discarded. A second method consists in the use of an ordinary sweeping-net of light material. A quantity of Hymenoptera are collected from flowers and driven to the bottom of the net, and secured as in the preceding method. The portion of the net containing the insects is then, by means of a pair of forceps, thrust bodily into a large collecting bottle. After a few minutes the insects are stupefied and may be readily examined.

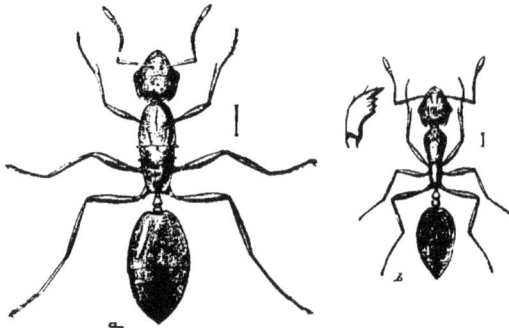

Fig. 62.—The Little Red Ant (*Monomorium pharaonis*). *a*, female; *b*, worker enlarged.

## COLLECTING COLEOPTERA.

GENERAL DIRECTIONS.—Owing to their hard outer skeleton, Coleoptera can be collected, handled, and preserved with greater safety and with less trouble than most other orders of insects. From this fact, and from their very great diversity in form, Coleoptera have, next to the Lepidoptera, always been favorites. As a consequence, there are now more species described in this than in any other order, and in the large museums they are much better represented than other insects. This rich material has been studied by numerous and competent specialists, and the classification of Coleoptera is at present more advanced and more accessible than that of the other orders. This fact gives stimulus to neophytes, and though the literature of our North American fauna is much scattered and we are still in want of comprehensive works (with the exception of the general "Classification" by Drs. Le Conte and Horn), yet, except in a few hitherto neglected families and smaller groups, the species are fairly well worked up.

On the other hand, our knowledge of the earlier states of Coleoptera is yet very imperfect as compared with the Lepidoptera. Coleopterous larvæ are, with few exceptions (notably Coccinellidæ and some Chrysomelidæ), much more difficult to find and rear, and their distinguishing characters are more difficult to study. The few comprehensive works on Coleopterous larvæ that have been published are based on rather scant material and none of them deal with the North American fauna.

Coleoptera occur in all climates and in all localities. Species are known from the highest northern latitudes ever reached by man, and in the tropics they occur in an embarrassing richness of forms. They are found in the most arid desert lands, in the depths of our subterranean caves, and on our highest mountains up to the line of eternal snow. The open ocean and the open water of our Great Lakes are the only regions free from them. As a rule, the number of species gradually increases from the Arctic regions toward the tropics, but it would be difficult to decide, speaking of North America, whether or not the fauna of the Middle States is poorer in the number of species than that of the Southern States; or whether the beetles of the Atlantic slope outnumber those of the Pacific States or those of the Central region. On the Pacific slope the influence of the seasons on insect life

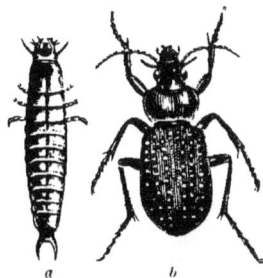

Fig. 63.—A Ground-beetle (Calosoma calidum). a, larva; b, adult.

is greater than on the Atlantic slope. While in the latter region a number of species may be found the whole year round, there is, in the more arid regions of the West, an abundance of insect life during and shortly after the rainy season, with great scarcity during the dry season, except, perhaps, on the high mountains.

Few persons have had a more extended experience in collecting Coleoptera than Mr. E. A. Schwarz, one of my assistants, and the following account has been prepared by him at my request and is given *in extenso*.

WINTER COLLECTING.—There are more species of Coleoptera hibernating in the imago state* than in any other order and winter collecting is therefore most profitable in many respects. For instance, great swampy tracts which are inaccessible in the summer season harbor an abundance of rare Coleoptera, which either can not be found in summer time or are found at that season with the greatest difficulty. At the approach of winter, however, all or most of these species will leave the swamp and seek drier ground, where they hibernate under old leaves, under bark of trees, or in rotten stumps near the edge of the swamp. Such places will, therefore, give a rich harvest to the Coleopterist late in the fall, during warm spells in midwinter, and in very early spring. If the temperature is below the freezing point, or if the ground is frozen hard, no winter collecting should be attempted, first, on account of sanitary

*There are a few species of Coleoptera known in Europe which belong to the true "winter insects," i. e. such as appear in the imago state only during winter time, but whether or not we have such species in our own fauna has not yet been ascertained.

considerations, and also because the Coleoptera then retreat more deeply into the ground and can not be found so easily as when the ground is free from frost. Other good collecting places in winter are the accumulated old leaves along the edges of forests or under the shrubbery along water courses, thick layers of moss, and the loose bark of dead or dying trees, and, finally, also under the bark of certain living trees, *e. g.* Pines, Sycamore, Shellbark Hickory. Digging in the ground at the base of large trees or rocks also yields good returns. The only instruments necessary for winter collecting are the sieve, the chisel, and the trowel.

SPRING COLLECTING.—With the first days of spring, collecting becomes a little more varied. The methods used for winter collecting can still be continued with good success. Certain spring flowers, notably Willow blossoms, will furnish many valuable species, which are not seen again during the rest of the season.

*Myrmecophilous and Termitophilous species.*—The early spring is also the best time for collecting the Myrmecophilous and Termitophilous Coleoptera. Termitophilous species have in North America hitherto been found only in connection with the White-ants (*Termes flaripes*), and the inquilinous beetles are found running among the White-

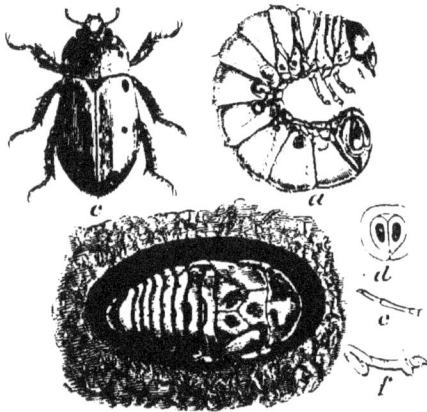

FIG. 64.—A Lamellicorn (*Pelidnota punctata*). *a,* larva; *b,* pupa; *c,* beetle; *d, e, f,* enlarged parts.

ants in the colonies under stones, loose bark of trees, and more numerously in the interior of old infested trees. Myrmecophilous Coleoptera are by far more numerous in species than the Termitophilous species and are found among many species of ants which have their nests either under stones or loose bark of trees, in stumps or logs, or which construct larger or smaller hills. Upon uncovering a colony of ants under a stone, the underside of the latter as well as the galleries of the ants in the ground should be carefully examined for inquilines, which from their greater or slighter resemblance to the ants are liable to be overlooked by an inexperienced collector. If such colony of ants harbors a rare beetle the subterranean part of the colony itself should be dug out and sifted, but since from the stony nature of the ground this is not always practicable it is to be recommended to carefully replace the stone under which the colony has been found. Upon revisiting the spot again the next day or even a few hours after the first visit additional specimens of the inquilines are usually to be obtained on the stone or in the superficial galleries of the ants. Ant colonies in hollow trees and in rotten logs should be sifted and there is no particular difficulty connected with this operation. Owing to the pugnacious character of the hill-constructing ants it would seem to be a rather unpleasant task to examine a strong and vigorous colony for inquilinous beetles, but the collector must not mind being bitten and stung by the infuriated ants, and after a little experience he will find that it is not such a difficult thing after all to attack even the largest ant-hill. The only thorough way of investigating such ant-hills is to sieve the same, which can be easily done if the hill is composed of sticks and other vegetable débris. If it is built of earth or sand the process of sifting is more difficult and tedious. Another method of securing specimens of these inquilinous beetles is to place flat stones or similar objects on the surface of the ant-hill and to examine them occasionally, when the beetles will be found on the underside of the traps.

*Spring Flights of Coleoptera.*—On the first really warm days of spring commences the "swarming" season of Coleoptera, when all winged species are flying about.

especially toward evening. On favorable days the number of specimens and species that can thus be found is astonishingly great, and this is one of the few occasions when the Coleopterist can advantageously use a light butterfly net. The flying beetles preferably alight and rest on the top of wooden fences (especially newly made ones), on the railings of bridges, etc., where they can be easily seen and secured, or they are attracted in great numbers by the white-painted surface of buildings. This flying season lasts in the latitude of Washington from the end of April to the middle of June, but favorable days are not of frequent occurrence, since a peculiar combination of atmospheric conditions appears to be necessary to induce the Coleoptera to fly about in great numbers.

*Beach collecting.*—Along the shores of the ocean, and the Great Lakes untold numbers of Coleoptera and other insects fall at this season into the water, and, if the tides, the currents, and the winds be favorable, they are washed ashore by the waves on the sandy beaches, where they often form windrows several inches in height and width. If the collector is happy enough to be at the right place on the right day he has then the opportunity to pick up hundreds of rare species within a very short time and without any trouble. Many of the specimens thus washed ashore are dead and decayed, but the majority are alive and in excellent condition. This "beach collecting" affords also an excellent opportunity for the Hymenopterist and Hemipterist to secure large numbers of rare species, but favorable days are also here of rare occurrence.

*Attracting by Lights.*—On the beaches, day and night flying insects can thus be captured. Away from the beach night-flying Coleoptera can best be collected at the electric lights of our cities; but, as in the Lepidoptera, not all night-flying species are attracted by the light. Gas and other lights also attract Coleoptera, and the various "light traps" that have been devised and described can advantageously be used for collecting these insects.

*Traps.*—The method of "sugaring," so important to the Lepidopterist, is by far less favorable for collecting Coleoptera. Still, certain rare Carabidæ, Elateridæ, and Cerambycidæ are attracted by this bait, and the Coleopterist should not entirely ignore this mode of collecting. There are a few other methods of trapping certain Coleoptera. By laying out dead mammals, birds, fishes, snakes, etc., on suitable places and so that they are protected from dogs, rats, etc., the carrion-feeding Coleoptera can be found in great abundance, but a cleaner and less disagreeable method of obtaining them is to bury in the ground tin cans or glass jars so that the top is even with the surrounding ground and to bait them with pieces of meat, fried fish, boiled eggs, etc. Many Curculionidæ, Scolytidæ, and numerous other wood-inhabiting species can be successfully trapped in the following way: A number of branches, preferably of only one kind of tree, are cut and tied up into bundles of convenient size. The bundles are then laid on the ground in a shady place or firmly fastened on trunks of trees. When the cut branches begin to get dry they will attract many of these Coleoptera, which can then be readily collected by shaking the bundles out over the collecting cloth.

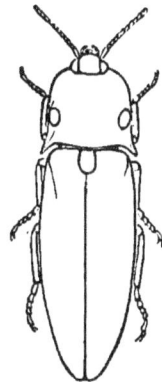

FIG. 65.—An Elaterid (*Pyrophorus noctilucus*). (From Packard.)

*Freshets.*—Freshets usually take place in springtime in most of our rivers and creeks, and furnish the means of obtaining a multitude of Coleoptera, among which there will be many species which can not, or only accidentally, be found otherwise. These freshets, sweeping over the low banks or inundating wide stretches of low land, carry with them all insects that have been caught by the inundation. Intermingled with, and usually clinging to, the various floating débris, these insects are eventually washed ashore by the current at various points and the Coleopterist should not miss this rare opportunity, but go out to the river bank at a time when the water is still rising, or at least when it has attained its highest point. Among, or on the washed up débris, a multitude of Coleoptera of various families can be found, and the specimens can either be gathered up on the spot or a quantity of the débris be put in sacks and taken home, where it can be examined more thoroughly and with greater leisure than out of doors. A day or so after the floods have receded the washed up specimens will have dispersed and only a few will remain in the débris for a longer period. Still more profitable than the spring floods are the summer freshets, because a larger and more diversified lot of Coleoptera is then brought down by the water. A similar opportunity for collecting is offered near the seashore if unusually high tides inundate the low marshes along the bayous and inlets.

SUMMER COLLECTING.—During the latter part of spring and throughout the whole summer, when the vegetation is fully developed, every possible collecting method can be carried on with success, so that the beginner hardly knows what particular method to use. There are stones to be turned over; old logs, stumps, and hollow trees to be investigated; newly felled or wounded trees to be carefully inspected; here a spot favorable for sifting claims attention; promising meadows and low herbage in the woods invite the use of the sweeping net; living or dead branches of all sorts of trees and shrubs to be worked with the umbrella; the mud or gravel banks of ponds, lakes, rivers, and creeks afford excellent collecting places; the numerous aquatic beetles are to be collected in the water itself; the dung beetles to be extracted from their unsavory habitations; in the evening the electric and other lights are to be visited, the lightning beetles chased on meadows and in the woods, or the wingless but luminous females of some species of this family to be looked for on the ground, and the trees and shrubs are to be beaten after dark in search of May beetles and other nocturnal leaf-feeding species which can not be obtained at daytime; and, finally, some of the rarest Scarabæidæ and some other species fly only late at night or again only before sunrise.

Fig. 66.—A Longicorn (*Prionus laticollis*).

In view of this embarrassing multitude of collecting opportunities in a good locality, the beginner is apt to be at a loss what course to pursue. Experience alone can teach here, and only an expert collector is able to decide, at a glance at the locality before him, what collecting method is likely to produce the best results, and his judgment will rarely be at fault.

It is impossible to go into details regarding the various collecting methods, just mentioned, and only a few general directions can be given regarding those methods which have not previously been alluded to.

*Collecting under Stones.*—Turning over stones is a favorite method among beginners and yields chiefly Carabidæ, the larger Staphylinidæ, certain Curculionidæ, and a multitude of species of other families. Stones on very dry ground are productive, only early in spring or in the fall, while those on moist ground, in the shade of woods, are good at all seasons. In the Alpine regions of our mountainous districts, especially above the timber line, collecting under stones becomes the most important method, and is especially favorable along the edges of snow fields. In often frequented localities the collector should carefully replace the stones, especially those under which he has found rare specimens. The neglect of this rule is one of the principal causes for certain rare species having become extinct in the vicinity of our cities.

*Collecting in rotten Stumps and Logs.*—Success in collecting in rotten stumps depends much upon the more or less advanced stage of decay as well as upon the situation of the log and upon the particular kind of wood. If the decay is very much advanced neither the loose bark nor the interior of the log will harbor many Coleoptera excepting a multitude of *Passalus cornutus* and its larvæ. If the decay is less advanced, but if such log is exposed to the scorching rays of the sun, it will be far less productive than a log in a shady situation. The investigation of the bark of a favorably situated log in the right stage of decay does not need any special instruction, but the decayed wood itself should be pried off with a chisel or trowel, put in the seive and sifted on the collecting cloth. This is the best way of obtaining the numerous species of rare Micro-coleoptera of various families that inhabit such places. A "red rotten" oak or beech log is more favorable for this mode of collecting than a "white rotten" of the same or other kinds of trees.

*Collecting in dying or dead Trees.*—Dying or dead trees almost always harbor a large number of Coleoptera and offer an excellent collecting opportunity until the wood becomes thoroughly dry, which usually takes place in large trees two or three years after the death of the tree, and in less time with smaller ones. The bark of such trees is the best collecting place for Cucujidæ, Colydiidæ, Scolytidæ, Histeridæ, etc., and it will be found that the shady side of the tree is more profitable than the side exposed to the sun. The numerous Buprestidæ, Elateridæ, Ptinidæ, Cerambycidæ, Melandryidæ, etc., which breed in the wood can be obtained only with difficulty. Some specimens may be cut out from their holes by a skillful use of the knife or hatchet; others (especially the Buprestidæ) may be found resting on or crawling over the trunk in the bright sunshine, while the more nocturnal species may be found on the tree toward evening or after dark, when, of course, a lantern must be used. A large proportion of the species living in the trunks of dead trees also breed in the dead branches of otherwise healthy trees from which they can be beaten into the umbrella, or where the use of the knife is more practicable than in the large trunks. The trunks of freshly felled trees attract numbers of Cerambycidæ and Buprestidæ and have to be carefully looked over, while the drying foliage of such trees affords an excellent opportunity for the use of the umbrella.

*Beating living Trees, Shrubs, and Vines.*—The success of beating into the umbrella branches of living trees and shrubs depends on the particular kind of tree or shrub, on the condition and situation of these, and largely also upon the season. Pine trees are very productive from early in the spring to early in the summer, but much less so in midsummer and later on. Young Oak trees or Oak shrubs are much more preferred by the leaf-eating Coleoptera peculiar to this tree than the older trees. The Beech, which, next to the Oak, is the best tree for wood-boring species, harbors but few leaf-eating species. The leaves of the Chestnut are also generally not attacked by Coleoptera; still a surprising number of species can be beaten from this tree when it is in blossom. There is not a single species of Coleoptera known to live in the wood or to feed on the leaves of the Holly (*Ilex glabra*); still it will pay the Coleopterist to beat this tree when it is in bloom. Trees, shrubs, and vines in the interior of unbroken forest districts are, as a rule, unproductive, while the edges of the woods, narrow strips of hedges, and especially solitary trees are excellent collecting places. In the Rocky Mountains, especially in the more southern sections, long stretches of mountain slopes are occasionally perfectly bare of vegetation with the exception of a few solitary, sickly-looking, and dwarfed trees, but every one of these is a veritable gold mine to the Coleopterist with his umbrella.

*Sweeping.*—The use of the beating net continues profitable from spring till fall, a different set of species appearing with each season. Low and swampy meadows, meadows on the slopes of mountains or surrounded by woods, low underbrush, and herbage in smaller patches of woods are very good beating grounds. Dry and sandy meadows are less productive, but harbor usually a different set of species on account of the difference in the flora. Pastures and meadows much frequented by cattle and horses are much less productive, and where a large number of sheep are kept there is usually no chance for using the beating net, since neither grass nor specimens are left. The lawns in our parks and gardens are usually poor collecting ground on account of the limited variety of plants in such places; but the few species found there occur in enormous number of specimens. The endless stretches of our western prairies swarm at the right season (in June) with numerous Coleoptera (mostly Ma-

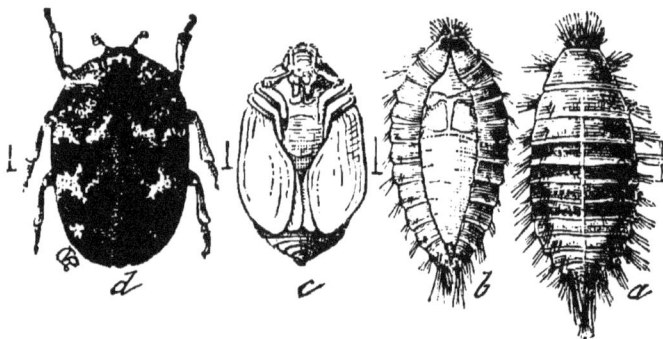

Fig. 67. A Dermestid (*Anthrenus scrophulariæ*). *a*, larva, dorsal view; *b*, larva, ventral view; *c*, pupa; *d*, adult—all enlarged.

lachiidæ, Chrysomelidæ, Mordellidæ, Curculionidæ, etc.), provided prairie fires have not swept too frequently over the place. Fires and cattle produce a remarkable change in the flora and fauna of the prairies; many indigenous species disappear or become scarce and are replaced by a much smaller number of imported species.

Sweeping may commence in the forenoon as soon as the dew has disappeared; it is less profitable in the heat of the midday, but produces the best results late in the afternoon and more especially in the short interval from just before sunset until dark. At this time many rare Pselaphidæ and Scydmænidæ, species of the genera *Colon* and *Anisotoma*, and other small Silphidæ can be beaten from the tips of grasses, all being species which can not, or only accidentally, be found during daytime, when they hide between the roots of plants.

*Collecting on mud and gravel Banks.*—The mud or gravel banks of rivers, creeks, and stagnant bodies of water are inhabited, especially early in summer, with an astonishing multitude of Coleoptera. Countless specimens of smaller Carabidæ (*Dyschirius, Clivina, Bembidium, Tachys,* etc.) and Staphylinidæ (*Tachyusa, Philonthus, Actobius, Stenus, Lathrobium, Trogophlæus* and many other genera) will be seen actively running over the mud or sand; many other specimens are hiding under the pebbles in company with other species (*Cryptohypnus, Georyssus,* etc.) or in little subterranean galleries (*Dyschirius, Bledius, Heterocerus*). All these beetles must be collected by picking them up with the fingers, an operation which, owing to the activity of the specimens, requires some little practice. The beginner will at first crush or otherwise injure many of the delicate specimens, the capture of which is moreover by no means facilitated by the rapidity with which most of them are able to take wing. The collector must necessarily kneel down and he must not mind getting covered with mud. A good device for driving these species out of their galleries or from their hiding places under stones or in cracks of the ground is to pour water over the banks, and this can in most cases be done with the hand. Larger stones and pieces of wood or bark lying on the bank are favorite hiding places of certain larger Carabidæ (*Nebria, Chlænius, Platynus,* etc.), and should of course be turned over. Finally, the moss growing on rocks and logs close to the water's edge, and in which, besides other beetles, some rare Staphylinidæ and the Byrrhid genus *Limnichus* can be found, should be scraped off and investigated on the collecting cloth or on the surface of a flat rock, if such be conveniently at hand.

*Collecting aquatic Beetles.*—The fishing for water beetles in deeper water by means of the water net has already been alluded to (p. [32]), but many species live in shallow brooks with stony or gravelly bottom, where the water net can not be used. The Dytiscidæ and Hydrophilidæ living in such places usually hide under stones, and can in most cases be easily picked up with the hand, or a little tin dipper or a spoon will be found convenient for catching them. The species of the family Parnidæ are found on the underside of rough stones or logs which are either partially or entirely submerged. They are more numerous, however, in the moss or among the roots of other plants that grow in the water. Such plants have to be pulled out and examined over the collecting cloth.

*Collecting at the Seashore and on sandy Places.*—A large number of species belonging to various families live exclusively in the vicinity of the ocean, some on the open beach, others along the inlets, bayous, or salt marshes, and still others on the dry sand dunes. The Cicindelæ are actively running or flying about close to the water's edge and have to be captured with the butterfly net. The remaining maritime species live hidden under the seaweed and other débris cast up by the waves, or in the sand (sometimes quite deep below the surface) beneath the débris or between the roots of the plants growing on the dunes. The majority of the maritime species do not appear before June (in the Middle States), but the collecting remains good until September.

In dry sandy places away from the seashore, the collecting at the roots of plants is especially to be recommended, and the plants, and more especially the bunches of coarse grasses usually growing

Fig. 68.—A Tiger Beetle (*Cicindela limbata*), drawn by Miss Sullivan—enlarged.

in such places, should be pulled up and shaken out over the collecting cloth. This mode of collecting acquires a great importance in the arid regions of the West and Southwest, where, in the warm season, nearly all Coleoptera are hiding during daytime in the ground at the roots of plants.

*Collecting Dung-beetles.*—The collecting of the numerous species (*Hydrophilidæ*, *Staphylinidæ*, *Histeridæ*, *Scarabæidæ*, etc.) which live in the droppings of various animals is by no means an agreeable task. The collector should provide himself with a pointed stick and collecting tweezers, and must manage to pick up the specimens as best he can. The larger specimens are best collected in alcohol, while the more delicate species can be collected in a cleaner condition by removing the droppings and sifting the ground beneath the same. Some species hide deep in the ground beneath the droppings and have to be dug out. Summer freshets, when

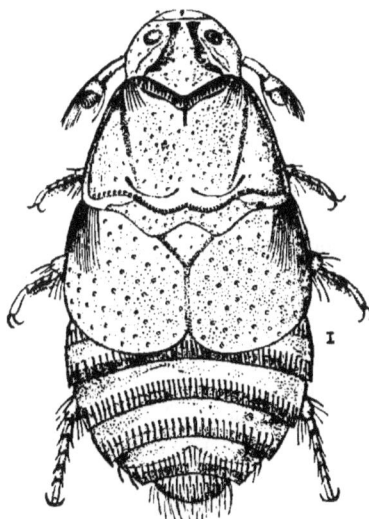

Fig. 69.—The Beaver Parasite (*Platypsyllus castoris*), adult—greatly enlarged.

pasture lands are inundated, offer an excellent opportunity for collecting the dung-inhabiting species in a clean condition.

*Night Collecting.*—The beating of trees and shrubs after dark is a good method of obtaining Lachnosternas and other species, and here the collector will do well to secure the assistance of a companion, who takes charge of the lantern and the collecting bottles, while the collector himself works the umbrella.

FALL COLLECTING.—From the first of August the number of species gradually diminishes, but late in the summer or early in fall quite a number of other species make their appearance, e. g., some Chrysomelidæ, Cerambycidæ, and many Meloidæ. Many of these frequent the blossoms of Golden-rods, umbelliferous and other late-flowering plants. The fall is also the best season for collecting Coleoptera living in fungi. Although puff-balls, toadstools, and the numerous fungi and moulds growing on old trees, etc., furnish many species of Coleoptera also earlier in the season, yet most fungi, and more especially the toadstools, flourish best in the fall, and consequently there is then the greatest abundance of certain species of Coleoptera. Decaying toadstools are especially rich, and should be sifted, and the collector should also not omit to examine the soil beneath them.

During the "Indian summer" there is usually a repetition of the "spring flight" of Coleoptera, though on a smaller scale, and collecting on the tops of fence posts and on whitewashed walls again becomes good. The first really sharp frost causes these late species to disappear, and winter collecting commences again.

## COLLECTING LEPIDOPTERA.

In this order the importance of collecting the early states and of rearing the adult insects rather than of catching the latter should, if the collector has the advancement of knowledge and the greatest pleasure in mind, be insisted upon. Collected specimens, in the majority of cases, will be more or less rubbed or damaged and unfit for permanent keeping, and will always be far inferior to freshly reared specimens. All Lepidopterists, therefore, rely to a great extent upon breeding rather than upon field collecting. There are, however, many species of which the early states are still unknown, and these can only be taken by field collecting, and by attracting to various lights or traps. This subject, therefore, naturally falls into two categories—(1) the general collecting of the adult, and (2) collecting the early stages and rearing the perfect insects.

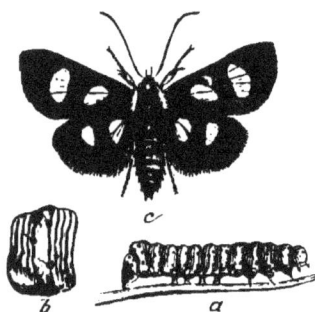

FIG. 70.—The Eight-spotted Forester (*Alypia octomaculata*). *a*, larva; *b*, enlarged segment of same; *c*, moth.

*Collecting the Adult.*—The implements for the general collecting of butterflies comprise the collecting net, and in some cases the beating net, although the use of the latter will not often be called for. The Rhopalocera or Diurnals may be taken about flowers, and the best season is in the early spring. Most of them are double-brooded, and the second brood will be in the greatest abundance during July and August. They are, however, to be found throughout the summer. They are also to be looked for in the neighborhood of the food-plants of their larvæ, and in the case of many species, examination of such plants

affords the most satisfactory means of collecting. The food of butterflies
is almost exclusively the nectar of flowers, but strangely enough they
are also attracted to decaying animal matter, and many species, including rare forms, may be taken about decaying animal matter or resting
on spots where dead animals have lain, or beneath which they have been
buried. Moist spots of earth are also frequented
by them, especially in dry seasons. Many of
the larger butterflies, whose larvæ feed on the
taller shrubs and the foliage of trees, will be
found fluttering about the open spaces in forests,
but by far the larger number, as the Browns,
the Blues, the Yellows, and the Whites, which
develop on the lower herbaceous and succulent
plants, will be found flying over fields, prairies,
and gardens. Crepuscular and nocturnal Lepidoptera, comprising most of the Heterocera,
the Sphingidæ, Bombycids, Noctuids, etc., have

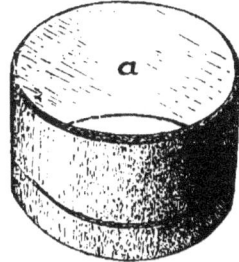

FIG. 71.—Collecting Pill-box.
a, glass bottom (original).

different habits. The Sphingidæ or Hawk Moths fly in early evening,
and may be collected in quantity about such plants as the Honeysuckle,
Thistle, Verbena, Petunia, etc. The Bombycids and many Noctuids also
fly in the early evening, but mostly at night. The former, however, do
not frequent flowers, except such as are the food-plants of their larvæ,
as their mouthparts are rudimentary, and they take no nourishment.

Collecting by the aid of strong light is a favorite means for moths
as well as other insects, and
nowadays the electric lights in
all large cities furnish the best
collecting places, and hundreds
of species may be taken in almost
any desired quantity. In woods
or in other situations they may
be attracted to a lantern or to a
light placed in an open window.
Various traps have been devised,
which comprise a lamp with apparatus for retaining and stupefying the insects attracted to the
light. The common form is made

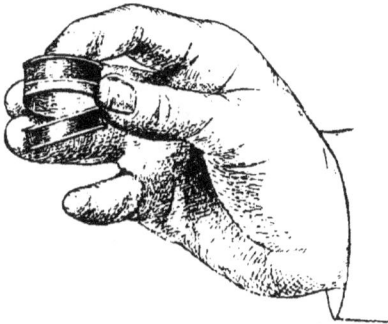

FIG. 72.—Method of holding and manipulating collecting pill-box in capturing (original).

by providing a lantern with a strong reflector. Under the light a funnel several inches larger than the lantern reaches down into a box or
bottle containing the fumes of chloroform, ether, or benzine.

Mr. Jerome McNeill describes at length and figures in the *American
Naturalist*, Vol. XXIII, p. 268–270, an insect trap to be used in connection
with electric lights. It consists of a tin pail or can charged with cyanide after the manner of a collecting bottle, which is attached beneath
the globe of the electric light.

The insects attracted by the light strike against a vertical tin screen fixed above the can and fall into a tin funnel the small end of which enters and closes the mouth of the can, and they are thus conducted into the last. A support or post in the center of the can bears a hollow tin cone, the apex of which is pierced with a number of small holes to admit light, and enters and partly closes the lower end of the funnel. The entire interior of the can is painted black and the chief light comes through the holes in the apex of the interior cone. The entrapped insects endeavor to escape by crawling up the central post towards the light coming through the small holes in the end of the cone rather than by the entrance slit about the latter and fall back repeatedly until overcome by the cyanide.

Many of the Lepidoptera will be ruined by the beetles and other insects or by their own ineffectual attempts to escape, but Coleoptera, Hymenoptera, Neuroptera, and Hemiptera are secured in satisfactory condition.

Many of the devices are very complicated and can not be described in this connection. The nocturnal species, also, fly into our houses, and this is especially the case in the country, and an open window, with a strong light reflected onto a table covered with either a white paper or a white cloth will keep one busy, on favorable nights, in properly taking care of the specimens thus attracted.

Another favorite method of collecting moths early in the evening, or as late as or later than midnight, is by sugaring. This consists in smearing a mixture of sugar and vinegar, or some similar compound, on the bark of trees or on the boards of fences, and visiting the spot from time to time to collect the moths attracted to the bait. It has been found that the use of beer or some other alcoholic liquor, as rum or brandy, with the sugar or molasses water, greatly adds to its efficiency in attracting the moths. This method of collecting moths will be found especially efficient on warm, moist, cloudy nights. The collector should be provided with a dark lantern and a good net, and a number of wide-mouthed cyanide collecting bottles. The smearing should be done just before dark, and I have always found that better success attends this method of collecting when two are engaged in it—one to hold a bull's eye lantern while the other bottles the specimens. Experience will soon teach the surest way of approaching and capturing the specimens.

For collecting Microlepidoptera, in addition to the ordinary net, some special apparatus will be found very essential. Lord Walsingham makes use of a special glass-bottomed pill-box, with which to capture specimens, and the satisfactory nature of the work done with this box, and the dexterity acquired by practice with it, I can vouch for by personal experience. These glass pill-boxes are useful, also, in admitting of the examination of specimens, so that worthless or common species can be discarded and only desired forms kept. The method of holding these boxes is illustrated in the accompanying illustrations. (Figs.

72, 73.) A drop of chloroform on the bottom of the box at once stupefies the capture so that it can be taken out and otherwise disposed of.

The necessity of rearing to obtain perfect specimens is even more
important in the case of the Microlepidoptera than with the larger forms,
and many species are very
easily reared and can thus
be obtained in quantity.
The Micros are abundant
from early spring to late fall
about shrubbery, in open
fields, and along the edges
of woods. They are, for the
most part, day fliers, being
on the wing chiefly in the
latter part of the day and
early evening. As soon as
collected they should be

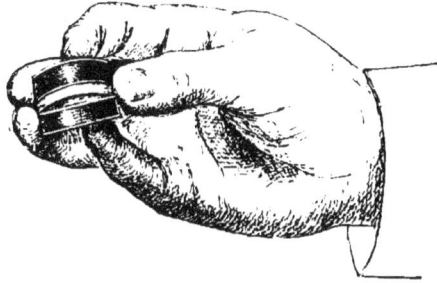

Fig. 73.—Same, showing method of closing pill-box after
the specimen is secured (original).

transferred to pill-boxes and the greatest care should be exercised to
avoid mutilating them, as the slightest touch will denude them of a
portion of their scales or break their limbs or antennae. Lord Walsingham thus gives his experience in collecting Micros:

I go out with a coat provided with large pockets inside and out, containing an
assortment of pill-boxes, generally of three sizes, glass-bottomed pill-boxes preferred,
a bag slung over my shoulder, and a net. Unless searching for particular day-flying
species, I prefer the last three hours before dark. As the sun goes down many species
move which do not stir at other times. I watch the tops of the grass, the stems of
the flowers, the twigs of the trees; I disturb leaves and low-growing plants with
a short switch and secure each little moth that moves, taking each out of the net in
a separate pill-box, selected according to the size of the insect, as he runs up the net
to escape. Transferring the full boxes to the bag I continue the process until moths
cease flying or night sets in. Many species can be taken with a lamp after dark.

*Collecting the early States.*—The careful entomologist who prides himself on the appearance of his specimens, will, as stated above, rely
largely on collecting the early states and on rearing the insects, for his
material. The Macrolepidoptera have either a single or two broods, or
more, in a season, and the collection of the early states will be greatly
facilitated if a knowledge of the insect's life-habits is first obtained.
The eggs are often found on the food plants of the species, and where
they are deposited in masses they afford a very easy method of getting
the larvae in numbers. In many cases, however, the eggs are deposited
singly and their discovery then becomes a difficult matter.

More satisfactory in some respects is the method of obtaining the eggs
from captured gravid females, and the general collector should always
be on the lookout for females of rare species from which he may be
able to obtain eggs. A single battered female may, in this way, be the
source of large numbers of excellent reared specimens. Many rare Lepidopterous larvae may be obtained by the use of the beating net and by

beating foliage over an umbrella. A very satisfactory method consists in collecting pupæ, which may frequently be found in numbers about the bases of the trees on which the larvæ feed. Many larvæ of the large family of Owlet Moths (*Noctuidæ*) are found either on the surface of the ground or under various substances, while others burrow into the stems of the different herbaceous plants, some being subaquatic and feeding on the underside of leaves or in the stems of aquatic plants. In the case of Microlepidoptera, their habit as larvæ, of mining leaves or tying or webbing them together, affords an easy means of detecting their presence in most cases. The miners are easily noticed by the discolored spots on the leaves or the wavy, pale, or brown lines marking their burrows. The presence of others is indicated by the leaves being drawn together and united with webs, or withered and brown from being skeletonized by the larvæ. Many species are case-bearers, and live upon the leaves and branches of trees and plants, dragging their cases along with them. Others burrow in grasses or in the stems of plants or the trunks of trees, or in fungi. In the case of the leaf-miners and leaf-tiers, little difficulty is experienced in rearing the imagoes.

The care of the larvæ, the outfit required, and the methods of breeding will be described in later sections.

COLLECTING HEMIPTERA.

For the most part the directions for collecting Coleoptera will apply to this order of insects equally well, especially so far as concerns the first section of the order (Heteroptera), and the higher families of the second section (Homoptera). A few directions may be given for the lower forms, including the Aphididae, Coccidae, Aleurodidae, and Psyllidae, and the suborder Parasita, including the degraded forms which infest man and the lower animals. The Plant-lice or Aphides should always be collected in connection with their food-plants, and it is very essential also to collect the same species at different seasons of the year to obtain the different forms or generations, which frequently present very marked differences. It is also very necessary to secure the winged forms, which are usually produced toward autumn, and without which the species are not easily identified. The Bark-lice or Scale-insects should also be collected in connection with the leaves or twigs which they infest. The males of these insects are minute and, as a rule, two-winged, resembling small gnats, and may be bred from the male scales. The females are for

FIG. 74.—A Pentatomid (*Stiretrus anchoraga*).

FIG. 75. The Blood-sucking Cone-nose (*Conorhinus sanguisuga*). *a*, mature bug; *b*, pupa.

the most part stationary. being fixed to the plant by the protecting, waxy, excretion or scale. The Flea-lice (*Psyllidæ*) frequently produce galls, and these should always be collected with the insect architects.

Some species do not produce galls, and may be collected by sweeping. The Hackberry is infested by large numbers of species of Psyllids, and these produce a great variety of interesting galls. The Aleurodidæ (Fringe-scales) are delicate insects, and easily injured in the taking; they are therefore best reared from their stationary and fringed larvæ and pupæ, which occur on the leaves of many plants.

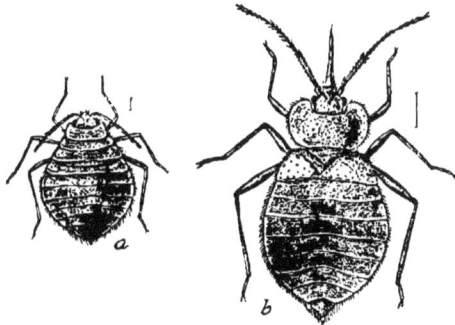

Fig. 76.—The Bed-bug (*Acanthia lectularia*). *a*, young; *b*, adult—enlarged.

Leaves bearing the latter should also be collected and pinned or preserved in alcohol. The Parasita, the

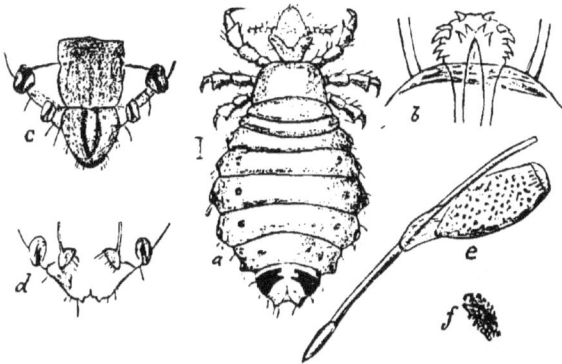

Fig. 77. The Short-nosed Ox-louse (*Hæmatopinus eurysternus*). *a*, female; *b*, rostrum; *c*, ventral surface, last segments of male; *d*, female; *e*, egg; *f*, surface of egg greatly enlarged.

lowest representatives of the order, may be obtained from the domestic and wild animals which they infest.

## COLLECTING DIPTERA.

Most Diptera frequent flowers and may be collected with a sweeping net without much difficulty. The best season is from April to June, and the bloom of the Willow, Alder, Plum, Cherry, Dogwood, Black berry, etc., will ordinarily yield a bountiful supply of specimens and species. Parasitic and saprophytic forms may also readily be obtained by breeding, the former as in the case of the parasitic Hymenoptera, and the latter from decaying vegetable matter and fungi. The Diptera require the most delicate treatment, and the greatest care must be exercised both in collecting and handling. A light sweep net is the best implement for collecting and the contents of the net should frequently be emptied into bottles provided with blotting paper to absorb the excess of moisture. Very small Diptera should not be killed when they can not be immediately pinned, and hairy flies should never be taken from the net with the hand, but should be handled with fine forceps. A pair of special collecting shears has been used by Lord Walsingham very successfully. It is represented in the accompanying figure, and consists of a pair of screen covered disks, between which the fly is caught. The insect is at once pinned through the screen and may be removed and transferred to a box containing a sponge soaked in chloroform. The use of this implement is especially advisable in the case of the Bee-flies (*Bombiliidæ*) and other hairy forms which are liable to be rubbed when

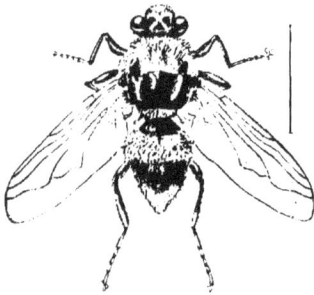

FIG. 78. Ox Bot-fly (*Hypoderma boris*) enlarged. (After Brauer.)

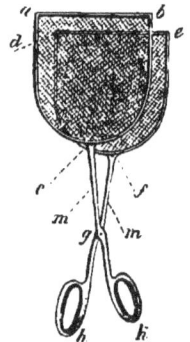

FIG. 79.—The Collecting Shears. (After Kiesenwetter.)

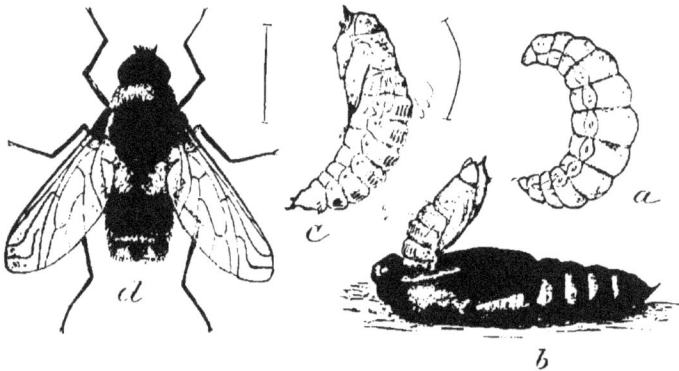

FIG. 80.—A Bee-fly (*Anthrax hypomelas*). *a*, larva from side; *b*, pupal skin protruding from cutworm chrysalis; *c*, pupa; *d*, imago—all enlarged).

collected in the ordinary net. The Gall-making Diptera (*Cecidomyidæ*) are of little value unless accompanied with their galls, and the aim should always be to collect the galls and rear the insects rather than the keeping of specimens taken in the course of general collecting with a sweep net. The rearing of Cecidomyidæ is, however, a delicate task, and requires considerable experience. Some knowledge of the habits

of the species is very essential to success. From immature galls no
rearings need be expected. A good plan is to examine the galls from
time to time and collect them when it is found
that the larvæ are beginning to abandon them.
In the case of species like the common Cone Gall-
gnat of the Willow, the larvæ of which do not
leave the gall to undergo transformation in the
earth, it is advisable not to gather the galls
until the transformation to the pupa state takes
place, which, in this species, occurs in early
spring. The various leaf-mining and seed inhabiting species can be
treated as in the case of the Microlepidoptera.

FIG. 81.—A Syrphus-fly.

## COLLECTING ORTHOPTERA.

The insects of this order may all be collected by the use of the sweeping net. Some of the families are attracted to light, as certain of the
roaches and green locusts, or Katydids (*Locustidæ*). Our common
roaches (*Blattidæ*) are cosmopolitan insects, and infest dwellings.
Certain species are also found about ponds, under rotten logs, the bark of
trees, and particularly in decaying vegetable matter. In the tropics the
species are very abundant, but aside from the domestic forms, they
occur rarely in northern latitudes. The collection of the egg-cases
(oötheca) is important as they furnish many interesting characters.
The Mantidæ, of which the Preying Mantis *(Phasmomantis carolina)* is

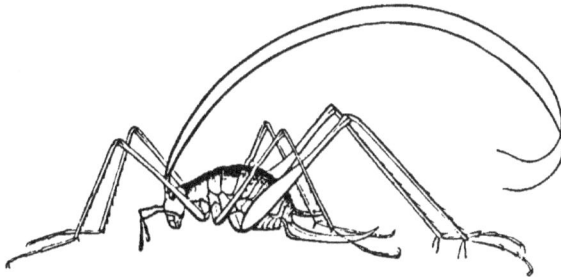

FIG. 82.—A blind Cricket (*Hadenœcus*) from Mammoth Cave. (From Packard.)

a type, are sluggish, carnivorous insects frequently found about houses
and may best be collected by general sweeping of vegetation. The
Phasmidæ or Walking-sticks are herbivorous and may be collected in the
m'dst of vegetation by sweeping or by the hand. The crickets (*Gryl-
lidæ*) frequent, for the most part, moist situations. Certain forms, like
the Mole-cricket and the Jumping Water-crickets (*Tridactylus* spp.).
burrow in moist soil and occur in numbers near the edges of ponds and
water courses. The katydids and locusts are abundant on low shrubs
or trees and in pasture and meadow land, but are most numerous in
the somewhat dry, arid regions of the West. Most of these insects

mature in late summer and fall and should be collected at this season. The Forficulidæ or Earwigs are very odd looking insects, resembling somewhat the Rove-beetles (*Staphilinidæ*), and are provided with a prominent anal forceps. They are very rare in the United States, are nocturnal in habit; and, flying about at dusk, may be attracted to light or may be secured by sweeping after nightfall. They feed on flowers and fruit.

### COLLECTING NEUROPTERA.

As indicated in the preliminary outline of classification, this large order has been divided into many orders by later entomologists. It has also been divided, as indicated, into two grand divisions, the Pseudo-neuroptera, comprising those insects with incomplete transformations, and the Neuroptera proper, comprising those insects whose metamorphoses are complete. It will be convenient to discuss these insects under these two heads.

*Pseudoneuroptera.*—Spring-tails, Bird-lice, Stone-flies, White-ants, Dragon-flies, May-flies.

The Spring-tails, Fish-moths, etc., representing the primitive stock from which the higher forms have developed, have a varied habit and hence are to be found in divers situations. The Spring-tails (*Collembola*, etc.), occur in damp and moist places, usually in immense numbers. The Fish-moths and Book-mites are common household pests, but also occur outdoors under logs, boards, bricks, and rubbish of all sorts. In houses they feed on the starch paste beneath wall-paper and also on the starch in bookbindings and other domestic articles. They may be collected at all seasons and a sieve is the only implement necessary.

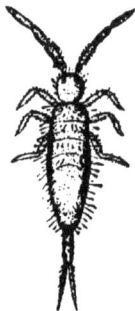

Fig. 83. A Spring-tail (*Degeeria lanuginosa*).

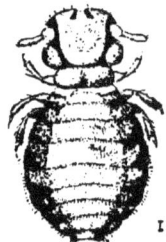

Fig. 84.—A Mallophagan (*Trichodectes latus*). (After Denny.)

The Bird-lice or Mallophaga may be collected at all seasons on birds and mammals. A number of species infest domestic animals, horses, cattle, etc., but the majority of them can be found only by the examination of domestic fowls and wild birds. The Stone-flies (*Perlidæ*) are found in the neighborhood of water courses and ponds, are very sluggish in flight, and easily captured with the sweep-net. They are also attracted to light. The Psocidæ are a small family of certain degraded wingless forms, comprising the Book-lice, which, as the name implies, infest books, feeding on the starch of the binding. Others have ample wings and closely resemble large Aphides. They occur on the trunks of trees and on foliage, and feed on lichens and other dried vegetable matter. They are gregarious in habit and frequently occur in immense numbers together. In the case of the Termitidæ or White-ants, their abundance renders their collection an easy matter. Effort, however, should be made to discover the different forms, the females and soldiers as well as the workers. The former may be found in rotten tree trunks, but are very rarely met with. In the tropics many species occur and construct curious nests, either attaching them to the boughs of trees or building them in the form of pyramids on the ground. The Dragon-flies (*Libellulidæ*,) are collected in the same way as the Diurnal Lepidoptera. They are very swift flyers, and are practically always on the wing. Their collection requires some degree of skill in the use of the net. A good method consists in visiting, in the early morning, water courses in which the larval and pupal states are passed, and capturing the adults just as they issue from their pupal skins at the edges of the pond or stream. In cold weather they are less active and may frequently be found clinging to trees and plants, particularly in the vicinity of their breeding places. May-flies (*Ephemeridæ*) occur in immense numbers near their breeding places in ponds and streams and

Fig. 85.—*b*, a May-fly (*Palingenia bilineata*); *c*, its larva: *a*, a Caddis-fly (*Macronema zebratum*).

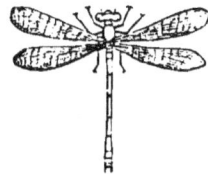

Fig. 86.—A Dragon-fly (*Libellula*). (From Packard.)

are also attracted in large quantities to electric lights. Their collection is therefore an easy matter, but on account of the very fragile nature of these insects the utmost care must be employed in handling them. The early states of all the aquatic forms mentioned above may be obtained for breeding by the use of the dip net by dragging it forcibly against water plants.

*Neuroptera proper* (Hellgrammites, Lace-wings, Ant-lions, Caddis-flies, etc.)—Among the largest insects of this order are the Sialidæ, which includes the enormous Hellgrammite Fly, *Corydalus cornutus*. The larvæ of this insect are carnivorous and occur in streams, under stones, etc. The adults may be collected in neighboring situations and are also attracted to light. The Lace-wing flies (*Chrysopa*), Ant-lions, etc., are carnivorous as larvæ, and occur, the former among the Aphides which infest various plants and the latter

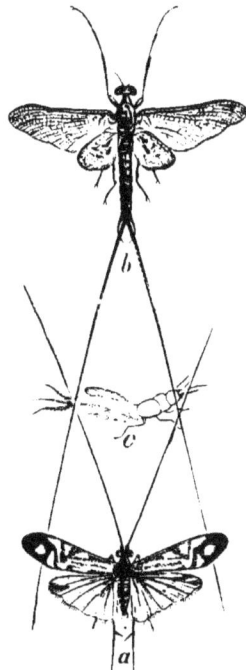

Fig. 87.—A Dragon-fly (*Agrion*). (From Packard.)

at the bottom of pits in loose, sandy soil. The adults may be obtained by general sweeping and are also attracted to light. The most interesting insects of this order are the Caddis-flies, on account of the peculiar and frequently very beautiful cases constructed by their larvæ, which it is important to collect. The Caddis-flies breed in ponds and lakes and the adults may be collected in such situations or at light. The larvæ may easily be reared, and should be collected for this purpose. Most of the insects named in this order are extremely delicate and require great care in handling.

FIG. 88.— An Ant-lion, adult (*Myrmeleon*). (From Packard.)

## KILLING AND PRESERVING INSECTS.

Between the collecting of the specimens and their final disposition in a well-arranged cabinet, a good deal of mechanical work is necessary, involving a skill and dexterity which can be thoroughly acquired only by practice.

FIRST PRESERVATION OF LIVING SPECIMENS.—Larvæ, pupæ, or imagoes, intended for rearing purposes, must be kept alive, and are best placed, after capture, in tin boxes of various sizes, according to the number of specimens to be put in each and according to the size or nature of the food plant, etc., on or in which the specimens are found, and of which a quantity must always be taken home. For larger tin boxes those known as "Seidlitz powder boxes," described and figured below, which can be made to order at any tinner's shop, are well adapted, and smaller tin boxes of a convenient round form can be obtained of the watchmaker. The collector will find it advisable to take with him on his longer jaunts a larger tin collecting box as well as the smaller boxes, and for this purpose nothing is better than a good botanist's collecting can or vasculum. All tin boxes used for entomological purposes should be tight, and the cover should so fit that it neither drops off too readily nor closes too tightly. Larvæ of Lepidoptera and Tenthredinidæ should be placed in a box with a quantity of the leaves of the plant on which they were found. Larvæ, especially of Coleoptera, found in the earth or in decayed wood, should be placed in a box filled with such earth or wood, so as to prevent shaking or rattling about. Larvæ found in roots or stems of living plants can generally be reared to maturity only if the whole plant with a quantity of the surrounding soil is taken home, and for this purpose the large collecting box, just mentioned, is very useful. Most Coleopterous or other larvæ found under bark or in solid wood can be reared only if large sections of the wood are obtained and the larvæ are full grown or nearly so. This holds true, also, of species breeding in seeds and with most leaf-mining species. The greatest difficulty is experienced with carnivorous Coleopterous larvæ, and care should be taken with such not to inclose two or more specimens in one box. Most larvæ die quickly if placed in an empty box, and this is especially true of predaceous species; so that it is always advisable to pack the box with moist soil, decaying wood, leaves or other similar substance. Aquatic larvæ should be carried in tin boxes filled with wet moss or some water plant, for, if placed in corked vials with water, they die quickly.

KILLING SPECIMENS.—Specimens not intended for rearing should be killed immediately after capture unless for each specimen a separate vial or box can be provided. If a number of miscellaneous insects are put in the same vial the stronger specimens will, in a short time, crush or otherwise injure the more delicate ones or the predaceous species will devour any others they can master. But even where the specimens are killed immediately the following rule should be observed: Do not put large and small specimens in the same vial, but provide a larger bottle for the larger specimens, and one, or still better, several, smaller vials for the medium-sized and very small specimens. The importance of this rule is recognized by all experienced collectors.

There are several methods of killing insects, each having its own peculiar advantages and drawbacks.

*Alcohol.*—The use of alcohol will, on the whole, prove the most satisfactory method of killing Coleoptera, many Hemiptera, some Neuroptera, and larvæ of all sorts. Only the best quality of alcohol should be used, but it should be diluted with from 30 to 40 per cent of pure water, the greatest care being taken to keep the alcohol as clean as possible. During the collecting a mass of débris and dirt is apt to be thrown into the bottle, and when this is the case the alcohol should be changed even during short excursions. At any rate, upon the return from the excursion, the specimens should be at once taken from the bottle and washed in pure alcohol in a shallow vessel. The larvæ and other material intended for permanent preservation in alcohol should be transferred to suitable vials and the material to be mounted cleansed with chloroform or acetic ether and then prepared for the cabinet. If it is inconvenient or impossible to mount the Coleoptera, etc., soon after the return from the excursion they should be washed, dried, and placed in pill boxes between layers of soft paper, or they may be replaced in a vial with pure alcohol. On longer collecting trips, lasting several days or weeks, specimens will keep thus very well, provided they are not shaken up, and this can be prevented by filling the empty space in the vial with cotton or soft paper. If the bottle is a large one and contains many large specimens the alcohol should be renewed three or four times at intervals of eight or ten days; otherwise the specimens are liable to decompose. Small and delicate specimens, if they are to be kept in alcohol, should be treated with still greater care. Upon the return from the excursion they should also be cleaned in pure alcohol and placed in small vials into which a very few drops of alcohol, just sufficient to keep the contents moist, are poured. The vial should be corked as tightly as possible and the specimens will keep pretty well for an indefinite time.

The drawbacks to the use of alcohol are: 1st, that all hairy specimens are liable to spoil; 2udly, that all Coleoptera with soft integuments spread the wing-cases apart if kept too long in it. The advantage of the alcohol is that it is the simplest and least troublesome fluid for naturalists traveling in distant countries who are not specialists in entomology. Specimens killed in alcohol are also less liable to be attacked by verdigris when pinned than those killed by some other method. Rum, whisky, or similar strong alcoholic liquors may be used as substitutes where no pure alcohol can be obtained, but are not especially to be recommended.

*Chloroform and Ether.*—Killing with the fumes of *chloroform* or *ether* (sulphuric or acetic) or *benzine*, or some other etheric oil, is often practiced and advocated by those who, for any reason, dislike the use of alcohol or object, on account of its poisonous nature, to the use of cyanide of potassium, and they are of especial value in the case of butterflies and moths, Hymenoptera and Diptera. "A small and stout bottle of chloroform or ether, with a brush securely inserted into the cork (Fig. 89), will be found very serviceable. A slight moistening through the air net will stupefy most insects caught in it, and facilitate their removal to the cyanide bottle; while a touch or two with the wet brush under the head and thorax, will kill the more delicate specimens outright, without in the least injuring them. Another way of using chloroform is by means of a small, hollow tube passed through the cork, what is called jeweler's hollow wire answering the purpose. The liquid evaporates more readily in such a bottle, and

FIG. 89.—Chloroform bottle with brush.

I altogether prefer the first mentioned. Some large insects, and especially female moths, whose size prevents the use of the ordinary cyanide bottles, are difficult to kill. With these, fluttering may be prevented by the use of chloroform, or they may be killed by puncturing the thorax or piercing the body longitudinally, with a needle dipped in liquid cyanide, or oxalic acid. A long bottle with a needle thrust into the cork may be kept for this purpose; but the needle must be of ivory or bone, as those of metal are corroded and eaten by the liquids. * * *

"For killing small and delicate moths which have been bred, I find nothing more handy than chloroform. They may be caught in turned wooden boxes which are kept by every druggist; and a touch of the chloroform on the outside of the box immediately stupefies them. It has a tendency to stiffen them, however, and they are best set immediately after death."

A piece of heavy blotting paper or heavy cloth soaked with chloroform or ether or benzine and placed at the bottom of a jar or bottle makes an excellent killing bottle for large-sized insects. For smaller specimens the collecting vial should be half filled loosely with narrow strips of soft paper, upon which a few drops of the liquid are poured, not so much, however, as to wet the paper. While collecting, the vial must be kept closed as much as possible. Some collectors prefer chloroform, others ether. If this method of killing is practiced with the necessary care, there

FIG. 90.— Bottle with liquid cyanide.

is no objection whatever to it: the specimens are not wetted as they are in alcohol, and remain cleaner than those killed by any other method. The drawback is that the substances mentioned evaporate very rapidly and have to be renewed even on short excursions. On account of this great volatility, one can never be certain that all the specimens in the collecting bottle are dead after a given time and there is always some danger that one or the other of the hardier insects may regain activity. What mischief such revived specimens are capable of doing, many collectors have experienced to their sorrow. Another disadvantage of these volatile substances is that if used in too large quantities they will, in delicate specimens, especially beetles, cause an extension of the soft ligaments between the head and prothorax or between the latter and the mesothorax, and thus bring the specimen into an unnatural position, or cause the head, or head and thorax to drop off.

FIG. 91.—The Cyanide bottle with paper strips to give support to the insects.

*Cyanide of Potassium.*—The method of killing which, of late years, has found most favor with collectors, is the use of cyanide of potassium. For killing large sized specimens they are simply put in what is now universally known as the "cyanide bottle." This may be constructed as follows:

Take a 2-ounce quinine bottle, or still better a shorter bottle with a wide mouth; break up a quantity of cyanide of potassium into pieces of convenient size (about a cubic centimeter); put these pieces in the bottle so that they form an even layer at the bottom; mix in a convenient vessel a quantity of plaster of Paris with water just sufficient to make the mixture semifluid and then pour it over the cyanide so as to cover this last to a depth of about 5 millimeters. The bottle is then left open for an hour or two until the plaster is thoroughly dry. The walls of the bottle are then cleansed from particles of the plaster which may have splashed on them, and the bottle is ready for use. If not used too frequently, especially in warm weather, it will last for an entire year or longer. Bottles or vials of different sizes can be prepared in the same way, and a very small cyanide vial which can be carried in the vest pocket will be found most convenient for use on all occasions. Fig. 92 represents a medium-sized chemist's test tube, converted into a very convenient cyanide bottle, in which, however, a cotton wad has been used to keep the poison in place. When the collected specimens have been removed from the bottle the latter should be carefully wiped clean with a piece of cloth or paper. The surface of the plaster soon becomes dirty and, on account of the hygroscopic property of the cyanide, more or less moist, especially during warm weather. The cyanide bottle is, therefore, not well adapted for the killing and temporary preservation of small and delicate specimens. This difficulty can be altogether obviated by placing a circular piece of blotting paper, cut to neatly fit the interior of the bottle, on the surface of the plaster. This can be

FIG. 92.—Pocket cyanide bottle.

renewed once a week or so, or oftener if it becomes necessary. It will frequently be advisable, also, especially in the collection of Diptera, Hymenoptera, and other delicate insects, to put a strip of blotting paper partially round the inner side of the bottle. This will absorb any moisture which may gather on the inside of the bottle and which would otherwise wet and injure the specimens. The accompanying figure (Fig. 93) illustrates a bottle arranged as described above. A similar result is attained by some collectors by partially filling the bottle with narrow strips of bibulous paper to support and separate the insects as shown at Fig. 91.

For delicate specimens, also, the collecting bottle may consist of a test-tube of about the size of Fig. 92. This is half filled with loose, thin strips of soft white paper. A piece of cyanide about the size of a pea is then wrapped carefully in paper and so placed in the middle of the strips that it can not come in contact with the sides of the glass.

Some prefer to pin the paper containing the cyanide to the lower surface of the cork. The latter should be rather short and tapering toward its lower end. It is longitudinally perforated through its center by a round hole just large enough to insert a goose-quill, which is cut straight at the lower end and obliquely at its upper end. By means of this goose-quill the specimens may be introduced into the bottle without taking off the cork. This form of cyanide bottle lasts for only one day's collecting, except in cold weather, and in very warm weather it is advisable to take two prepared bottles along, so that the first used can be stowed away as soon as the cyanide begins to moisten the paper strips. Most insects are quickly killed in such a bottle, but some Coleoptera must be left in for five or six hours, while others resist death for a still longer time. This is especially true of the Coleopterous families Curculionidæ, Trogositidæ, and Tenebrionidæ.

Submersion in alcohol will prove a satisfactory method of killing these or other beetles with similar vitality.

*Other Agents.*—Prof. E. W. Claypole has found the use of benzine or gasoline very cheap and satisfactory for killing Lepidoptera, as the largest are at once killed thereby without injury to their scales. (*Can. Ent.*, XIX, p. 136.) He squirts it onto the specimen within the net or in the open air by means of a druggist's dropping tube.

Fig. 95.—The cyanide bottle with blotting-paper lining (original).

Hot water kills rapidly and leaves the specimens in good flexible condition for mounting. The heads of large insects may be held for a few moments in the water, while smaller specimens should first be thrown into a corked bottle and the bottle submitted to heat. Where the laurel grows its bruised leaves may be used in place of cyanide; they kill less quickly. The leaves of the Laurel-cherry (*Prunus laurocerasus*), a plant commonly grown in England for screens and hedges, are also used for this purpose.

Some collectors, with indifferent olfactory sense, moisten the cork of their boxes with creosote. Its killing power lasts for several days. A few whiffs from a cigar, when nothing else is at hand, will also kill many of the more tender insects.

SPECIAL DIRECTIONS FOR DIFFERENT ORDERS.—A few brief directions for the special treatment of different orders may be given. Certain Coleoptera, notably those of the Curculionid genus Lixus, are covered with a yellowish pruinosity resembling pollen, which is of an evanescent nature, so that if the specimens are collected and killed by the ordinary methods, the pruinosity is completely lost. To preserve the natural beauty of such species it is necessary to put each specimen alive in a small vial and to kill it at once by means of a lighted match held under the vial for a few seconds. In pinning or otherwise mounting the specimen it should not be handled between the fingers.

Many Hymenoptera and Lepidoptera, especially species with yellow markings, if kept for any length of time in a cyanide bottle, will become discolored, the yellow changing to reddish, and hence such insects should not be left longer than necessary in the bottle. If care is exercised in this respect, no danger of discoloration need ordinarily be feared. The chloroform collecting bottle may be used with these insects if discoloration is anticipated. All the more delicate insects, including Hymenoptera, Diptera, the smaller Lepidoptera, and the Neuroptera, require special care in killing. Large numbers should not be thrown into a killing bottle together, and plenty of bibulous paper should be kept in the bottle to prevent moisture from accumulating and wetting and ruining the specimens. It is frequently advisable to pin Diptera, especially the hairy forms (as the Bee-flies), in the net and transfer them at once to a cigar box containing a sponge moistened with chloroform. When the collecting shears are used, the insects are always thus pinned at once, which is, in fact, the only method of securing them. This is also necessary in the case of many Lepidoptera. Delicate Neuroptera may be killed by the use of the cyanide bottle, or, preferably, placed at once in a vial of alcohol, as these insects, in many instances, cannot be kept securely if pinned or mounted. Large Lepidoptera, as the Bombycids, may be killed by pouring benzine, naphtha, or chloroform over the thorax and abdomen. These substances evaporate rapidly and do not appreciably injure the vestiture of the insects. Some collectors, in the case of butterflies, seize them dexterously between the thumb and finger, and give a sharp pinch on the sides of the thorax. This will prevent the fluttering of the insect when transferred to the cyanide bottle, and, if carefully done, the scales need not be rubbed off. It is objectionable, however, because the thorax is distorted and subsequent anatomical study interfered with, and, in the case of moths, should never be practiced, as the thorax affords important characters used in classification. Orthoptera may be killed by the use of the cyanide bottle but should be transferred at once to the vials of alcohol. If placed in a cyanide bottle, especially in the case of Locusts (Acrididæ), they are apt to exude colored juices from the mouth, so that the specimens become soiled. Hence the use of vials of alcohol is preferable, and these insects should never be thrown into vials containing delicate insects of other orders. Plant-lice, together with the plant which they infest, should be placed at once in vials of alcohol, and specimens of the Aphides, representing all the forms present, should be mounted on slides for microscopic examination. The fixed forms of Coccids, comprising the majority of the species, require no special treatment, and the leaves, twigs, or bark on which they occur may be pinned at once and placed in the collection. The free forms are treated as in the case of plant-lice.

## ENTOMOTAXY.

Under this term may be considered the preparation of insects for the cabinet.

### CARE OF PINNED AND MOUNTED SPECIMENS.

*Insect Pins.*—In mounting insects for the cabinet, expressly made entomological pins should be used. These come from three different sources: Kläger pins, made by Hermann Kläger, Berlin, Germany; Karlsbad pins, made by one or several firms in Karlsbad, Bohemia, Austria; and Vienna pins, made by Miller, Vienna, Austria.* These three kinds of pins have each their own slight advantages and disadvantages, so that it is difficult to say which is the best. All have the disadvantage that the pinned specimens are liable to be ruined by verdigris, and to obviate this japanned ("black") insect pins are made by Kläger and Miller. These black pins are, however, much softer than the "white" pins, and therefore more difficult to handle. A pin of 35 millimeters in length will be found most convenient for pinning all insects excepting the larger Lepidoptera and other heavy-bodied insects, for which a longer pin may advantageously be used. According to the different degrees of fineness, the pins are numbered from No. 00 (the finest in the trade) to No. 7 or 8, but the numbers used by the different manufacturers do not correspond with each other. In experience, pins of Nos. 1, 2, 3, and 4 (Kläger numbers) are more often needed than the others. The long pins of the finer numbers (Nos. 0 and 00) are difficult to handle in the collection and, for this reason, not to be recommended.

For many small insects, especially Microlepidoptera and Microdiptera, which *must* be pinned, even the finest ordinary insect-pins are too large, and two special makes of pins are in use for this purpose. The "elbow pin" (formerly made and sold by Dr. Kuenow, of Königsberg, Prussia, Germany) consists of a piece of fine silver wire, pointed at one end, and with a coil loop at the other end, into which a longer pin (No. 3 or No. 4) is thrust. This pin is illustrated in Fig. 94. Still more satisfactory are the "Minutien-Nadeln" (pins for minute insects) manufactured by Mr. Miller, of Vienna, Austria, and which consist of a straight piece (about 14ᵐᵐ. long) of extremely fine steel wire which is pointed at

---

* In North America, Kläger pins and Karlsbad pins can be obtained through Mr. John Ackhurst, 78 Ashland Place, Brooklyn, N. Y., and possibly also through Messrs. Blake & Co., 55 North Seventh street, Philadelphia, Pa. The Vienna pins and the Minutien-Nadeln have to be ordered direct through the manufacturer, Mr. Miller.

one end, and which is used in connection with a piece of pith or cork. The mode of using this pin is shown in Fig. 101. These fine and elbow pins may be obtained either "white" or japanned.

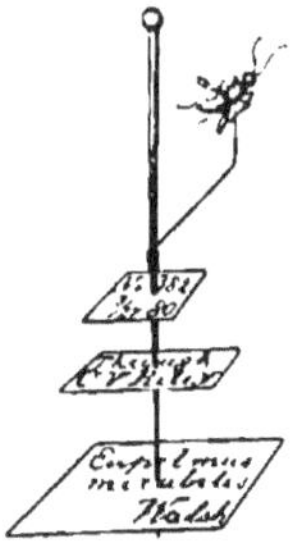

"Many English entomologists use short pins, very much like those of ordinary make, and my late friend Walsh never gave up the custom, and most vehemently opposed the use of what he ridiculed as 'long German skewers.' But the only advantage that can possibly be claimed for the short pins is that they are less apt to bend, consequently more easily stuck into the bottoms of boxes, and require less room; while, compared with the long pins, they have numerous disadvantages.

Long pins admit of the very important advantage of attaching notes and labels to the specimen; render it more secure from injury when handled, and from museum pests in the cabinet; and on them several rows of carded duplicates may be fastened, one under the other, so as to economize room."

I have seen few old collections in better condition than that of the late E. Mulsant, of Lyons, France; and he used iron wire, cut slantingly, of the requisite length—a common custom in France. These wires bend so easily and have such dull points that they require much more careful manipulation than the pins, and the claim made for them that they do not verdigris would, perhaps, be offset by their rusting in moist climates or near the sea. Silver wire or silver-plated wire is also used.

*Preparation of Specimens.*—Upon the return from an excursion the specimens should be prepared for the collection as soon as practicable. If they have been collected in the forenoon they should be mounted the same evening, and those collected during an afternoon or evening excursion should be mounted the following morning, or, at any rate, before they get dry and brittle. Even specimens collected in alcohol should be attended to as soon as possible.

Specimens are taken from the collecting bottle, spread out on a sheet of white blotting paper and cleaned from adhering impurities either with a soft dry brush, or, in the case of species with hard covering, by washing them with chloroform or ether or benzine where necessary. Theoretically the best way of mounting would be to pin all specimens, since the under side with its important characters then remains free for examination. Pins adapted for pinning even the smallest insects have been described above, but this pinning is such a delicate operation and requires so much time that considering the large number of small specimens that may be collected on a single short excursion it is next to impossible to carry out this method, and therefore only the larger specimens need be pinned and the smaller may be glued onto the paper points described later. If the work is done with proper

FIG. 94.—Insect mounted on "elbow-pin."

care all insects can be prepared for the cabinet so that both the upper and under surface of the specimen may be examined without further manipulation.

*Pinning.*—"Insects should be pinned through the middle of the thorax, when, as is more generally the case, this portion (the mesothorax) is largely developed. Beetles (*Coleoptera*) and Bugs (*Hemiptera*), should, however, be pinned, the former through the right elytron or wing-cover (Fig. 95), and the latter through the scutel or triangular piece behind the thorax, the pin issuing between the middle and hind legs (Fig. 96). The specimens look very pretty with all the legs neatly spread out, but for practical purposes it is better to let them dry in the natural, partly bent position. It is a saving of time and space, and the limbs are not so apt to break. The legs

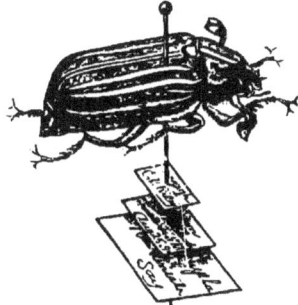

FIG. 95.—Method of pinning and labeling Coleoptera (original).

must also not reach too far downward or they will interfere with the proper labeling and the secure pinning of the specimen in the cabinet. Moreover, the antennae and legs must be brought into such position that they will not obstruct the view of any important part of the under-surface. The pin should always project about half an inch above the insect to facilitate handling, and uniformity in this regard will have much to do with the neat appearance of the collection. In pinning very large and heavy insects on a No. 4 or No. 5 pin, it is a good plan to first flatten the pin by a few blows of a hammer, in order to prevent the specimen from subsequently turning round on the pin."

FIG. 96.—Method of pinning Hemiptera (original).

In pinning specimens which have a flat or nearly flat undersurface and short legs (as in many Coleoptera and Hemiptera and some Hymenoptera. *e. g.* the Saw-flies) the specimens are laid on a piece of cork and held in place there with the fingers or with a forceps. The pin is then pushed through the insect at the proper point, care being taken not to strike one of the legs or coxae, and that the pin passes through the specimen in a vertical direction.

After the pin has been pushed through the specimen it is taken out of the cork and the specimen is pushed up to its proper height. This can be done either by holding the specimen between the fingers or by placing it on the upper edge of a thick book. A piece of cardboard provided with a small hole may also be used for this purpose. The perforations in ordinary sheet-cork, or the lapel of one's coat, will answer the same purpose. In pinning Lepidoptera or Hymenoptera the specimen should lie lightly in the angle formed by the thumb and first two fingers of the left hand and the pin be carefully thrust through at the proper angle. In pinning all insects the pin should be so inserted that the insect is nearly at right angles with the pin, the posterior end being slightly depressed.

*Mounting on Points.*—Most insects which are too small to be pinned on a No. 2 pin may be fastened to cardboard by means of gum tragacanth, gum shellac, or any good glue. It is not always easy to determine whether to pin a medium specimen or to glue it to a triangle. Pinned specimens are more secure, and not so apt to fall or be knocked off, but they are liable to become corroded by verdigris and ultimately lost, especially in families the larvæ of which are endophytous or internal feeders. It is better to glue wherever there is doubt. A drop of corrosive sublimate added to the water in which the gum tragacanth is dissolved will indefinitely prevent its souring, but should not be used where the gum is to come in contact with the pin, as it inclines the latter to verdigris. In such cases a little spirits of camphor mixed with the gum tragacanth is best. Shellac should be dissolved in alcohol and this requires some time. This glue is not affected by moisture, and if it is desired to remove the specimens, they must be immersed in alcohol until the shellac is again dissolved.

A number of different kinds of glue are used by entomologists. The requirements of a good glue are that it be colorless, and, what is of greater importance, that the specimens adhere firmly to the paper points so that there is little or no danger of their being jarred off. Those glues which are readily soluble in cold or lukewarm water are perhaps more convenient than those which require alcohol or chloroform for dissolving. Gum arabic and gum tragacanth have the disadvantage that they are more liable to attract mites and are more brittle, so that they do not hold specimens as well as some of the liquid glues that are on the market. Spalding's glue answers a very good purpose, as also the preparation known to European entomologists as Leprieur's gum. White bleached shellac, while requiring alcohol to dissolve it, has the advantage that a very minute quantity suffices. In olden times the method employed was simply to glue the specimen by the ventral side to the middle of a quadrangular piece of cardboard, which was then pinned on a No. 3 or No. 4 insect pin. This method is still in vogue with English entomologists, but can not be recommended except for mounting duplicates. Much better are the small isosceles triangles which, before mounting the specimen, are pinned through near the base on a No. 2 or No. 3 insect pin. Only the best and finest cardboard should be used for this purpose, since that of poor quality is liable to be broken while passing the pin through it and will yellow with age. "Reynolds's Superfine Board," which may be ordered through any dealer in artist's supplies of Devoe & Co., Fulton street, New York City, is perhaps the best for this purpose. Some of the neatest mounting which I have had done by any of my agents or assistants is by Mr.

Albert Koebele, who has used mica or gelatine instead of cardboard, the object being not only to show the whole of the under side of the specimen, but to obscure less of the light from the labels and to render the triangles less conspicuous in the cabinet. These have been in use in the museum collection only for the last two or three years, and whether they will eventually tend to corrode the pins is not yet settled. Mica and isinglass are also used for the same purpose. The points used in mounting may easily be cut by hand to a convenient size, say one-fourth of an inch (6–8$^{mm}$) long by one-sixteenth or less at the base, and tapering to a point. The point may be narrower or wider to accommodate insects of different sizes.

For cutting these triangles or points, various forms of punches similar to the appended figure (Fig. 97) known to the trade as conductor's punches may be used, and points thus cut are to be preferred to those made by other means, on account of the greater uniformity secured.

An experienced hand, however, will cut these points very rapidly and accurately with a pair of shears, and most collectors use no special instrument for this purpose.

The punches mentioned may be obtained of the manufacturers* of such instruments at from $2 to $3. Care should be observed in ordering to state explicitly the length, width at base and point, or, what is better, to inclose sample of the size of point it is desired to cut; but above all, to state that the block of paper to be cut out is the result desired, and that the instrument should cut clean and even, with no ragged edges.

For mounting different forms and sizes the fastidious collector uses four or five sizes of points, but for all practical purposes one to cut a card point not less than 1.3$^{mm}$ at the base and prolonged as nearly as possible to a point, and another

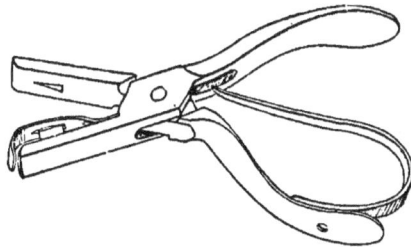

FIG. 97.—Insect punch for cutting triangles or points (original).

a trifle wider at the base, say 1½ or 1$\frac{3}{4}$$^{mm}$ and with a point about 1½$^{mm}$ in width will suffice.

For mounting most long-bodied insects, e. g., Staphylinidæ and Elateridæ, an oblong card say 1½$^{mm}$ in width is

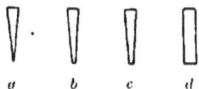

FIG. 98.—Points for mounting insects (original).

desirable. With a little care these may be cut with sufficient uniformity with scissors. Seven and one-half millimeters may be taken as a standard of length, as this is about the size used by the majority of our best collectors.

Shorter points, say 6$^{mm}$ or one-quarter inch long, are sometimes preferred, where economy of space is a desideratum.

*Montgomery & Co., 105 Fulton street, New York City.

A series of four points of different sizes for mounting insects is shown in the accompanying illustration. The sharp-pointed one, *a*, is designed for the minutest forms and the larger points for large insects. The largest should be mounted on points of a nearly rectangular shape, shown at *d*. The dimensions of these points as adopted by most entomologists, are as follows:—

| | Length. | Breadth. | Point. |
|---|---|---|---|
| *a* ..... | 7.5 mm. | 1.5 mm. | .0 mm. |
| *b* ..... | 7.5 | 1.5 | .4 |
| *c* ...... | 7.5 | 1.5 | .6 |
| *d* ..... | 7.5 | 1.6 | 1.6 |

The point or triangle should be mounted on the pin and directed to the left, the height from the top of the pin varying somewhat with the specimen, but averaging about one-half an inch. The insect is then glued to the point with the head pointed forward. In the case of Coleoptera and Hymenoptera, and in fact of most insects, the specimen is mounted with the back uppermost, but in the case of the smaller Hymenoptera it is advisable to mount some of the specimens, at least, on the left side (see Fig. 99). This directs the legs toward the pin, as a matter of safety, prevents their being broken in handling, and also gives opportunity for subsequent examination of the back, side, and venter of the specimen. Coleopterists always mount speci-

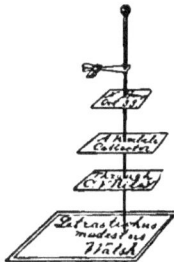

FIG. 99.—Insect mounted on cardboard triangle.

mens on the venter, and in the case of a correctly mounted specimen the whole underside of the body should be available for examination except the right half of the metasternum, as shown in figure 100.

In mounting minute insects a few precautions are necessary. The beginner usually uses too much glue or shell-lac, and the result is that the mounted specimens are more or less covered with the fluid, so as to render them unfit for examination. If, on the other hand, too little of the glue is used, the specimens are not securely fastened to the paper point, and are liable to be jolted off by the slightest jar. Before mounting specimens the legs and antennæ must be brought into the proper position by means of a brush or with a dissecting needle, so that they may easily be seen. A supply of paper points should always be at hand, and after selecting one of the proper size for the specimen, with an acute

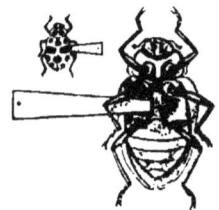

FIG. 100.—Method of gluing beetle on paper point (original).

tip for a very small specimen and with a more obtuse point for a larger one, a small quantity of glue is applied to the tip by means of a pointed stick, such as a toothpick, the amount varying with the size of the specimen. The tip of a moistened brush may be used to transfer the specimen to the point, or one will soon become dextrous enough to do this without the aid of the brush. The specimens are then allowed to dry in a horizontally placed box. If the drying box is placed in a vertical position the specimens, especially long-bodied ones, are liable to topple over before the glue has become firm.

Delicate flies and Microlepidoptera, which it will not do to fasten with mucilage, may first be mounted on the fine pins described above and these thrust into oblong or triangular bits of pith or cork, which are mounted on larger pins as shown in Figures 101 and 102. This affords a very satisfactory method of mounting, particularly as the different sexes may be brought together on the same bit of pith, or the adult and puparium in Diptera, as shown at Figure 101. Strips of stout cardboard with the pins run through the narrow edge may also be used. The method of mounting minute Hymenoptera and Diptera and other insects on a bent wire, men-

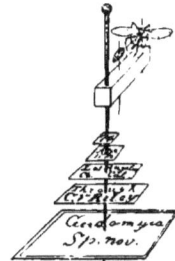

FIG. 101.—Cecidomyiid mounted on pith (original).

tioned above, is illustrated at Figure 94. This method has not proved so satisfactory, as the wires are apt to become loose on the pin.

*Mounting Duplicates.*—If the collector finds more specimens of a rare species than he cares to have in his collection, the excess may be mounted as duplicates. If the species happens to be of a large size the specimens are pinned in the ordinary way, but if small enough to be gummed,

FIG. 102.—Microlepidoptera mounted on pith (original).

there is a most convenient method of rapidly mounting the specimens so that they may be sent through the mail with much less risk of getting broken or knocked off than if glued on paper points, and will also take up very little room in the duplicate boxes. It consists in gluing the specimens in a transverse row on a strip of white card paper with one of the glues soluble in water, care being taken that between the individual specimens some space be left, and further that the heads and antennæ do not project beyond the edge of the paper. The width of the paper strip must be somewhat

FIG. 103.—Method of mounting duplicates (original).

greater than the length of the specimen, so that below the latter there is sufficient room for inserting a pin through the paper. After the glue has become dry the row of specimens is cut with scissors into several smaller rows of convenient size, so that on each of these rows there are two or three or more specimens, according to the size of the species. A locality label is pushed high up on a No. 3 or No. 4 pin, and one of the mounted rows of specimens is then pinned and pushed up

near the locality label; a second row is then pinned and pushed near the first row, and the same process continued with the third row and so on. A single pin will thus bear five or six rows, and in giving away or sending away specimens the lowest row is taken from the pin and repinned for mailing. The accompanying figure (Fig. 103) illustrates the mounting of a moderate-sized species in rows of two specimens each. This method of mounting duplicates may be adopted not only for Coleoptera, but also for Heteroptera, Homoptera (excepting Aphididae and allied families), smaller Orthoptera, and Hymenoptera. It is, however, impracticable for Lepidoptera, Diptera, and most Neuroptera.

*Temporary Storage of Specimens.*—If the entomologist is prevented from mounting his captures soon after returning from an expedition, or if, on extended collecting trips, time does not offer for this purpose, specimens of almost all orders except the Lepidoptera, Orthoptera, and Neuroptera may be placed in a small, tightly closing pill box, care being taken to keep the larger specimens apart from the small ones. In this way specimens will keep for an indefinite period, provided they are properly packed. In the case of the traveling collector, where the material is to be carried from point to point at great risk of breaking, specimens should be packed very carefully to prevent any shaking or rattling about in the boxes. This may be done by placing a round piece of soft paper on the top of the specimens in the pill box. This paper should be gently pressed down and the empty space above filled with other layers of paper or with cotton. The packing of specimens between cotton is not recommended, as it is a difficult and tedious task to afterwards free them from the adhering fibers. Layers of soft paper or, yet better, velvet, are preferable.

*Envelopes for Lepidoptera, etc.*—On an extended trip, it will be found impracticable to mount and prepare insects requiring cumbersome apparatus for spreading, as Lepidoptera or Neuroptera, and a very excellent plan consists in folding the wings of the insect so that the lower surfaces come together and then placing it in a triangular envelope, as shown in the accompanying illustration. The collector should be provided with a quantity of paper of the requisite dimensions for making these envelopes, and specimens, as they are taken from the collecting bottle, may be rapidly inclosed in them, labeled, and packed away in a tight wooden (not tin) box containing a supply of naphthaline, the specimens thus occupying the minimum

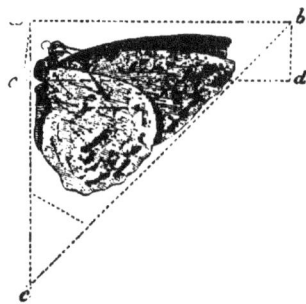

FIG. 104.—Method of preserving Diurnal Lepidoptera in paper envelopes. (After Kiesenvetter.)

of space. Specimens secured in this way may be kept without further manipulation indefinitely or until time is found to relax and set them.

This is also an excellent method of sending diurnal Lepidoptera and Dragon-flies through the mails and is preferable in some respects to mailing spread specimens.

*Directions for Spreading Insects.*—"For the proper spreading of insects with broad and flattened wings, such as butterflies and moths, a spreading board or stretcher is necessary. One that is simple and answers every purpose is shown at Fig. 105. It may be made of two pieces of thin whitewood or pine board, fastened together by braces at the ends. but left wide enough apart to admit the bodies of the insects to be spread; strips of cork or pith, in which to fasten the pins, may then be tacked or glued below so as to cover the intervening space. The braces must be deep enough to prevent the pins from touching anything the stretcher may be laid on, and by attaching a ring or loop to one of them the stretcher may be hung against a wall,

Fig. 105. Spreading board for Lepidoptera.

out of the way. For ordinary-sized specimens I use boards 2 feet long, 3 inches wide, and ⅜ inch thick, with three braces (one in the middle and one at each end) 1½ inches deep at the ends, but narrowing from each end to 1¼ inches at the middle. This slight rising from the middle is to counteract the tendency of the wings, however well dried, to drop a little after the insect is placed in the cabinet. The wings are held in position by means of strips of paper (Fig. 105) until dry. For stretching the wings and for many other purposes, a handled needle will be found useful. Split off, with the grain, a piece of pine wood 3 or 4 inches long; hold it in the right hand; take a medium-sized needle in the left hand; hold it upright with the point touching a walnut table, or other hard-grained wood, and bring a steady pressure to bear on the pine. The head of the needle will sink to any required distance into the pine, which may then be whittled off, and you have just the thing you want (Fig. 106). To obtain uniformity in the position of the wings, a good rule is to have the inner margins of the front wings as nearly as possible on a straight line. When the specimens are thoroughly stiff and dry, they should be taken

Fig. 106. Needle for spreading insects.

from the stretcher and kept for several weeks in the drying box before being permanently placed in the cabinet. The drying box is simply a box of any required dimensions, containing a series of shelves on which to pin the specimens, and without a solid back or front. The back is covered on the inside with fine gauze and on the outside with coarser wire, and the door in front consists of a close-fitting frame of the same material, the object being to allow free passage of air, but at the same time to keep out dust and prevent the gnawings of mice and other animals. The shelves should be not less than 2 inches deep, and if made in the form of a quadrangular frame, braced with two cross-pieces on which to tack sheet cork, they will serve for the double purpose of drying spread specimens and for the spreading of others, as there are many insects with long legs which are more conveniently spread on such a board, by means of triangular pieces of stiff cardboard braces or 'saddles,' than on the stretcher already described. Two of these braces are fixed on the setting board, by means of stout pins, at sufficient distances apart to receive the body between them. The wings are then spread upon them and kept in place until dry by means of additional braces. In the case of bees, wasps, etc., the pin may be thrust well into the cork or pith so that the wings may be arranged in the proper position and braced and supported by strips of stout cardboard. This method is especially recommended in the case of the Fossorial wasps, the legs of which, if mounted in an ordinary spreading board, can not be properly arranged.

In spreading Lepidoptera I have used, in the place of a number of paper strips pinned across the wings, blocks of glass of various sizes to hold the wings in position. My method of mounting, with a large amount of material on hand to be attended to, consists in pinning a row on the spreading-board and fixing the wings in position with spreading needles, fastening them with a single narrow strip of paper placed next the body. The entire spreading-board is filled with specimens in this way, a single long strip of paper on either side answering to keep the wings of all the specimens in position. Then, instead of pinning additional strips to hold the wings flat and securely in position, the pieces of glass referred to are used, placing them on the wings of the insect. With the use of glass the spreading-board must always be kept in a horizontal position and must never be disturbed. The advantage of the glass is that the wings can be seen through it and more truly adjusted.

Spreading-boards may be made as described above, or it may be of advantage, when a good deal of work is to be done, to adopt a somewhat different method. Five or six spreading-boards may be made together, forming a sort of shelf. A number of these shelves may be constructed and the whole combined in a case with a screen cover to exclude insects. The individual shelves may be arranged with grooves to slide on tongues in the side of the case. A screen covered case for spreading-boards is always desirable, as the insects are otherwise very liable to be eaten by roaches or other insects. A spreading-case of the form described is shown at Fig. 107.

*A new Apparatus for Spreading Microlepidoptera.*—For the spreading of Microlepidoptera my assistant, Mr. Theo. Pergande, has devised an apparatus, represented in the accompanying illustration, which he finds very convenient. It consists of a small spreading-block represented at

*B* and the support with attachment shown at *A*. The former is made in a long strip of the shape shown in the illustration, having a square groove, *c*, cut in the top. Over this is glued a thin strip of wood, *b*, say $\frac{1}{8}$ inch thick, and a narrow slit is sawed in the center of this above, cutting through into the groove *c*. This is then sawed up into pieces of uniform length, say $1\frac{1}{2}$ to 2 inches, and the block is completed by the insertion of a rectangular

Fig. 107.—Spreading-case (original).

strip of pith or cork into the groove. The Micro is pinned on a short black pin, and the pin is thrust down into the narrow opening made by the saw and is held firmly by the pith or cork. This block is then slid into the groove in the setting-board *A*, which narrows slightly from *c*, and pushed along until firmly secured (*d*). The operator can then rest his hands and arms on either side of the support, and, if necessary, bring a large hand lens over the object by means of a support with ball-and-socket joint shown at *e*. The wings may thus be easily and accurately arranged and fixed in position with pins or strips of paper, as in the ordinary mounting of such insects. Two or three specimens may be mounted on each of these blocks. The construction of the support is indicated in the annexed drawing. One side is attached by clamps, shown enlarged at *f*, which afford means of adjusting the width of the slit in which the small sawed blocks slide and correct the shrinking or swelling which may take place in moist or dry seasons. The advantage of the apparatus is that the operator has the setting block firmly fixed before

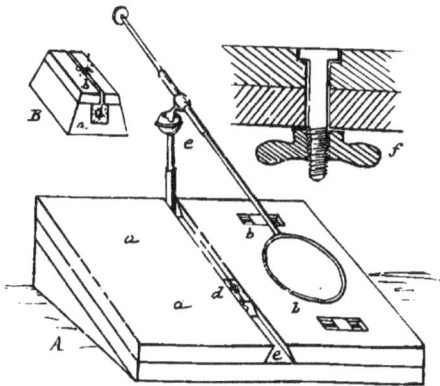

Fig. 108.—Spreading apparatus for Microlepidoptera (original).

him and has both hands free to manipulate the wings of the insect in addition to having the lens in a convenient position, the use of which is necessary in the preparation of the very minute forms.

*Spreading Microlepidoptera.*—The mounting of Microlepidoptera is about the most delicate work in entomotaxy, and I can not do better than quote the explicit directions given by Lord Walsingham on the subject.

Returning to camp I put a few drops of liquid ammonia on a small piece of sponge and place it in a tin canister with such of the boxes as do not contain the smallest species, and put these and the remainder away until morning in a cool place. In the morning I prepare for work by getting out a pair of scissors, a pair of forceps, my drying-box containing setting-boards, a sheet of white paper, and some pins.

First, I cut two or three narrow pieces of paper from 3 to 6 lines wide, or rather wider, according to the size of the largest and smallest specimens I have to set. I then double each of these strips and cut it up into braces by a number of oblique cuts. Now I turn out the contents of the canister and damp the sponge with a few drops of fresh ammonia, refilling with boxes containing live insects. Those which have been taken out will be found to be all dead and in a beautifully relaxed condition for setting. Had the smallest specimens been placed in the canister over night there would have been some fear of their drying up, owing to the small amount of moisture in their bodies.

If the weather is very hot there is some danger of killed insects becoming stiff while others are being set, in which case it is better to pin at once into a damp cork box all that have been taken out of the canister, but under ordinary circumstances I prefer to pin them one by one as I set them.

Taking the lid off a box, and taking the box between the finger and thumb of the right hand, I roll out the insect on the top of the left thumb, supporting it with the top of the forefinger and so manipulating it as to bring the head pointing toward my right hand and the thorax uppermost. Now I take a pin in the right hand and resting the first joint of the middle finger of the right against the projecting point of the middle finger of the left hand to avoid unsteadiness, I pin the insect obliquely through the thickest part of the thorax, so that the head of the pin leans very slightly forward over the head of the insect. After passing the pin far enough through to bring about one-fourth of an inch out below,[*] I pin the insect into the middle of the groove of a setting board so that the edge of the groove will just support the under sides of the wings close up to the body when they are raised upon it. The board should be chosen of such a size as will permit of the extension of the wings nearly to its outer edge. The position of the pin should still be slanting a little forward. The wings should now be raised into the position in which they are intended to rest, with especial care in doing so not to remove any scales from the surface or cilia of the wings. Each wing should be fastened with a brace long enough to extend across both, the braces being pinned at the thick end, so that the head of the pin slopes away from the point of the brace; this causes the braces to press more firmly down on the wing when fixed. The insect should be braced thus: The two braces next the body should have the points upwards, the two outer ones pointing downwards and slightly inwards towards the body, and covering the main portion of the wings beyond the middle. Antennæ should be carefully laid back above the wings, and braces should lie flat, exercising an even pressure at all points of their surface. The fore wings should slope slightly forwards so that a line drawn from the point of one to the point of the other will just miss the head and palpi. The hind wings should be close up, leaving no intervening space, but just showing the upper angle of the wing evenly on each side. I can give no more precise directions as to how this desirable result may most simply and speedily be attained; no two people set alike. Speed is an object; for I have often had to set twelve dozen insects before breakfast. A simple process is essential, for a man who is always pinning and moving pins, and rearranging wings and legs, is sure to remove a certain number of scales and spoil the appearance of the insect, besides utterly destroy-

---

[*] This applies to the use of short pins, which should subsequently be connected through strips of pith with longer pins. For some of the larger micros the long pins may be used directly and a different spreading board employed.

ing its value. I raise each of the fore wings with a pin, and fix the pin against the inner margin so as to keep them in position while I apply the braces. Half the battle is really in the pinning. When an insect is pinned through the exact center of the thorax, with the pin properly sloped forward, the body appears to fall naturally into its position on the setting board, and the muscles of the wings being left free are easily directed and secured; but if the pin is not put exactly in the middle it interferes with the play of the wings. Legs must be placed close against the body or they will project and interfere with the set of the wings. Practice, care, and a steady hand will succeed. When all the insects that have been killed are set the contents of the canister will be found again ready, twenty minutes being amply sufficient to expose to the fumes of ammonia. Very bright green or pale pink insects should be killed by some other process, say chloroform, as ammonia will affect their colors.

Insects should be left on the setting boards a full week to dry; then the braces may be carefully removed and they may be transferred to the store box.

In my own experience I have found that a touch or two of the chloroform brush on the pill-box containing small moths is sufficient to either kill or so asphyxiate them that they can easily be mounted. I have also found that strips of corn pith or even of soft cork, with grooves cut into them, are very handy for the pinning and spreading, and that by means of a small, broad-tipped, and pliable forceps the smallest specimens can be deftly arranged in the groove and kept in place until pinned. In fact, for all persons who have not very great experience and dexterity this method is perhaps more to be recommended than that of holding them between the thumb and fingers. Where chloroform is used either to kill or deaden specimens, it is important that after they are once spread and in the drying box they should be subjected to an additional asphyxiation, as the larger species may revive and are apt to pull away from the holding strips, and thus rub off their scales.

Microlepidoptera, together with Microhymenoptera and Diptera may be conveniently pinned on fine, short pins, and these thrust into an oblong bit of cork or pith. This form of mounting has already been described and is represented in figure 102. The neatest mounting of Microlepidoptera which I have seen is the work of my assistant, Mr. Albert Koebele, who mounts these insects on an oblong strip of pith. This is very light and presents no difficulty in pinning. The strips may be made of considerable length and both sexes may be pinned on the same block (see Fig. 103). Most Lepidoptera present on the under surface an entirely different aspect from that on the upper surface, and, in such cases, it is a good plan to mount a number of specimens obversely.

*Relaxing.*—It will frequently be desirable to re-spread insects which have been incorrectly mounted, or to spread specimens which have been collected and stored in papers, or pinned and allowed to dry without being prepared for the cabinet. Such specimens may be relaxed by placing them in a tight tin vessel half filled with moist sand to which a little carbolic acid has been added to prevent molding. Small specimens will be sufficiently relaxed to spread in twenty four hours. Larger specimens require from two to three days. More rapid relaxing may be caused by the use of steam, and a flat piece of cork with the specimens laid or pinned thereon and floated on the top of hot water in a closed vessel constitutes an excellent relaxing arrangement.

*Inflation of the Larvæ of Lepidoptera.*—The larvæ of Lepidoptera preserved in alcohol are excellent for anatomical and general study, but are not very suitable for use in economic displays. This means of preservation also has the disadvantage of not generally preserving the natural color and appearance of the specimens. These objections may be avoided, however, by the dry method of preserving larvæ, viz. by blowing or inflation. The process may be described as follows: The larva may be operated upon alive, but should preferably be first killed by dipping in chloroform or alcohol, or in the cyanide bottle. It is then placed on a piece of blotting paper and the alimentary canal caused to protrude from one-eighth to one-fourth of an inch, by rolling a pencil over the larva from the head to the posterior extremity. The protruding tip is then severed with a sharp knife or pair of dissecting scissors, and the contents of the abdomen are forced out by passing a pencil, as before, a number of times over the larva. Great care should be exercised in expressing the fluids not to press the pencil too strongly against the larva or to continue the operation too long, as this will, especially in delicate larvæ, remove the pigment from the skin, and the specimen when dried will show discolored spots and be more or less distorted. The larva should be moved from place to place on the blotting paper during the operation, so as not to become soiled by its own juices. A straw, or a glass tube drawn to a point at the tip, is then inserted in the protruding portion of the alimentary canal. If a straw is used the larva may be fastened to it by thrusting a pin through the wall of the canal and the straw. In the case of the glass tube the alimentary canal can be caused to adhere by drying for a few minutes and this operation may be hastened and the fastening made more secure by touching the point of union with a drop of glue. The straw or glass tube is then attached to a small rubber bag, previously inflated with air, the ordinary dentist's or chemist's gas bag answering admirably for this purpose. The larva is now ready for drying, and for this purpose a drying oven is required into which it is thrust and manipulated by turning it from side to side, to keep it in proper shape and dry it uniformly until the moisture has been thoroughly expelled. An apparatus which I have found very convenient for this purpose is represented at Fig. 109. It consists of a tin box with mica or glass slides. *c*, to allow the larva to be constantly in sight. It has also a hinged top, *b*, which may be kept closed or partly open, or entirely open, as may be necessary, during the operation. The ends of the box are prolonged downward about 5 inches, forming supports for it. *g*. Beneath it is placed an alcohol lamp, *f*, which furnishes the heat. In the end of the box is a circular opening, *d*, for the introduction of the larva, and this may be entirely or partly closed by a sliding door, *a*. It will be found of advantage to line the bottom of the box (inside) with a brass screen of very fine mesh to distribute and equalize the heat. This apparatus can be very easily made by any tinsmith and will answer every purpose.

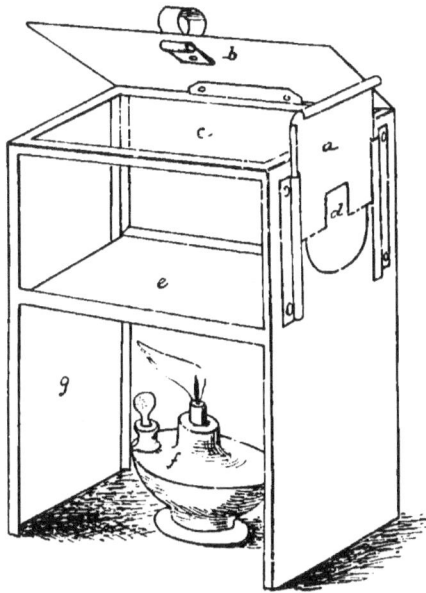

Fig. 103.—Drying oven for the inflation of larva (original).

The larvæ of Microlepidoptera or young larvæ may be dried without expressing the body contents, and will keep, to a great extent, their normal shape and appearance. The method consists in placing them on a sand bath, heated by an alcohol lamp. The vapor generated by the heat in the larvæ inflates them and keeps the skin taut until the juices are entirely evaporated. They may then be glued at once to cardboard and pinned in the cases.

In the mounting of large inflated larvæ I have adopted the plan of supporting them on covered copper wire of a size varying with the size of the larva. A pin is first thrust through a square bit of cork and the wire brought tightly about it and wrapped once or twice, compressing the cork and giving a firm attachment to the pin. The wire is then neatly bent to form a diamond-shaped loop about one-sixth of an inch in length and again twisted loosely to the end—the length of the twisted portion about equalling that of the larva to be mounted. This is then either thrust into the blown skin of the larva through the anal opening, the larva being glued to the wire by the posterior extremity, or the larva is glued to the wire by the abdominal legs and venter, thus resting on the wire as on a twig. This style of mounting is illustrated in Pl. I. With a little experience the operator will soon be able to inflate the most delicate larvæ and also the very hairy forms, as for instance *Orgyia leucostigma*, without the least injury, so that the natural colors and appearance will be preserved.

Another very good method, and still safer, is to blow with straw, cut the straw square off at the anus, and then preserve the thoroughly dried and blown specimen in a glass tube of about the same length and diameter as the larva. This arrangement in conjunction with the tube holder, which will be described further on, is one of the most satisfactory for the preservation of inflated larvæ.

For the biological-display collection, larvæ may be blown in various natural positions, to be subsequently fastened on leaf or twig or in burrows which they have occupied. Fastened to artificial foliage in which nature is imitated as much as possible, such blown larvæ are quite effective.

*Stuffing Insects.*—Large larvæ may sometimes be satisfactorily preserved for exhibition purposes by stuffing them with cotton. The method consists simply in making a small slit with the dissecting scissors or a short scalpel between the abdominal prolegs, and removing the body contents. Powdered arsenic or some other preservative should be put in the body of the larva with the cotton used in stuffing it, and the slit closed by a few stitches, when the larva may be dried and mounted on a twig or leaf. This method of stuffing with cotton is also applicable in the case of certain large-bodied insects which, if mounted and put away without preparation, would be liable to decompose, as, for instance, the larger moths, grasshoppers, etc. A slit can be made in the center of the abdomen or near the anus beneath, and the body contents removed and replaced with cotton. Stuffing in this way with cotton is of especial advantage in the case of certain of the large endophytous insects which grease badly. The cut will not be noticed after the insect has dried, or it may be closed by a stitch or two.

*Dry Preservation of Aphides and other soft-bodied Insects.*—Difficulty has always been experienced in preserving soft-bodied insects, particularly Aphides, in a condition serviceable for subsequent scientific study. Kept in alcohol or other antiseptic fluid, they almost invariable lose much of their normal appearance, and many of the important characteristics, especially of color, are obscured or lost. The balsam mount is also unsatisfactory in many respects, as the body is always more or less distorted and little can be relied upon except the venation and the jointed appendages. A method of preserving soft-bodied insects by means of the sudden application of intense heat was communicated to the *Entomologische Nachrichten*, Vol. IV, page 155, by Herr D. H. R. von Schlechtendal. It is claimed for this method that the Aphides and other soft-bodied insects can be satisfactorily preserved in form and coloring, the success of the method being vouched for by a number of well-known German entomologists, Kaltenbach, Giebel, Taschenberg, Mayr, and Rudow. A condensed translation of the method employed by Schlechtendal is given by J. W. Douglas in the *Entomologists' Monthly Magazine* for December, 1878, which I quote:

The heat is derived from the flame of a spirit or petroleum lamp. Above this is placed a piece of sheet-tin, and over this the roasting proceeds. A bulging lamp cylinder, laid horizontally, serves as a roasting oven. In this the insect to be dried, when prepared as directed, and stuck on a piece of pith, is to be held over the flame; or the cylinder may be closed at the lower end with a cork, which should extend far inwards, and on this the insect should be fastened; the latter mode being preferable because the heat is more concentrated, and one hand is left free. The mode of procedure varies according to the nature of the objects to be treated. For the class of larger objects, such as Hemiptera, Cicadina, and Orthoptera, in their young stages of existence, the heat must not be slight, but a little practice shows the proper temperature required. If the heat be insufficient, a drying up instead of a natural distention ensues. The insect to be roasted is to be pierced by a piece of silver wire on the under side of the thorax, but it is not to be inserted so far as to damage the upper side, and the wire should then be carried through a disk of pith, placed beneath the insect, on which the legs should be set out in the desired position. But with some objects, such, for instance, as a young *Strachia*, the drying proceeds very quickly, so that if distention be not observed then the heat is too great, for the expansion of the air inside will force off the head with a loud report; also, with softer, thicker Pentatomidæ care must be taken to begin with a heat only so strong that the internal juices do not boil, for in such case the preparation would be spoiled. It is of advantage to remove the cylinder from time to time, and test, by means of a lens, if a contraction of the skin has taken place on any part; if so, the roasting is to be continued. The desired hardness may be tested with a bristle or wire.

For *Aphides* the *living Aphis* is to be put on a piece of white paper, and at the moment when it is in the desired position it is to be held over the flame, and in an instant it will be dead and will retain the attitude. Then put it, still on the paper, into the oven; or, still better, hold it over the heated tin, carefully watching the drying and moving the paper about in order to prevent it getting singed. The roasting is quickly accomplished in either way, but somewhat slower out of the oven especially in the larger kinds, such as Lachnus. If the paper turn brown it is a sure sign that caution is requisite. To pierce these brittle preparations for preservation is hazardous, and it is a better way to mount them with gum on card, placing some examples on their back.

For Cecidomyidæ, Agromyzidæ, Cynipidæ, and other small insects liable to shrink, yet containing but little moisture, such as Poduridæ, Pediculidæ, Psyllidæ, etc., another method is adopted. Over the insect, mounted on a wire, etc., as above directed, a thin chemical reagent glass or glass rod, heated strongly at one end, is held, and the heat involved is generally sufficient to bring about the immediate drying and distention, but if the heat be too little the process must be repeated; and, although by this method the danger of burning is not obviated, yet the position of the legs is maintained much better than by the aforesaid roasting.

Larvæ of all kinds, up to the size of that of *Astynomus ædilis*, even when they have long been kept in spirits, may be treated successfully by the roasting method; but with these objects care must be taken that the heat is not too strong or else the form will be distorted. For small larvæ it is preferable to use a short glass, in order better to effect their removal without touching the upper part, which becomes covered with steam, and contact with which would cause the destruction of the preparation. Larvæ of Coleoptera, which contain much moisture or have a mucous surface, must be on a bed of paper or pith in order to prevent adhesion and burning, and these may be further avoided if the cylinder be slightly shaken during the process, and the position of the object be thereby changed.

Many Aphides and Coccids are covered with a waxy secretion which interferes very materially with their easy examination. Mr. Howard has overcome this difficulty by the following treatment:

"With Aphides and Coccids which are covered with an abundant waxy secretion which can not be readily brushed away, we have adopted the plan of melting the wax. We place the insect on a bit of platinum foil and pass it once over the flame of the alcohol lamp. The wax melts at a surprisingly low temperature and leaves the insect perfectly clean for study. This method is particularly of use in the removal of the waxy cocoon of the pupæ of male Coccidæ, and is quicker and more thorough

than the use of any of the chemical wax solvents which we have tried."
(*Insect Life*, I, p. 152.)

*Mounting Specimens for the Microscope.*—The study of the minuter forms of insect life, including Parasites, Thysanura, Mallophaga, the newly hatched of most insects, etc., requires the use of the microscope, and some little knowledge of the essentials of preparing and mounting specimens is needed. The subject of mounting the different organs of insects and the preparation for histological study of the soft parts of insects opens up the immense field of microscopy, the use of the innumerable mounting media, the special treatment of the objects to be mounted, staining, section-cutting, and many other like topics, a full description of which is altogether out of place in the present work. Anyone desiring to become thoroughly versed in the subject should consult some of the larger manuals for the microscopist, of which there are many. For the practical working entomologist, however, a knowledge of all these methods and processes is not essential, and in my long experience I have found that mounting in Canada balsam will answer for almost every purpose. The softer-bodied forms will shrink more or less in this substance, and it is frequently necessary to make studies or drawings of them when freshly mounted; or, if additional specimens are preserved in alcohol, they will supplement the mounted specimens and the material may be worked up at the convenience of the student. The materials for the balsam mounts may be obtained of any dealer in microscopical supplies. They consist of glass slides, 3 inches by 1 inch, thin cover-glasses of different dimensions, and the prepared balsam. The balsam is put up very conveniently for use in tin tubes. A sufficient quantity is pressed out on the center of the glass slide, which has previously been made thoroughly clean and dry, the insect is removed from the alcohol, and when the excess of liquor has been removed with bibulous paper, it is placed in the balsam, the limbs and antennæ being arranged as desired by the use of fine mounting-needles. A cover-glass, also made thoroughly clean and dry, is then placed over the specimen and pressed gently until the balsam entirely fills the space between the cover and the glass slide. The slide should then be properly labeled with a number referring to the notes on the insect, preferably placed on the upper edge of the slide above the cover-glass, and also a label giving the number of the slide and the number of the slide box. On the opposite end of the slide may be placed the label giving the name of the specimen mounted and the date. If a revolving slide table is employed to center the mounts, the appearance of the slide may be improved by adding a circle of asphalt or Brunswick black. With the balsam mounts, however, this sealing is not necessary. The slide (Fig. 110) should then be placed in a slide case with the mount uppermost, and should be kept in a horizontal position to prevent sliding of the cover-glass and specimen until the balsam is thoroughly dried. For storing slides I have found very convenient the box shown at Fig.

111. It is constructed of strong pasteboard and is arranged for holding twenty-six slides. The cover bears numbers from 1 to 26, opposite which the name of each insect mounted, or the label on the slide, may

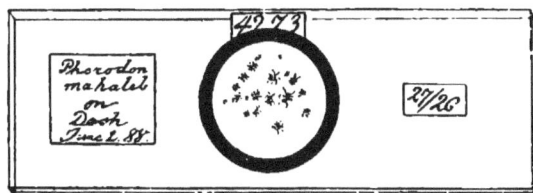

FIG. 110.—Balsam mount, showing method of labeling, etc. (original).

be written. This box when not in use is kept in a pasteboard case, on which may be placed the number of the box. These slide cases may be stored in drawers or on shelves made for the purpose. In mounting specimens taken from alcohol it is advisable to put a drop of

FIG. 111.—Slide case, showing method of labeling case and of numbering and labeling slides (original).

oil of cloves upon them, which unites with the balsam and ultimately evaporates. The occurrence of minute air bubbles under the cover-glass need occasion no uneasiness, for these will disappear on the drying of the balsam.

In mounting minute Acarids or mites it has been found best to kill the insects in hot water, which causes them to expand their legs, so that when mounted these appendages can readily be studied. If mounted living, the legs are almost invariably curled up under the body and can not be seen. This method may also be used in the case of other minute insects. Some insects, such as minute Diptera, are injured by the use of hot water, and for these dipping in hot spirits is recommended.

In the mounting of Aphides the same difficulty is avoided in a measure by Mr. G. B. Buckton, author of "A Monograph of the British Aphides," by first placing a few dots of balsam on the glass slide, to which the insect is transferred by means of a moistened camel's-hair brush. The efforts of the insect to escape will cause it to spread out its legs in a natural position and a cover glass may then be placed in position and a drop of the balsam placed at the side, when, by capillarity, it will fill the space between the slide and cover glass and the limbs will be found to have remained extended. If three or four drops of the balsam are put on the glass the wings may also be brought down and caught to them so that they will remain expanded in shape for examination.

*Preparing and Mounting the Wings of Lepidoptera.*—The student of Lepidoptera will frequently find it necessary in the study of the venation of wings to bleach them or denude them of their scales in some way. Various methods of bleaching and mounting the wings of these insects have been given, and a few of them may be briefly outlined.

The simplest and quickest, but perhaps the least satisfactory, method is to remove the scales with a camel's-hair brush. This will answer for the larger forms and where a very careful examination is not required. For more careful examination and study the wings are first bleached by the action of some caustic solution and then mounted in balsam for permanent preservation. Chambers's method for Tineina, Tortricina, Pyralidina, and the smaller moths generally, is as follows: The wing is placed on a microscopic slide in from 3 to 4 drops of a strong solution of potash, the amount varying according to the size of the wing. A cover of glass is then placed in position on the wing as in ordinary mounting.

The quantity of liquid should be sufficient to fill the space beneath, but not sufficient to float the cover glass. The mount is then placed over an alcohol flame, removing it at the first sign of ebullition, when the wing will be found denuded, if it be a fresh specimen. An old specimen, or a larger wing, will require somewhat more prolonged boiling. The fluid is drawn off by tilting the glass or with bibulous paper, and the potash removed by washing with a few drops of water. The cover glass is then removed and the wing mounted either on the same slide in balsam or floated to another slide, or at once accurately sketched with the camera lucida. Permanent mounting, however, is always to be recommended.

The Dimmock method of bleaching the wings of Lepidoptera, given in Psyche, Vol. 1, pp. 97–99, is as follows: He uses for bleaching a modification of the chlorine bleaching process commonly employed in cotton bleacheries, the material for which is sold by druggists as chlorate of lime. The wings are first soaked in pure alcohol to dissolve out the oily matter, which will act as a repellant to the aqueous chlorine solution. The chlorate of lime is dissolved in 10 parts of water and filtered. The wings are transferred to a small quantity of this solution and in an hour or two are thoroughly bleached, the veins, however, retaining a light brown color. If the bleaching does not commence readily in the chlorine solution the action may be hastened by previously dipping them in dilute hydrochloric acid. When sufficiently decolorized the wings should be washed in dilute hydrochloric acid to remove the deposit of calcic carbonate, which forms by the union of the calcic hydrate solution with the carbonic dioxide of the air. The wings are then thoroughly washed in pure water and may be gummed to cards or mounted on glass slides in Canada balsam, first washing them in alcohol and chloroform to remove the moisture. If either of the solutions known as *eau de labaraque* and *eau de jacelle* are used in place of the bleaching powder, no deposit is left on the wings and the washing with acid is obviated. This process does not dissolve or remove the scales, but merely renders them transparent, so that they do not interfere with the study of the venation.

Prof. C. H. Fernald (*American Monthly Microscopical Journal*, I, p. 172, 1880). mounts the wings of Lepidoptera in glycerin, after having first cleared them by the Dimmock process. After bleaching and washing, the wings are dried by holding the slides over an alcohol flame, and a drop of glycerin is then applied and a cover glass put on at once. By holding the slide again over the flame until ebullition takes place the glycerin will replace the air under the wings and no injury to the structure of the wings will result, even if, in refractory cases, the wing is boiled for some little time. The mount in this method must be sealed with some microscopic cement, as asphalt or Brunswick black.

A method of mounting wings of small Lepidoptera for studying venation, which I have found very convenient, is thus described by Mr. Howard in *Insect Life*, Vol. I, p. 151:

"Some years ago we used the following method for studying the venation of the wings of small Lepidoptera. We have told it since to many friends, but believe it has not been published. It is in some respects preferable to the so-called 'Dimmock process,' and particularly as a time-saver. It is also in this respect preferable to denudation with a brush. The wing is removed and mounted upon a slide in Canada balsam, which should be preferably rather thick. The slide is then held over the flame of an alcohol lamp until the balsam spreads well over the wing. Just as it is about to enter the veins, however, the slide is placed upon ice, or, if in the winter time, outside the window for a few moments. This thickens the balsam immediately and prevents it from entering the veins, which remain permanently filled with air and appear black with transmitted light. With a little practice one soon becomes expert enough to remove the slide and cool it at just the right time, when the scales will have been rendered nearly transparent by the balsam, while the veins remain filled with air. We have done this satisfactorily not only with Tortricidæ and Tineidæ, but with Noctuids of the size of *Aletia* and *Leucania*. The mounts are permanent, and we have some which have remained unchanged since 1880. Prof. Riley had for some years before this been in the habit of mounting wings in balsam, in which of course the scales cleared after a time."

Prof. John B. Smith recommends a modification of the Dimmock process of bleaching the wings of Lepidoptera, publishing it in Insect Life, Vol. i, pp. 291, 292, as follows:

"By the Dimmock process the wings are first acted upon by a saturated solution of the chloride of lime, chlorine being, of course, the bleaching agent. Afterward they are washed in water to which hydrochloric acid has been added, to get rid of the slight deposit of lime. The process is a slow one for thickly scaled, dark-colored insects, and it occurred to me to try a mixture of the chloride and acid, liberating the chlorine gas. The method was absolutely successful, the wings decolorizing immediately and being ready for the slide within two minutes. In fact, very delicate wings can scarcely be taken out quick enough, and need very little acid. The advantage is the rapidity of work and the certainty of retaining the wings entire, the chloride of lime sometimes destroying the membrane in part before the bleaching is complete. The disadvantage is the vile smell of the chlorine gas when liberated by the combination of the two liquids. For quick work this must be endured, and the beauty and completeness of the result are also advantages to counterbalance the discomfort to the senses."

For further special directions for mounting, for microscopic purposes, different insects and the different parts of insects, representing both the external chytinous covering and the internal anatomy, the student is referred to special works.

### PRESERVATION OF ALCOHOLIC SPECIMENS.

APPARATUS AND METHODS.—The collections of most value, especially to our various agricultural colleges and experiment stations will be largely of a biologic and economic character, and the interest attaching to a knowledge of the life history of insects will induce many collectors to build up independent biologic collections. Very much of this biological material will be alcoholic, and though many immature states of insects may be preserved by dry processes, still the bulk must needs be kept in liquid. This material may, when not abundant, be kept with the general systematic collection, but experience has shown that it is better to make a separate biological collection, and this is recommended especially for State institutions where the collections may be expected to attain some considerable proportions. In the case of such collections it is very desirable to adopt some method of securing the vials in such a

manner that they can easily be transferred from one place to another and
fastened in the boxes or drawers employed for pinned insects. For
directions in this regard I reproduce from an article on the subject in
*Insect Life*, Vol. II, pp. 345, 346, which was republished, with slight
changes, from my annual report for 1886 as Honorary Curator.*

*Vials, Stoppers and Holders.*—The vials in use to preserve such specimens as must be left in alcohol or other liquids are straight glass tubes
of varying diameters and lengths, with round bottom and smooth even
mouth. The stoppers in use are of rubber, which, when tightly put into
the vial, the air being nearly all expelled, keep the contents of the vial
intact and safe for years.

Various forms of bottles are used in museums for the preservation of
minute alcoholic material. I have tried the flattened and the square and
have studied various other forms of these vials; but I am satisfied that
those just described, which are in use by Dr. Hagen in the Cambridge
Museum, are, all things considered, the most convenient and economical. A more difficult problem to solve was a convenient and satisfactory method of holding these vials and of fastening them into drawers
or cases held at all angles, from perpendicular to horizontal. Most alcoholic collections are simply kept standing, either in tubes with broad
bases or in tubes held in wooden or other receptacles; but for a biologic
collection of insects something that could be used in connection with
the pinned specimens and that could be easily removed, as above
set forth, was desirable. After trying many different contrivances I
finally prepared a block, with Mr. Hawley's assistance, which answers
every purpose of simplicity, neatness, security, and convenience. It is,
so far as I know, unique, and will be of advantage for the same purpose
to other museums. It has been in use now for the past six years, and
has been of great help and satisfaction in the arrangement and preservation of the alcoholic specimens, surpassing all other methods for ease
of handling and classifying.

The blocks are oblong, one-fourth of an inch thick, the ends (*e e*, Fig.
112) beveled, the sides either beveled or straight, the latter preferable.
They vary in length and breadth according to the different sizes of
the vials, and are painted white. Upon the upper side of these blocks
are fastened two curved clamps of music wire (*b b*), forming about two-
thirds of a complete circle. The fastening to the block is simple and
secure. A bit of the wire of proper length is first doubled and then
by a special contrivance the two ends are bent around a mandrel so as
to form an insertion point or loop. A brad awl is used to make a slot in
the block, into which this loop is forced (*c*, Fig. 112, 5), a drop of warm
water being first put into the slot to soften the wood, which swells and
closes so firmly around the wire that considerable force is required to
pull it out. Four pointed wire nails (*d d d d*), set into the bottom so as

to project about one-fourth inch, serve to hold the block to the cork bottom of the case or drawer in which it is to be placed. The method of use is simple and readily seen from the accompanying figures, which represent the block from all sides.

The advantages of this system are the ease and security with which the block can be placed in or removed from a box; the ease with which a vial can be slipped into or removed from the wire clamps; the security with which it is held, and the fact that practically no part of the contents of the vial is obscured by the holder—the whole being visible from above.

The beveled ends of the block may be used for labeling, or pieces of clean card-board cut so as to project somewhat on all sides may be used for this purpose, and will be held secure by the pins between the block and the cork of the drawers.

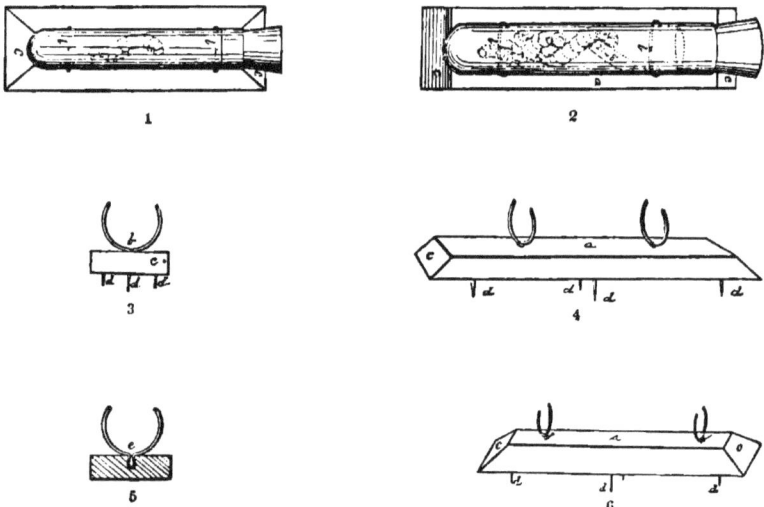

Fig. 112.—Vial holder: 1, block, with vial, beveled on all sides; 2, do., beveled only on ends; 3, block, end view; 5, do., section; 4, 6, do., side views; *a*, block; *b*, spring-wire clamps; *c*, beveled ends of block; *d*, pointed wire nails; *e*, point of insertion of clamp. (Lettering on all figures corresponds.)

The use of rubber stoppers in this country was first instituted by Dr. H. A. Hagen in connection with the Cambridge biological collection, and he has made some very careful records to determine the durability of such stoppers. From an examination of some seven thousand vials with rubber stoppers, two-thirds of which had been in use for from ten to twelve years, he comes to the conclusion that less than one in a thousand gives out every year after twelve years' use, and in the first six years probably only one out of two thousand. Stoppers of large size keep much longer than those of small size. American rubber stoppers are all made of vulcanized India rubber and have the disadvantage of forming small crystals of sulphur about the stopper, which become loosened and attach themselves to the specimens. It is supposed that pure rubber-stoppers used for chemical purposes would not present this disadvantage, which may be obviated, however, or very much reduced, if the stoppers are washed or soaked, preferably in hot water, for an hour or two at least.

If stoppers are stored for a considerable time and exposed to the air they become very hard and unfit for use, and Dr. Hagen has drawn attention to a method recommended by Professsor W. Hemple, of Dresden, Saxony, of preventing them from becoming thus hardened. He says that to keep rubber stoppers or rubber apparatus of any sort elastic, they should be stored in large glass jars in which an open vessel containing petroleum is placed. This treatment prevents the evaporation of the fluids which are fixed in the rubber in the process of vulcanization. It is better also to keep the light from the jar. To soften stoppers which have already become hardened, they should be brought together in a jar with sulphuret of carbon until they are pliable and afterward kept as recommended above.

In the use of the rubber stopper the novice may find some difficulty in inserting it in a vial filled with alcohol. The compression of the alcohol, or alcohol and air when the vial is not completely filled, forces the stopper out, and this is true whether of rubber or cork. If a fine insect pin is placed beside the cork when this is thrust into the bottle, the air or liquid displaced by the cork will escape along the pin and the latter may then be removed and the cork remains securely in position.

If cork stoppers have been used the vials may be stored in large quantities together in jars filled with alcohol. This will prevent evaporation of the alcohol from the vials, and the specimens may be preserved indefinitely. This is only desirable in the storage of duplicate specimens and unarranged material and is not recommended as a substitute for the use of the rubber stopper. With cork stoppers evaporation can be in a measure prevented if the cork is first anointed with the petroleum preparation known as vaseline. This substance is practically unaffected at ordinary temperature and is sparingly soluble in cold alcohol. Experiments with it have shown that at ordinary spring and summer temperatures there is no appreciable loss of alcohol from vials and jars.

My old method of keeping alcoholic specimens, which I abandoned for the method outlined above, was fairly serviceable, inexpensive, and warrants description.

I had special folding boxes constructed resembling in exterior appearance a large insect box. The bottom of the box was solid and was made by gluing together two 1½-inch planks.

Holes extending nearly through the lower plank and of various sizes to accommodate vials of different diameters were bored as closely together as the wood justified without splitting or breaking.

The holes were numbered consecutively and the vials when placed in them were numbered to correspond; the box also had its number, and in the notes the vial was referred to by number of box and vial thus, $\frac{3}{73}$ (box 3, vial 73). The vial should project one-half to 1 inch above the hole, and should be loose enough to provide for the swelling of the wood in moist weather.

To protect the vials a cover having a depth of about 1½ inch was hinged to the back and secured in front by hook-and-eye fastenings.

This method of storing vials is satisfactory enough for private collections, but for larger public collections is not so suitable.

A rather convenient and inexpensive method of storing vials is that used by Dr. Marx. In this method the vials are stored in a wooden

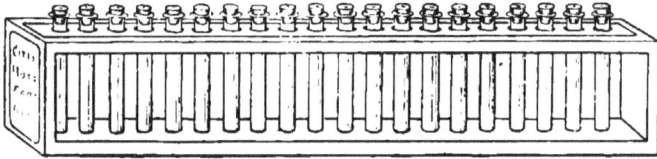

Fig. 113.—The Marx tray for alcoholic specimens (original.)

frame, shown at Fig. 113. The top piece of the tray into which the vials are thrust has a cork center, in which holes corresponding to the size of the vials are made with a gun-wad punch. The outer end of the tray bears a label or labels describing the material in the tray. The vials used by Dr. Marx are of thinner glass than those which I recommend and flare slightly at the top, as shown in the accompanying illustrations. They are made in various sizes to accommodate larger

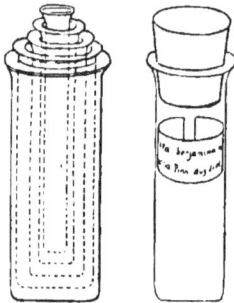

Fig. 114.—Vials used in the Marx tray (original.)

and smaller specimens. A vial thrust into the hole punched in the cork rests on the bottom piece of the tray, the flange or neck preventing it from sliding through. These trays are arranged on shallow shelves in a case or cabinet, especially constructed for the purpose and a large quantity of material may be stored by their use in small compass. The use of the cork center piece in the upper part of the tray is not a necessity, and a wooden piece may be used in which holes are bored with a bitt of proper size.

*Preserving Micro-larvæ in Alcohol.*—The following is quoted from Packard's "Entomology for Beginners," for which it was translated from the "*Deutsche Ent. Zeitg.*," 1887, Heft 1:

"Dr. H. Dewitz mounts the larvæ and pupæ of Microlepidoptera, and also the early stages of other small insects, in the following way: The insects are put into a bottle with 95 per cent alcohol. Many larvæ turn black in alcohol, but boiling them in alcohol in a test tube will bleach them. They may then be finally placed in glass tubes as small and thin as possible, varying from 0.003 to 0.006 meter in diameter, according to the size of the insects. About 0.07 meter's length of a tube is melted over a spirit lamp, and the tube filled three-quarters full with 95 per cent alcohol, the insects placed within and the contents of the tube heated at the end still open, and then closed by being pulled out with another piece of glass tubing. After the glass has been held a few minutes in the hand until it is slightly cooled off, the end closed last is once more held over the lamp so that the points may be melted together, and this end of the glass may be finished. During the whole time from the closure of the tube until the complete cooling of the glass it should be held obliquely in the hand, so that the alcohol may not wet the upper end, for if the tube is too full it is difficult

FIG. 115.—Method of preserving minute larvæ etc. (After Dewitz.)

to melt it, as the steam quickly expanding breaks through the softened mass of glass. The tube may be mounted by boring a hole through a cork stopper of the same diameter as the glass. The stopper is cut into the shape of a cube, a strong insect pin put through it, and the glass tube inserted into the hole. It can then be pinned in the insect box or drawer, near the imago, so that the free end of the glass may touch the bottom, while the other end stands up somewhat; while to keep the tube in place the free end resting on the bottom may be fastened with two strong insect pins. The specimens thus put up can easily be examined with a lens, and if they need to be taken out for closer examination the tube can be opened and closed again after a little practice."

PRESERVATIVE FLUIDS.—The principal liquids in which soft-bodied insects may be successfully preserved are the following:

*Alcohol.*—As indicated in the foregoing portions of this work, alcohol is the standard preservative used for soft-bodied specimens, and may be used either full strength or diluted with water. Diluted alcohol should always be first used with larvæ, since the pure alcohol shrivels them up. The weak spirits can afterwards be replaced by strong, for permanent preservation.

*Alcohol and White Arsenic.*—The method of preserving insects recommended by Laboulbène and quoted in Packard's Entomology for Beginners, consists in plunging the insects in the fresh state into a preservative liquid, consisting of alcohol with an excess of the common white arsenic of commerce. The larva placed in this mixture absorbs .003 of its own weight, and when removed and pinned is safe from the attacks of museum pests. This liquid is said not to change the colors, blue, green or red of beetles, if they are not immersed for more than twenty-four hours. This treatment is applicable to the orders Coleoptera, Hemiptera, and Orthoptera. If the insect is allowed to stay in this mixture for a considerable time, say three or four weeks, and then removed and dried, it becomes very hard and brittle and can not be used for dissection or study, but makes a good cabinet specimen.

The white deposit of arsenic which will appear on drying can be washed off with alcohol.

*Alcohol and Corrosive Sublimate.*—The same author recommends another preparation consisting of alcohol with a variable quantity of corrosive sublimate added, the strength of the solution varying from 100 parts of alcohol to 1 part of corrosive sublimate for the strongest, to one-tenth of 1 part of sublimate in 100 parts of alcohol for the weakest. The insects are allowed to remain in this mixture not longer than two hours before drying. The last-described preparation is said to preserve the specimens from mold. Both of these solutions are very poisonous and should be used with care.

*Two Liquids to preserve Form and Color.*—Professor Packard also quotes the formula of A. E. Verrill for preserving insects in their natural color and form. Two formulas are given; the first consists of 2½ pounds of common salt and 4 ounces of niter dissolved in a gallon of water and filtered. The specimens should be prepared for permanent preservation in this solution by being previously immersed in a solution consisting of a quart of the first solution and 2 ounces of arsenite of potash in a gallon of water. Professor Packard gives also the formula of M. H. Trois for preserving caterpillars, for which it is claimed that the colors of the caterpillars are preserved perfectly, even when exposed to strong light. The formula for this solution is as follows:

| | |
|---|---|
| Common salt ................................................grams.. | 2.35 |
| Alum ...........................................................do... | 55 |
| Corrosive sublimate....................................centigrams. | 18 |
| Boiling water.....................................................liters.. | 5 |

Allow the liquid to cool and add 50 grains of carbolic acid, and filter after standing five or six days.

*Glycerin.*—Glycerin, either pure or mixed with water or alcohol, is frequently used to preserve the larvæ of delicate insects. It preserves the color and form better than alcohol, but particularly in the case of larvæ, it causes a softening of the tissues which renders them unfit for study.

*The Wickersheim Preserving Fluid.*—This valuable preserving fluid has been known for some time, but is not very commonly used, on account of frequent disappointment due to the difficulty attending its preparation. It is claimed for it that animal or vegetable bodies impregnated with it will retain their form, color, and flexibility in the most perfect manner. The objects to be preserved are put in the fluid for from six to twelve days, according to their size, and then taken out and dried in the air. The ligaments remain soft and movable, and the animals or plants remain fit for anatomical dissection and study for long periods, even years. It is said to be especially valuable for the preservation of larvæ and soft-bodied insects. In order to perfectly preserve the colors, it is necessary to leave the specimens in the fluid, or, if they are taken out, they should be sealed up in air-tight vials or vessels. The formula for the fluid is as follows:

Dissolve 100 grams alum, 25 grams common salt, 12 grams saltpeter, 60 grams potash, 10 grams arsenious acid in 3,000 grams boiling water. Filter the solution, and when cold add 10 liters of the liquid to 4 liters of glycerin and 1 liter of methyl alcohol.

## LABELING SPECIMENS.

*General Directions.*—It matters little how much care and pains have been taken in the preparation and mounting of specimens, they will have little value unless accompanied by proper labels giving information as to locality and date of collection, name of collector, and a label or number referring to notebooks, if any biological or other facts concerning them have been ascertained. There should be pinned to the specimen labels referring to, or giving all the information obtainable or of interest concerning it. A somewhat different style of label will be found necessary in the case of the two forms of collections described in the foregoing pages, namely, the biological or economic collection, and the systematic collection. For the former, numbers may be attached to the specimens which will refer to the notes relating to the specimen or species. For the latter, in most cases, all necessary information may be recorded and made available by written or printed labels attached directly to the specimens. In most cases, however, I find a combination of these two systems convenient and desirable. The numbering system is very simple, and is the one which I have followed in all the species for which I have biological or other notes. It consists in giving each species, as it comes under observation, a serial number which refers to a record in a notebook. With this number may be combined, if convenient, the date of rearing or collection of the specimen, and also the locality and food-plant if known. The vast number of species represented in a systematic collection renders the numbering system entirely out of place and inadequate, and the labeling system alone is generally available. If it becomes necessary in the systematic collection to refer to food-plants or life-history or any other fact of interest, the numbering system should be used, and I recommend that the numbers be written in red ink on the labels, to distinguish at a glance the numbers referring to biological notes from other numbers that will occur in the collection.

*Labels for pinned Specimens.*—The following labels should be employed in the collection: (1) *Locality label*, which should be as explicit as possible. (2) *Date of capture*, which is very useful and sometimes quite important in various ways. It indicates at what time additional specimens of some rare species may be secured, and greatly assists in elaborating the life history of the species, and in other cases assists in the correct determination of closely allied insects, which differ chiefly in habit or date of appearance. (3) *A label to indicate the sex.* This label has recently acquired greater importance than formerly, on account of the value of the sexual differences in the distinction of species. The well-known signs for male, female, and worker, printed in convenient form, are well adapted for collections. (4) *The name of the collector.* This label is of less value, but sometimes becomes important in determining the history of the specimen or the exact place of capture. The name of the species is not necessarily attached to all the specimens in a collection, and ordinarily will be placed with the first specimen in a series in the cabinet. This and other labeling of insects in cabinet is discussed in another place. Other labels are useful to indicate type specimens, namely, those of which descriptions have been drawn up and published, and which should be designated by a special label written by the author himself. Determinations by an authority in a special group should be indicated, and the labels placed on specimens by such an authority should not be removed.

It will not be found necessary to use a separate label for each of the data indicated above, and a single label may be made to combine many of them, as, except for the specific names of the insects themselves (which should always be on the lowermost label), most other words will bear abbreviation, especially localities and dates. "A combination label, which has given general satisfaction to all to whom it has been communicated, is a two-line label printed in diamond type, on heavy writing paper. The upper line consists of the name of the locality, *e. g.,* 'Washngtn' (a name consisting of more than eight letters to be abbreviated), and the lower line has at the right-hand corner 'DC' (interpunctuation and spacing to be avoided so as to save space). This leaves on the second line sufficient room for inserting the date, which can be quickly and neatly written with ink if the labels are printed in columns of ten or more repetitions. The label thus combines locality with date of capture. Or the upper line reads 'Arizona' and the lower line 'Morrison,' the label thus combining locality with the name of the collector."*

In general I indorse the system of labeling suggested in the above condensation from Mr. Schwarz, but there is no particular disadvantage, and in fact many advantages, in special cases, in a larger label or in folded labels. Particularly in visiting large foreign collections I have found it convenient to use large labels of thin paper which will contain a good deal of information closely written in pencil and bear folding several times, so as not to occupy more than the ordinary label space when pinned to the specimens. This involves detaching the label when the specimen or species comes to be studied, but this additional labor is insignificant compared with the large amount of valuable information which in time is thus brought together in condensed availability for the student; for brief notes of opinions of experts, of comparison with types, of special studies, of reference to descriptions, etc., may thus be all brought together. Where there is not room to indicate the authority for a determination on the upper side of a label, I also find it convenient to do so on the lower side.

*E. A. Schwarz, Proc. Ent. Soc., Wash., II, No. 1, 1891.

*Labeling alcoholic Specimens.*—Alcoholic specimens, including alcoholic biologic material and collections of Arachnida and Myriopoda, are well adapted to the labeling system, as the vials are always of sufficient size to allow the insertion of one or more labels large enough to contain a pretty full record of the specimen. The label may consist of a number referring to notes, or of a number together with the other data indicated for the systematic collection. The label in my experience is preferably written in pencil, which, in alcohol, is practically permanent. Waterproof inks are sometimes used, and of these the oak-gall ink is undoubtedly the best. Dr. George Marx, in labeling his Arachnida, uses onion-skin paper and waterproof ink, such as Hig-

FIG. 116.—Cabinet for apparatus used in mounting and labeling. (Original).

gins's drawing ink. There is some danger, in placing a label in a vial, of its settling against the specimen and injuring it. This, however, can generally be avoided if a little care is used. The label may be long and narrow and folded lengthwise so as to occupy one side only of the vial, or short and inserted in such manner that it will pass around the inside of the vial, where it will be held by the natural adhesion to the glass in the upper portion of the vial, as shown at Fig. 114.

*Cabinet for Apparatus.*—The work of preparation of insects for the cabinet may be greatly facilitated if a convenient case is provided with drawers and compartments for the keeping of pins of different sizes, labels, braces, implements, tweezers, dissecting apparatus, and the like, with microscopical supplies – slides, cover glasses, mounting media, etc. I present a photograph of a cabinet of this sort used in my earlier work and found very convenient and serviceable (Fig. 116).

## INSECT BOXES AND CABINETS.

*General Directions.*—The boxes or cases which are used to keep insects in permanently may be made of any dimensions to suit the fancy, 12 by 16 inches inside being a convenient size and allowing economic use of cork. They must, however, be perfectly tight and should not be more than $2\frac{1}{2}$ inches deep on the inside. The bottoms should be lined with something which will hold the pins, and the whole inside covered with white paper, which, if delicately cross ruled, will facilitate the regular pinning of specimens. While the size and style of the box and cabinet may be left to individual taste, some choice must be had of material. *Red cedar should never be used.* I have learned, to my sorrow, the baneful effects of this wood, notwithstanding it is recommended—evidently by those who are guiltless of having used it—as having the advantage over other wood of keeping off museum pests. It seems impossible to get this wood so seasoned but that a certain amount of resin will continually exude from it; and insects in boxes of this material are very apt to soften and become greasy. Paper boxes are also bad, as they attract moisture and cause the specimens to mold. Well-seasoned pine and whitewood are the most satisfactory; and, in such boxes as have glass covers and are intended to form part of a neat cabinet for parlor ornament, the fronts may be of walnut or cherry.

The character of the boxes and cabinets used for storing insects will depend largely on the nature and extent of the collection and the object of the collector. For temporary use, nothing is more convenient and economical than a cigar box lined with cork or pith. Such boxes, however, should be employed only for the temporary storage of fresh specimens, as they afford free access to museum pests, and insects kept in them for any length of time are apt to be destroyed or rendered useless.

*The Folding-box.*—The use of folding-boxes for the working collector is to be especially recommended in the case of those orders comprising small insects like Coleoptera, Hymenoptera, etc. These boxes have the great advantage of being readily rearranged on the shelves and of being very easily used in study. The boxes of this type now manufactured by John Schmidt, of Brooklyn, N. Y., and John Burr, of Camden, N. J., based on the experience which I have had, have proved so serviceable

and satisfactory in this respect that I have employed them for the bulk
of the collection in the National Museum. These boxes (Fig. 117) are
constructed as follows:

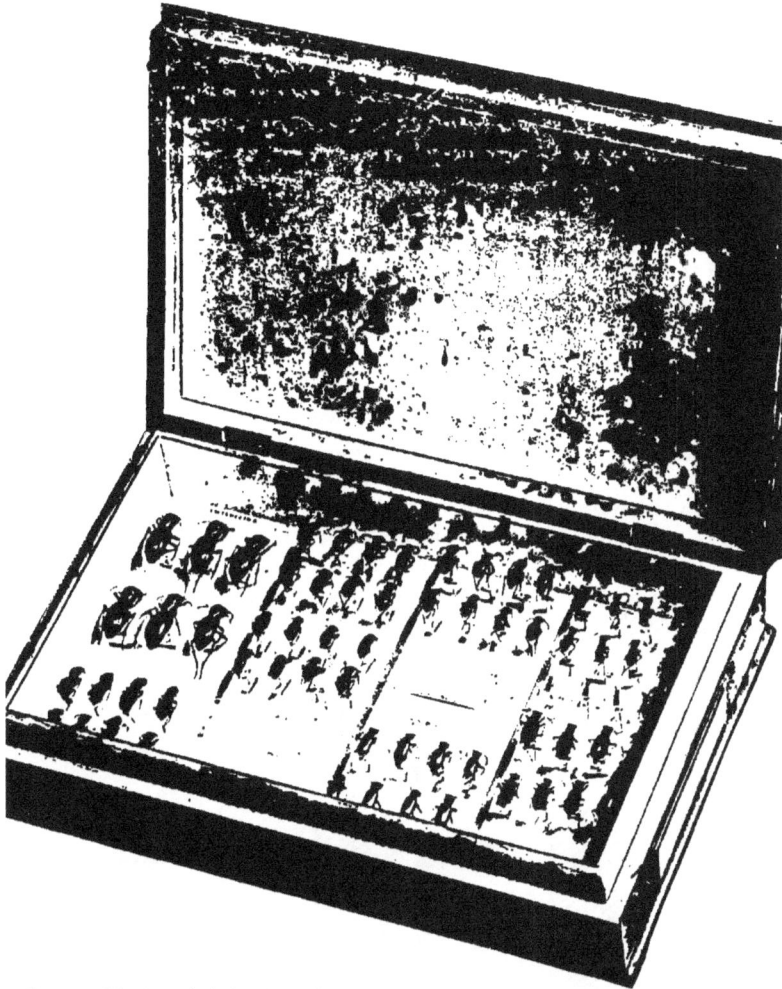

FIG. 117.—The Schmidt folding insect box, opened and showing arrangement of insects (original).

They are of white pine, shellacked and varnished, the bottom and
top double and crossgrained, to prevent warping, and projecting slightly
at all sides except the hinged back. They are 13 by 8¼ inches outside
measurement. The inside measurement is 11¾ by 7. The sides, back,
and front are five-sixteenths of an inch thick, with a machine joint,
which is neat and very secure. The boxes are 2⅜ inches in outside
depth, unequally divided, the lower portion 1½ inches outside depth,
lined inside with a thin whitewood strip, projecting three-fourths of an

inch above the rim of the outside box. Over this projecting lining
the lid closes as tightly as practicable and is kept from springing by
hooks and eyes. The bottom is cork-lined and covered with a fine,
white, glazed paper.

Similar folding boxes with both sides of equal depth and both lined
with cork, when properly covered, may be made to look like books and
be set on end in an ordinary bookcase, but the single lining is preferable, as there is less danger of the breakage of specimens and the boxes
may either be laid flat one on the other on shelves, or, what is more
convenient, placed side by side resting on the front edge, so that the
label is attached to one of the narrow ends. The rows of insects are
then pinned crosswise, not lengthwise, of the box, with the abdomens
turned toward the front which rests on the shelf.

All the boxes are furnished with neat brass label-holders, in which
a card containing a list of the contents can readily be placed and
removed at pleasure. The chief demerit of this box which I have en-
deavored to overcome by the above details is the tendency to warp and
crack in the trying steam heat of our Government buildings.

*The Cabinet.*—For larger insects, such as Lepidoptera, Neuroptera,
etc., a larger box is desirable, and for these orders I have adopted
for use in the National Museum a cabinet which resulted from a careful
study in person of the different forms and patterns used for entomological collections both in this country and Europe, whether by private in-

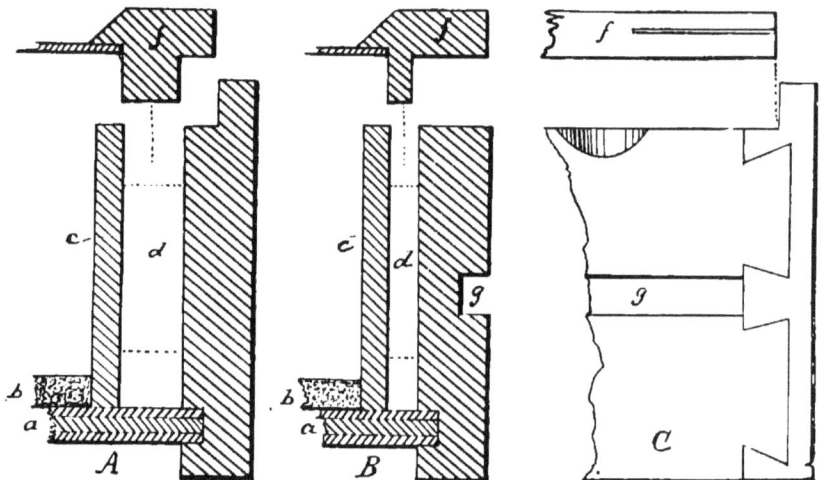

FIG. 118. Construction of insect cabinet drawer of the National Museum. A, cross-section f front;
B, same f side; C, view of front end of side, ⅔ natural size (original).

dividuals or public institutions. The drawer and cabinet are essentially after the pattern of those used in the British (South Kensington)
Museum, but adapted in size to our own requirements. In the use of the
National Museum these cabinets have proved eminently well adapted
to their object.

The drawers (Fig. 118, A, B, C) are square, with an outside measurement of 18 inches and an outside depth of 3 inches. The sides and back have a thickness of three-eighths of an inch, while the front is five-eighths of an inch thick. The pieces are firmly dovetailed together, the front being clean and the dovetailing blind. The bottom, $a$, is of three-ply crossgrained veneer, run into a groove at the sides, leaving a clear inside depth of $2\frac{1}{16}$ inches to the frame of the cover. The bottoms are lined in all but forty of the drawers with first quality cork, $b$, one-fourth of an inch thick. At a distance of one-fourth of an inch from the sides and back and three-eighths of an inch from the front there is an inside box of one-eighth inch whitewood, $c$, closely fitted, and held in place by blocks between it and the outer box. There is thus between the inner and outer box a clear space, $d$, all round, in which insecticides or disinfectants can be placed to keep out Museum pests, making it impossible for such to get into the inner box containing the specimens without first passing through this poison chamber. The entire inside is lined with white paper, or, in the case of the uncorked boxes, painted with zinc white. The front is furnished with a plain knob. The cover is of glass, set into a frame, $f$, three-fourths of an inch wide, three-eighths of an inch thick, with a one-fourth inch tongue fitting closely into the space between the inner lining and outer box, which here serves as a groove. This arrangement furnishes a perfectly tight drawer of convenient size and not unwieldy for handling when studying the collection.

The material of which these drawers are made is California red wood, except the cover frame, which is mahogany. The cabinets containing these drawers are 36 inches high, 40 inches wide, 21 inches deep (all outside measurements), and are closed by two paneled doors. Each cabinet contains twenty drawers in two rows of ten each, and the drawers slide by means of a groove, $g$, on either side, on hard-wood tongues, and are designed to be interchangeable.

*The Lintner display Box.*—For beauty and security and the perfect display of the larger *Lepidoptera*, I have seen nothing superior to a box used by Mr. J. A. Lintner, of Albany, N. Y. It is a frame made in the form of a folio volume, with glass set in for sides and bound in an ordinary book cover. The insects are pinned onto pieces of cork fastened to the inside of one of the glass plates and the boxes may be stood on ends, in library shape, like ordinary books. For the benefit of those who wish to make small collections of showy insects, I give Mr. Lintner's method, of which he has been kind enough to furnish me the following description:

Figs. A, B, and C represent, in section, the framework of the volume, $a$ showing the ends, $b$ the front, and $c$ the back. The material can be prepared in long strips of some soft wood by a cabinet-maker (if the collector has the necessary skill and leisure for framing it) at a cost of 60 cents a frame, if a number sufficient for a dozen boxes be ordered. Or, if it be preferred to order them made, the cost should not exceed 80 cents each.

Before being placed in the hands of the binder the mitering should be carefully examined and any defect in fitting remedied, so that the glass, when placed in position, may have accurate bearings on all the sides. The interior of the frame is covered with tin foil, made as smooth as possible before application, to be applied with thoroughly boiled flour paste (in which a small proportion of arsenic may be mixed) and rubbed smoothly down till the removal of the blisters, which are apt to appear. The tin foil can be purchased, by weight, at druggists', and the sheets marked off and cut by a rule in strips of proper width, allowing for a trifle of overlapping on the sides. Its cost per volume is merely nominal.

First-quality single-thick glass for sides must be selected, wholly free from rust, veins, air-bubbles, or any blemish. Such glass can be purchased at 15 cents a pane. The lower glass, after thorough cleaning, especially of its inner surface, with an alkaline wash, and a final polishing with slightly wetted white printing paper, is to be firmly secured in its place by a proper number of tin points; the upper glass is but temporarily fastened. The binder must be directed to cover the exposed sides of the frame with "combed" paper, bringing it over the border of the permanent lower glass and beneath the removable upper glass.

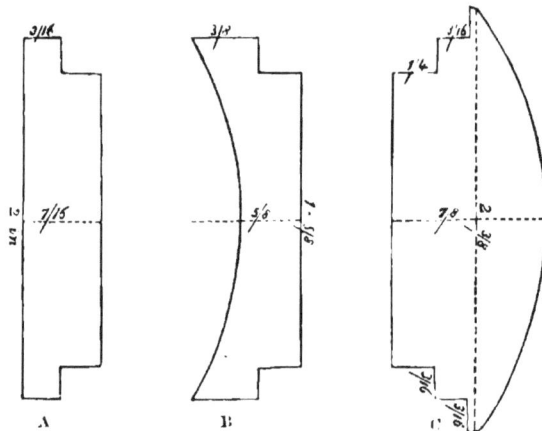

FIG. 119.—Construction of the Lintner box.

The covers of the volume are of heavy binders' board (No. 18), neatly lined within with glazed white paper. On one of the insides of the lids may be attached, by its corners, a sheet with the numbers and names of the species contained in the volume, or these may be placed on the pin bearing the insect. If bound in best quality of imitation morocco, with cloth covers, lettered and gilded on the back, the cost (for a dozen volumes) need not exceed $1 each. If in turkey morocco, it will be $1.50.

The lettering and ornamentation of the back will vary with the taste of the individual. The family designations may be permanently lettered, or they may be pasted on the back, on a slip of paper or gum label, as are the generic names, thus permitting the change of the contents of a volume at any time if desired.

The bits of cork to which the insects are to be pinned are cut in quarter-inch squares from sheet-cork of one-fourth of an inch in thickness. If the trouble be taken to trim off the corners, giving them an octagonal form, their appearance will be materially improved and much less care will be required in adjusting them on the glass.

The cement usually recommended for attaching the cork to the glass is composed of equal parts of white wax and resin. My experience with this has not been favorable, for, after the lapse of a few years, I have invariably been subjected to the serious annoyance of being compelled to renew the entire contents of the volume, clean the glass, and replace the corks with new cement. From some cause, inexplicable to me, a gradual separation takes place of the cork with its cement from the glass, first appearing at the angles of the cork, and its progress indicated by an increasing number of iridescent rings which form within until the center is reached, when, if not previously detached, the insect falls with the cork, usually to its injury and that of others beneath it.

A number of years ago I happened to employ, in attaching a single piece of cork in one of my cases, a cement originally made for other purposes, consisting of six parts of resin, one of wax, and one of Venetian red. Several years thereafter my attention was drawn to this piece by finding it as firmly united as when at first applied, and at the present time (after the lapse of twelve years) it is without the slightest indication of separation. Acting upon this hint, I have, of late, used this cement in the restoration of a number of my cases, and with the most satisfactory results. It is important that the cement, when used, should be heated (by a spirit lamp or gas flame) to as high a degree as it will bear without burning. An amount sufficient to cover the bottom of the small, flat metal vessel containing it to the depth of an eighth of an inch will suffice and prevent the cork from taking up more than its requisite quantity. It should be occasionally stirred to prevent the precipitation of its heavier portions. The cork may be conveniently dipped by the aid of a needle inserted in a handle, when, as quickly as possible, it should be transferred to the glass, for the degree of adhesion seems to depend upon the degree of fluidity of the cement. From some experiments made by me, after the corks had been attached as above, in heating the entire glass to such a degree as thoroughly to melt the cement until it spreads outward from beneath the weight of the cork, and then permitted to cool—the glass meanwhile held horizontally, that the corks might not be displaced—the results appear to indicate that the above cement, applied in this manner on glass properly cleaned, will prove a permanent one. It is scarcely necessary to state that this method is not available where the glass has been bound as above.

Preparatory to corking the glass for the specimens assigned to it, the spaces required for them are to be ascertained by arranging them in order on a cork surface or otherwise. On a sheet of paper of the size of the glass, perpendicular lines, of the number of the rows and at their proper distances, are to be drawn, and cross lines equal in number to the insects contained in the rows. The distances of these lines will be uniform, unless smaller specimens are to occupy some portion of the case, when they may be graduated to the required proportion. With the sheet ruled in this manner and placed beneath the glass, the points where the corks are to be applied are indicated by the intersections of the lines. The sheet, marked with the family of the insects for which it was used and with the numbers designating its divisions, may be laid aside for future use in the preparation of other cases for which it may be suitable. In a series of unbound cases in my collection, in which the glasses measure 11 by 14½ inches, I have used for my Lepidoptera and laid aside the following scales, the citation of which will also serve to show the capacity of the cases: 3 by 8, Catocalas; 2 by 7 and 3 by 9, Sphingidae; 4 by 11 to 4 by 14, Bombycidae; 5 by 13 to 6 by 16, Noctuidae; 8 by 16 and 8 by 20, Lycaenidae and Tortricidae.

The unbound cases above referred to are inexpensive frames, made by myself, of quarter-inch white wood or pine, the corners mitered, glued, and nailed with three-quarter inch brads, lined within with white paper (better with tin foil), and covered without with stout manila paper. The glasses are cut of the size of the frame, and when placed in position thereon are appressed closely to it by laying upon them, near each corner, a heavy weight, and strips of an enameled green paper, cut to the width of 1 inch, are pasted over their edges, extending a little beyond the thickness of the frame, and brought downward over the outside of the frame. On its back two gum labels, indicating the insects inclosed, are placed at uniform heights (7 and 12 inches), when, if all has been neatly done, they present a tasteful appearance upon a shelf. When there is reason to believe that the case will need to be opened for the change or addition of specimens, it will be found convenient to employ, for the fastening of the left-hand side of the upper glass, paper lined with a thin muslin, to serve as a hinge when the other sides have been cut.

Should it become desirable to bind these cases, outside frames may be constructed after the plans above given, with the omission of the inside quarter inch (the equivalent of these frames), in which these may be placed and held in position by two or three screws inserted in their sides.

*The Martindale Box for Lepidoptera.*—Mr. Isaac C. Martindale, in the October, 1891, number of *Entomological News*, pp. 126, 127, describes a new form of cabinet for butterflies, the drawers of which present some new features. They are for the same end as the Lintner box described above—namely, for the display of the upper and under surface of the wings of Lepidoptera, and promise to be more useful. The drawer is described as follows:

> The especial feature is the drawer itself, which, instead of having a cork bottom, as is usually the case, has both the top and bottom of glass. The top part of the drawer frame fits tightly over a ledge one inch in height, effectually preventing the intrusion of destructive insects, the pest of the entomologist; but it is readily lifted when it is desirable to add to the contents or change the location of the specimens. For the inside arrangement I have taken a strip of common tin, one inch wide, and turned up each side five-sixteenths of an inch, thus leaving three-eighths of an inch for the bottom. The length of the strip of tin, being about two inches longer than the width of the drawer, admits of each end being turned up one inch. Into this tin trough is tightly fitted a cork strip three-eighths of an inch square. The whole being covered with white paper, such as is usually used for lining drawers, conceals the inequalities of the cork and makes a fine finish. They should be made to fit neatly in the drawer, and can be readily moved about to suit large or small specimens. For *Lycænas, Pamphilas*, etc., as many as fifteen of these strips may be used in one drawer, and as few as five for *Morphos, Caligos*, etc. The upturned ends are fastened in place by using the ordinary thumb tacks that can be procured at any stationer's. The frame work of the drawers should be of white pine, well seasoned. Into this the thumb tacks are readily inserted and as easily withdrawn when a change in the position of the cork strips is needed.

*Horizontal vs. vertical Arrangement of Boxes.*—I have elsewhere discussed the availability of the upright vs. the horizontal arrangement of insect boxes.* In the case of Lepidoptera and large-bodied insects I have found the horizontal drawer or box to be preferable. If large-bodied insects are placed in a vertical position they are very liable to become loose on the pins, swing from side to side, and damage themselves and other specimens; but for the smaller insects of all orders, the vertical arrangement is quite safe and satisfactory. If the pin is slightly flattened, as described on p. 69, the danger of large specimens becoming loose is to a great extent avoided.

*Lining for Insect Boxes.*—The old lining of insect boxes was the ordinary sheet cork of commerce, and if a good quality of cork is procurable it will answer the purpose. A better substance, however, for the lining of insect boxes is the prepared or ground cork, which is now almost

_____
* *American Naturalist*, Vol. XV, p. 101, 1881.

exclusively used. It is simply ground cork mixed with a small amount of glue, compressed into sheets and covered with paper. This gives a very homogenous composition, and is much better than the ordinary cork, having a more uniform and neat appearance, and admitting the insertion of the pins more freely. It may be purchased from H. Herpers, 18 Crawford street, Newark, N. J.

A less expensive substitute is paper stretched upon a frame. Prof. E. S. Morse has given in the "American Naturalist" (Vol. i, p. 156) a plan which is very neat and useful for lining boxes in a large museum, which are designed to be placed in horizontal show-cases (Fig. 120). "A box is made of the required depth, and a light frame is fitted to its interior. Upon the upper and under surfaces of this frame a sheet of white paper (drawing or log paper answers the purpose) is securely glued. The paper, having been previously damped, in drying contracts and tightens like a drumhead. The frame is then secured about one-fourth of an inch from the bottom of the box, and the pin is forced down through the thicknesses of paper, and if the bottom of the box be of soft pine, the point of the pin may be slightly forced into it. It is thus firmly held at two or three different points, and

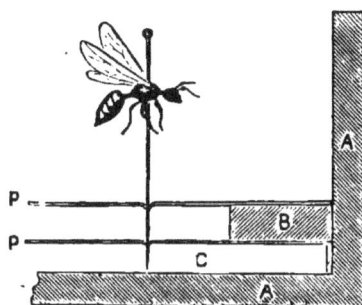

FIG. 120.—Paper lining for insect box. (After Marse.)

all lateral movemnts are prevented. Other advantages are secured by this arrangement besides firmness; when the box needs cleaning or fumigation, the entire collection may be removed by taking out the frame; or camphor, tobacco, or other material can be placed on the bottom of the box, and concealed from sight. The annexed figure represents a transverse section of a portion of the side and bottom of the box with the frame. A A, box; B, frame; P P, upper and under sheets of paper; C, space between lower sheets of paper and bottom of box."

Other substitutes are the pith of various plants, especially of corn. Palm wood and "inodorous felt" are also used, being cut to fit the bottom of the box.

Pita wood or the light porous wood of the Agave or Century plant when cut into proper strips also makes a very light and satisfactory lining, while good close bog-peat cut into proper thicknesses is not infrequently used in France and Germany. Druce & Co., 68 Baker street, London, W., England, have lately been manufacturing what is known as cork carpet, which seems to be a combination of ground cork and rubber. It comes in various colors and of the proper thickness, and makes a very smooth and desirable lining, holding the pins very firmly.

It cost 90 cents per square yard in England, and I have had one cabinet lined with it as an experiment, as there is a probability that the pins may corrode in contact with the rubber.

## ARRANGEMENT OF INSECTS IN THE CABINET.

*Systematic and biologic Collections.*—The permanent arrangement of specimens in boxes and drawers will vary somewhat with the nature of the insects. The almost universal custom of collectors, however, is to arrange the insects in vertical columns. In the case of the smaller forms, as Coleoptera, Hymenoptera, Diptera, 2½ to 3 inches in width is allowed for the columns; and for the larger insects, as Lepidoptera, Orthoptera, for which larger drawers are recommended, a greater width of column is needed and 4½ to 5 inches will be found necessary. With alcoholic material, a similar arrangement in columns may be followed.

In spacing or dividing insect boxes into columns for the arrangement of specimens, I have followed the plan of pinning narrow strips of colored paper in the boxes at regular distances to divide the columns of insects. A fine line made with a medium pencil will answer the same purpose and will not materially disfigure the box.

The appearance of the collection will largely depend on the care used in the alignment of the specimens, both vertically and horizontally. It is advisable to have at least four specimens of a species, which, entomologically speaking, constitute a set. The collector, however, should not limit the number of his specimens to four, as it is frequently necessary to have a larger number to represent, firstly, the sexes; secondly, varieties; and thirdly, geographical distribution.

In the systematic collection the species should be arranged serially in accordance with the latest catalogue or monograph, and if the collector intends making a complete study of the group, space should be left for the subsequent insertion of species not at present in his possession and also for new species. This will avoid the rearrangement of the entire collection at brief intervals.

*Economic Displays.*—In the case of economic displays, which will include pinned specimens, alcoholic material, early states and specimens illustrating the work of the insect—also the parasitic and predaceous enemies—the horizontal arrangement can be followed, and I have found it advisable, in making such displays, to arrange them in this manner, so that any needed width for the display of particular species may be had. A good idea of the system of arrangement adopted for an economic exhibit may be obtained from the accompanying illustration (Pl. 1). Every insect will require a somewhat different treatment, owing to its different habit, but the plan indicated in the illustration should, in the main, be followed. Prof. J. H. Comstock uses and recommends a sort of block system, which consists in pinning the insects and specimens showing their work, and alcoholic material, to blocks of soft wood. These are then arranged in the display cases. The advantage claimed for the system is facility in transferring and rearranging the exhibits. This method is somewhat cumbersome, and in making and handling economic exhibits I have found pinning specimens directly to the cork lining of the box, as already described, to be entirely satisfactory. A biologic exhibit should be carefully planned beforehand, and when once completed is permanent and does not require rearrangement, as is frequently necessary in a systematic collection, owing to the constant changes in classification. The only alteration necessary is a renewal of specimens which have become injured, or faded by exposure to light.

*Labeling Collections.*—I have already fully discussed the subject of labeling insects before placing them in their final resting place in the collection. In the collection certain additional labels are required, viz. labels for the order, family, subfamily, genus, species, and sometimes variety. The label for the order should be placed above the first species in the collection, and should be in large type, as should also be the name of the family, which is to be placed above the first species in the family. The genus label should be in prominent type, somewhat smaller than the family label, and should be placed at the head of the genus. Custom varies as to placing the label of the species. In my practice I have adopted the plan of placing the label below the series of specimens representing the species. Some entomologists reverse this plan and place the label above the series of specimens. Others recommend pinning the label to the first and best-determined specimen of the series. This has the advantage of always keeping the label with the species and preventing the danger of mistake or confusion of the latter. In the case of large insects, however, this plan has the disadvantage that the label can not be seen except by taking out the specimen, and, on the whole, the plan which I have adopted of placing the label below the series of specimens is preferable, but may be supplemented by the other, as in addition to the independent label, one of the specimens should have a label pinned with it. The labels should be neatly written on blanks printed for the purpose; but a better plan, perhaps, and one which I have followed, where possible, in labeling the national collection, is to cut the names neatly from a catalogue of the insects, which will furnish all the labels from order to species, and fasten them with short, inconspicuous pins in their proper places in the collection. Where it is not desired to keep the collection as compact as possible, or where one has limited space, I would advise labeling the species, not only with the recognized name, but also with the synonyms. This requires some space, and will hardly be followed except in public collections. It is also desirable to arrange together, and label as such, the varieties of any given species. The appearance of the collection will depend largely on the uniformity of the labeling, and too much care can not be exercised in this respect.

## MUSEUM PESTS, MOLD, ETC.

Unfortunately for the well-being of collections, dried insects are liable to the attacks of various museum pests, the most troublesome of which are themselves insects, but altogether out of their proper place and rôle in the general collection. Unless constant precautions are taken, the collector will discover after a few months that instead of the rare specimens with the preparations of which he has taken no little pains there remains only a series of fragmentary specimens, which a few years' neglect will reduce to little more than a mass of dust or powder. The price, then, of a good collection is eternal vigilance. Most insects, when exposed for any length of time to strong light, fade or lose color, and the only way to prevent such achromatism is to exclude the light.

Insect pests affecting collections include Psocidæ, Mites, Tineidæ, Coleoptera of the families Ptinidæ and Dermestidæ, these last being the most injurious.

The Psocidæ—degraded wingless insects already referred to in the classification (p. 24)—will find their way into the tightest boxes, but ordinarily do little if any damage, except in the case of delicate insects, such as Ephemerids, Microlepidoptera, and Microdiptera. The common forms found in collections are *Atropos dirinatorius* and *Clothilla pulsatoria*. Mites or Acari are rarely troublesome in collections, though Dr. H. A. Hagen reports having found a species (probably of Tyroglyphus) with imported insects, and considers them as liable to become dangerous enemies. Tineid larvæ are rarely found in collections, and only affect the larger moths. They are not easily discovered, since they make no dust, as do most other pests. Some persons have been considerably annoyed by one of the common clothes moths, *Tineola biselliella* (Fig. 121). Dr. Hagen found that it attacked freshly collected or newly spread insects, where the spreading-boards were left uncovered, but Mr. F. M. Webster has found it injurious to the general collections at Columbus, Ohio.

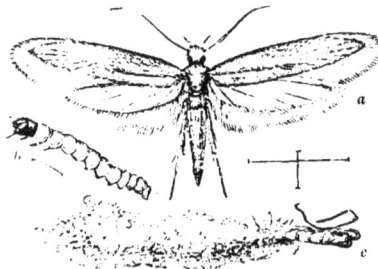

FIG. 121. *Tineola biselliella;* a, adult; b, larva; c cocoon and empty pupa—skin enlarged.

Of beetles, the Ptinidæ are sometimes found in collections but are not common. Two species are known to attack entomological specimens, namely, *Ptinus fur*, which is quite rare, in this country, but much more abundant in Europe, and *Tribolium ferrugineum*, a cosmopolitan species which, however, has several times been associated in injurious numbers with large collections of insects imported from the East Indies.

But by far the most dangerous enemies of insect collections are the

larvæ of some half dozen or more species of Dermestidæ belonging to
the genera Anthrenus, Attagenus, Trogoderma, and Dermestes. Of
these *Anthrenus varius* is the more common pest, in museums, especially in the North and East. In the South and West *Trogoderma tarsale*
and *T. ornatum* (?) replace Anthrenus. The European species *Anthrenus
musæorum*, is, on the authority of Hagen, rare in this country, and
probably occurs chiefly in collections of imported insects. It is the
common injurious species of Europe. *Anthrenus scrophulariæ* (see Fig.
67) occurs also in collections, Dr. Hagen stating that he has found it
nearly as common as *A. varius*, and certainly more dangerous. In my
own experience it is rarely found in insect collections. Two species of
Attagenus (*A. pellio* and *A. megatoma*) have also been found in collections. *A. megatoma* has been found by Dr. Hagen to do not a little
damage to insect collections in Cambridge, as well as to equal if not
exceed the Carpet Beetle in its disastrous attacks upon carpets and
household furniture. The other species, *A. pellio*, is rarely found in this
country, but is much more common and obnoxious in Europe than *A. megatoma*. *Dermestes lardarius* is sometimes found in collections, and is
attracted by the presence of animal matter such as skins, etc. The two
particularly destructive pests, as pointed out, are *Anthrenus varius* and
*Trogoderma tarsale*. These species, together with most of the others,
have no definite breeding period, but, in the uniform temperature of the
laboratory or museum, breed all the year round and present no definite
broods. It is the experience at the Museum that the boxes on the
lower tier of shelves are very much more subject to attack than those on
the upper tiers, from which it would seem that the parent beetle
deposits her eggs outside the boxes on the floor of the cases and that
the young larvæ work their way into the smallest crevices. The danger
of infection by these pests is greater in warm climates like that of Washington than in regions further north, as the warm season begins earlier,
lasts longer, and furnishes better conditions for breeding
and multiplication.

REMEDIES.—The following remedies and preventives
will prove efficient in checking or preventing the work of
these pests.

*Naphthaline.*—Where tight boxes are employed little fear
of the work of these destructive agents need arise, especially if the boxes are kept supplied with repellent naphthaline cones. These are hard cones of naphthaline,
mounted on pins for convenient placing in the boxes (see
Fig. 122), and may be obtained of dealers in entomological
supplies. Naphthaline cones act as repellents to these
insects and also to some extent retard the development of the larvæ in
all stages and particularly of the eggs.

Fig. 122.—
A naphthaline
cone.

Mr. Schwarz states (*Proc. Ent. Soc. of Washington*, Vol. 1, page 63)
that in place of these cones a form of naphthaline may be used which

is known in commerce as "white carbon," and is put up in the form of small square rods for use in intensifying the flames of gaslight. The material is very cheap, costing only 8 cents per pound wholesale, and may be broken up into small pieces, wrapped in paper, and pinned. The use of naphthaline cones is not advisable in boxes containing delicate specimens, as it leaves a deposit which dulls the colors and encourages greasing. The deliquescence of the naphthaline cones produces a blackish, oily residuum which will soil the lining of the box, and it is always advisable either to pin a piece of blotting paper beneath the cone or to wrap this in paper.

Constant watchfulness is necessary to see that the eggs which have been deposited and checked in development by the application of this insecticide do not ultimately hatch and start a new generation in the insect box.

*Bisulphide of Carbon.*—If the collection is found to be infested with insect pests, it may be renovated by pouring a little bisulphide of carbon into the boxes and closing them at once. This substance evaporates rapidly and will destroy all insect life, and does not injure specimens or pins nor stain the boxes. If infested specimens are received, these should be inclosed in a tight box and treated with bisulphide of carbon before being added to the general collection, and it is always well for those who are receiving pinned specimens by exchange or otherwise to keep a quarantine box of this kind on hand.

*Mercury Pellets.*—The use of mercury pellets is recommended to free boxes from Mites, Psoci, etc., and also to collect any particles of dust which may gain entrance. A few small pellets of mercury, placed free in the bottom of the horizontal box will, by the movement of the box, be caused to roll to and fro and accomplish the desired end.

*Carbolic Acid.*—Mr. A. T. Marshall (*Entomologist's Monthly Magazine*, Dec., 1873, p. 176) records that he washes the paper of his boxes with the common disinfecting solution of carbolic acid in two-thirds water, which dries without staining and protects the specimens from Psoci.

*A Means of preserving Insects in dry hot Countries.*—In the "*Horæ Societatis Entomologicæ Rossicæ,*" XXIV, pp. 233, 234 (1889), M. A. Wilkins, writing from Tachkent in Turkestan, alludes to the inefficiency of ordinary preservatives in Central Asia, on account of their rapid volatilization through the hot dry air, so that if a collection be neglected for only two or three months *Anthreni* are sure to be found in the boxes. He has hit upon a plan which he finds effective, and at the same time very simple. He employs India-rubber bands about 1½ inches in width and less than the length of the boxes to which they are to be applied. These bands are stretched over the opening line of the boxes, and effectually prevent the entrance of the most minute destroyers. Possibly a similar plan might be adopted in other countries with a like climate. At any rate, the method has the merit of extreme simplicity. (The *Ent. Mo. Mag.*, Apr., 1891, p. 107.)

Collections kept in damp places or in a moist climate are very liable to mold, and under such conditions it is difficult to avoid this evil. Carbolic acid is recommended, but Mr. Ashmead, who has kept a large collection in the moist climate of Florida, has found the use of naphthaline much more satisfactory. Mr. Herbert H. Smith who has had more extensive experience in the tropics prefers the carbolic acid. Moldy specimens may be cleansed by washing with carbolic acid applied with a fine camel's hair brush.

## VERDIGRISING AND GREASING.

The action of the acid juices in the bodies of certain specimens—as many of the Lepidoptera, Coleoptera, and Diptera—will cause the formation of verdigris about the pin, which in time accumulates and disfigures and distorts the specimen, and ultimately corrodes the pin, so that the slightest touch causes it to bend or break. There is no preventive yet known for this trouble other than the use of pins which have no brass to be corroded. Japanned pins are made for this purpose, and are, on the whole, satisfactory, but they bend easily and some caution is required in handling them. In place of these pins, which are somewhat more expensive than the steel pins, iron pins may be used. These are very soft and bend too easily for satisfactory use. The steel pins may be rendered available for use by an immersion in a silver bath, which is comparatively inexpensive.

Insects the larvae of which live in wood are particularly subject to verdigris, as the Cerambycidae and Elateridae in Coleoptera, the Uroceridae in Hymenoptera and Sesiidae in Lepidoptera. In Hymenoptera the families Formicidae, Mutillidae, and the endophytous Tenthredinidae verdigris very rapidly, and most Diptera also. With all these insects japanned or silvered pins should be used, or when not too large the insects should be mounted on triangles. This verdigrising is associated with what is known as greasing, and this, as just indicated, is also associated with endophytous larval life. The verdigris may be prevented by the methods indicated, and I would strongly advise, as a good general rule to be followed, the rejection of the ordinary pins for all species which, in the larva state, are internal feeders. But there is no way of preventing greasing or decomposition of the fats of the body, which may affect a specimen years after it has been in the cabinet. If the specimen is valuable the grease may be absorbed by immersion in ether or benzine, or by a longer treatment with powdered pipe-clay or plaster of Paris. Insects collected on seabeaches, and saturated with salt water, also corrode the common steel pin very quickly and should be mounted on japanned pins. It is also advisable to rinse such specimens thoroughly in fresh water before mounting.

The conviction has been forcing itself on my mind for some time that the naphthaline cones tend to promote greasing and verdigris, and carbolic acid in some small vessel secured to the cork, were, perhaps,

## THE REARING OF INSECTS.

*General Directions.*—The importance, even to the mere collector, of rearing insects to obtain specimens for the cabinet has been referred to from time to time in these pages. The philosophic study of entomology, however, requires much more than the mere collecting of specimens, and one of the most profitable and, at the same time, most fascinating phases of the study relates to the life-history and habits. In no branch of natural history are biologic studies more easily carried on, or the biologic facts more remarkable or interesting. The systematist by such study will be saved from the narrow and hair-splitting tendencies which study of slight difference of characters tends to, while to the economic entomologist it is most essential.

In the rearing of insects success will be attained in proportion to the extent to which the conditions of nature in the matters of temperature, moisture, food-supply, and conditions for pupation, are observed.

" In the hands of the careful breeder an insect may be secured against its numerous natural enemies and against vicissitudes of climate, and will, consequently, be more apt to mature than in a state of nature. The breeding of aquatic insects requires aquaria, and is always attended with the difficulty of furnishing a proper supply of food. The transformations of many others, both aquatic and terrestrial, can be studied only by close and careful outdoor observation. But the great majority of insect larvæ may be reared to the perfect state indoors, where their maneuverings may be constantly and conveniently watched. For the feeding of small species, glass jars and wide-mouthed bottles will be found useful. The mouths should be covered with gauze or old linen, fastened either by thread or rubber, and a few inches of moist earth at the bottom will furnish a retreat for those which enter it to transform and keep the atmosphere in a moist and fit condition.

*The Breeding Cage or Vivarium.*—" For larger insects I use a breeding cage or vivarium which answers the purpose admirably. It is represented in figure 123, and comprises three distinct parts: First, the bottom board *a*, consisting of a square piece of inch thick walnut with a rectangular zinc pan *ff*, 4 inches deep, fastened to it above, and with two cross pieces *gg* below, to prevent cracking or warping, facilitate lifting, and allow the air to pass underneath the cage. Second, a box *b* with three glass sides and a glass door in front, to fit over the zinc pan. Third, a cap *c*, which fits closely on to the box, and has a top of fine wire gauze. To the center of the zinc pan is soldered a zinc tube *d* just large enough to contain an ordinary quinine bottle. The zinc pan is filled with clean sifted earth or sand *e*, and the quinine bottle is for the reception of the food plant. The cage admits of abundant light and air, and also of the easy removal of excrement or frass which falls to the ground; while the insects in transforming enter the ground or attach themselves to the sides or the cap, according to their habits. The most convenient dimensions I find to be 12 inches square and 18 inches high: the cap and the door fit closely by means of rabbets, and the former has a depth of about 4 inches to admit of the largest cocoon being spun in it without touching the box on which it rests. The zinc pan might be made 6 or 8 inches deep, and the lower half filled with sand, so as to keep the whole moist for a greater length of time."

The sand or earth in the zinc pan at the bottom of the breeding cage should be kept constantly moistened, and in the case of hibernating pupæ the constant adding of water to the top of the earth or sand causes it to become very hard and compact. To overcome this objection it was suggested in the *Entomologists' Monthly Magazine* for June, 1876, page 17, that the base should be made with an inner perforated side, the water to be applied between it and the outer side, and I have for some years employed a similar double-sided base, which answers the purpose admirably (See Figure 124.). It is substantially the same as that made for the Department by Prof. J. H. Comstock in 1879. It consists of a zinc tray *a*, of two or three inches greater diameter than the breeding cage, which surrounds the zinc pan proper containing the earth, and the tube *d* for the reception of the food-plant. The lower portion of the inner pan *b* is of perforated zinc. Zinc supports, *c c*, are constructed about halfway between the bottom and the top of this pan, on which the breeding cage rests. In moistening the earth in the cage, water is poured into the tray, which enters the soil slowly, through the perforations in the zinc pan. I have found this modification of very decided advantage and use it altogether in the work of the Division, and heartily recommend it.

The base of the vivarium or breeding cage should never be made of tin, but always of zinc. If made of tin, it will soon rust out. Galvanized iron may be

Fig. 123.—Insect breeding-cage or vivarium.

used in place of the zinc, and will doubtless prove equally satisfactory.

"A dozen such cages will furnish room for the annual breeding of a great number of species, as several having different habits and appearance, and which there is no danger of confounding, may be simultaneously fed in the same cage. I number each of the three parts of each cage to prevent misplacement and to facilitate reference, and aside from the notes made in the notebook, it will aid the memory and expedite matters to keep a short open record of the species contained in each cage, by means of slips of paper pasted on the glass door. As fast as the different specimens complete their transformations and are taken from the cage the notes may be altered or erased, or the slips wetted and removed entirely. To prevent possible confounding of the different species which enter the ground, it is well, from time to time, to sift the earth, separate the pupæ and place them in what I call 'imago cages,' used for this purpose alone and not for feeding. Here they may be arranged with references to their exact whereabouts.

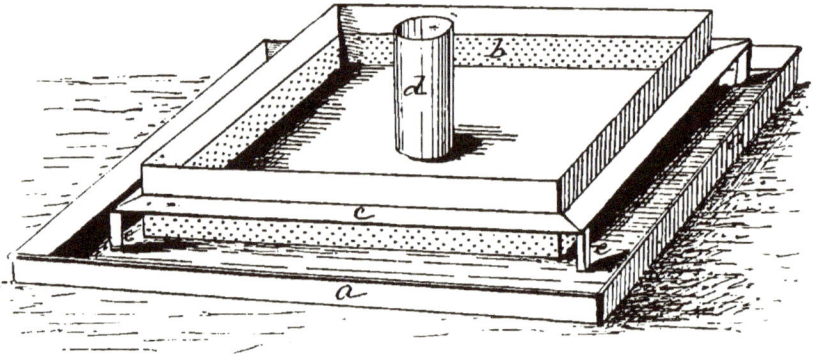

FIG. 124.—Improved base for breeding-cage (original).

"A continued supply of fresh food must be given to those insects which are feeding, and a bit of moist sponge thrust into the mouth of the bottle will prevent drowning, and furnish moisture to such as need it. By means of a broad paste brush and spoon the frass may be daily removed from the earth, which should be kept in a fit and moist condition—neither too wet nor too dry. In the winter, when insect life is dormant, the earth may be covered with a layer of clean moss, and the cages put away in the cellar, where they will need only occasional inspection, but where the moss must nevertheless be kept damp. Cages made after the same plan, but with the sides of wire gauze instead of glass, may be used for insects which do not well bear confinement indoors, the cages to be placed on a platform on the north side of a house, where they will receive only the early morning and late evening sun."

*Detailed Instructions for Rearing.*—In the rearing of insects every worker will develop a number of methods of value, and it is only by careful study and comparison of the experiences of all that the best system can be elaborated. For this reason I have, in what follows, quoted, in a more or less fragmentary way, the experiences of different entomologists.

As is remarked by Miss Murtfeldt, in an interesting paper read before the Entomological Club of the American Association for the Advancement of Science, August 20, 1890, "there is a great individuality, or rather specificality, in insects, and not infrequently specimens of larvæ are found for which the collector taxes his ingenuity in vain to provide. Not the freshest leaves, the cleanest swept earth, or the most well-aired cages will seem to promote their development."

The greatest care and watchfulness, therefore, are necessary to insure success in the rearing of larvæ. In many cases such larvæ can only be successfully reared by inclosing them in netting on their food-plant out of doors. It is a frequent device of Lepidopterists also to inclose a rare female in netting placed on the food plant of the species, where the male may be attracted and may be caught and placed in the bag with the female, when copulation usually takes place successfully, or a male may be caught in the field and inclosed with such female. Mr. W. H. Edwards, where the plant is a small one, uses for this purpose a headless keg covered at one end with gauze, which he places over the plant inclosing the female.

Mr. James Fletcher, of Ottawa, Canada, one of our most enthusiastic rearers of insects, has given some details of his methods in a recent very interesting account of "A Trip to Nepigon." One style of cage used by him in securing the eggs of large Lepidoptera " is made by cutting two flexible twigs from the willow or any other shrub and bending them into the shape of two arches, which are put one over the other at right angles and the ends pushed into the ground. Over the penthouse thus formed a piece of gauze is placed, and the cage is complete. The edges of the gauze may be kept down either with pegs or with earth placed upon them." This kind of cage is used for all the larger species which lay upon low plants. The species which oviposit on larger plants or trees are inclosed in a gauze bag tied over the branch. This is applicable to insects like *Papilio, Limenitis, Grapta*, etc. Care must be taken, however, that the leaves of the plant inside the net are in a natural position, for some species are very particular about where they lay their eggs. some ovipositing on the top of the leaves, others near the tip, and many others on the under surface. " When a bag made beforehand is used. the points must be rounded, and in tying the piece of gauze over the branch care must be taken to pull out all creases and folds, or the insect will be sure to get into them and either die or be killed by spiders from the outside of the bag. It is better to put more than one female in the same cage. I have frequently noticed that one specimen alone is apt to crawl about and settle on the top of the cage, and not go near the food plant. When there are two or three they disturb each other and are frequently moving and falling on the food plant, when they will stop for a moment and lay an egg. A stubborn female of *Colias eurytheme* was only induced to lay by having a male placed in the cage with her, and by his impatient fluttering and efforts to escape she was frequently knocked down from the top, and every time she fell upon the clover plant beneath, she laid an egg before crawling to the top again." Some insects, even with all care in making their surroundings as natural as possible, will persistently refuse to lay. Mr. Fletcher has successfully obtained eggs from some of these by a method which he says one of his correspondents styles " Egg-laying extraordinary." It consists simply in " gently pressing the abdomen of a female which has died without laying eggs, until one and sometimes two perfect eggs are passed from the ovipositor." Mr. Fletcher has secured a number of eggs from rare species in this way, and successfully reared the larvæ. The following directions for obtaining the eggs and rearing the larvæ of Lepidoptera, given in this paper by Mr. Fletcher, are excellent, and I quote them entire:

" There are one or two points which should be remembered when obtaining eggs and rearing larvæ. In the first place, the females should not be left exposed to the direct rays of the sun; but it will be found sometimes that if a butterfly is sluggish, putting her in the sun for a short time will revive her and make her lay eggs. Confined females, whether over branches or potted plants, should always be in the open air. If females do not lay in two or three days they must be fed. This is easily done. Take them from the cage and hold near them a piece of sponge (or, Mr. Edwards suggests, evaporated apple), saturated with a weak solution of sugar and water. As soon as it is placed near them they will generally move their antennæ towards it, and, uncoiling their tongues, suck up the liquid. If they take no notice of it the tongue can be gently uncoiled with the tip of a pin, when they will nearly always begin to feed. It is better to feed them away from the plant they are wanted to lay upon, for if any of the sirup be spilled over the flowerpot or plant it is almost sure to attract ants. I kept one female *Colias interior* in this way for ten days before eggs were laid. When eggs are laid they should, as a rule, be collected at short intervals. They are subject to the attacks of various enemies—spiders, ants, crickets, and minute hymenopterous parasites. They may be kept easily in small boxes, but do better if not kept in too hot or dry a place. When the young caterpillars hatch they must be removed with great care to the food plant; a fine paint brush is the most convenient instrument. With small larvæ or those which it is desired to examine often, glass tubes or jelly glasses with a tight-fitting tin cover are best. These must be tightly closed and in a cool place. Light is not at all necessary, and the sun should never be allowed to shine directly upon them. If moisture gathers inside the glasses the top should be removed for a short time. Larvæ may also be placed upon growing plants. These can be planted in flowerpots and the young caterpillars kept from wandering either by a cage of wire netting or, by what I have found very satisfactory, glass lamp chimneys. These can be placed over the plant, with the bottom pushed into the earth, and then should have a loose wad of cotton batting in the top. This has the double effect of preventing too great evaporation of moisture and keeping its occupants within bounds. Some larvæ wander very much and climb with the greatest ease over glass, spinning a silken path for themselves as they go. When caterpillars are bred in the study it must not be forgotten that the air inside a house is much drier than it is out of doors amongst the trees and low herbage, where caterpillars live naturally. The amateur will require some experience in keeping the air at a right degree of moisture when breeding upon growing plants. In close tin boxes or jars, where the leaves must be changed every day, there is not so much trouble. An important thing to remember with larvæ in jars is to thoroughly wash out the jars with cold water every day. If, however, a caterpillar has spun a web on the side and is hung up to moult, it must not be disturbed. In changing the food it is better not to remove the caterpillars from the old food, but having placed a new supply in the jar, cut off the piece of leaf upon which they are and drop it into the jar. If they are not near the moult a little puff of breath will generally dislodge them. Some caterpillars, as *Papilio turnus*, which spins a platform to which it retires after feeding, can best be fed upon a living tree out of doors, but must be covered with a gauze bag to keep off enemies. A piece of paper should be kept *attached* to each breeding jar or cage, upon which regular notes must be taken *at the time*, giving the dates of every noticeable feature, particularly the dates of the moults and the changes which take place in the form and color at that time."

The necessity of outdoor work is further felt in the determination of the facts in the life-history of some insects which have an alternation of generations, as some Gall-flies (*Cynipidæ*), and most Aphides. To successfully study these insects constant outdoor observation is necessary, or the species must be inclosed in screens of wire or netting outdoors on their food-plant. Many insects which breed on the ground or on low herbage may be very successfully watched and controlled by covering the soil containing them or the plant on which they feed with a wire screen or netting. The use of wire screens is also advisable in the case of wintering pupæ or larvæ out of doors. Many species can be more easily carried through the winter by placing them outdoors under such screens during the winter, which insures their being subjected to the natural conditions of climate, and then transferring them to the breeding cage again early in the spring. This is advisable in the case of Microlarvæ and pupæ. Species which bore in the stems of plants may be easily cared for and leaf-mining and leaf-webbing forms can be secured under screens or covers out of doors for the winter in sheltered situations. Many species which, if kept in a warm room can not be reared, will, if subjected to freezing weather under slight protection in the open air, emerge successfully the following spring.

The greatest care is necessary in the breeding of Tenthredinidæ, as most of them transform under ground and are single brooded, the larvæ remaining in the ground from midsummer until the following spring. Nothing but constant care in maintaining uniform moisture and temperature of the soil will insure the success of such breeding. Some species bore into rotten wood or the stems of plants to undergo their transformations, as for instance the Dogwood Saw-fly (*Harpiphorus varianus*). This species, unless supplied with soft or rotten wood in which to bore, will wander ceaselessly round the cage, and in most cases eventually perish.

Where a small room can be devoted to the purpose, an excellent wholesale method of obtaining wood-boring insects (*Coleoptera, Lepidoptera*, etc.) is to collect large quantities of dead or dying wood of all sorts or any that indicates the presence of the early states of insects, and store it in such apartment. The following spring and summer the escaping insects will be attracted to the windows and may be easily secured. The objection to this method is that, in many cases, it will be impossible to determine the food habit of the insect secured, owing to the variety of material brought together.

*The Root Cage.*—For the study of insects which affect the roots of plants a root cage has been devised by Prof. J. H. Comstock which is of sufficient importance to warrant full description. It consists of a zinc frame (Fig. 125*a*) holding two plates of glass in a vertical position and only a short distance apart, the space between the plates being filled with soil in which seeds are planted or small plants set. Outside of each glass is a piece of zinc or sheet iron (*b*) which slips into grooves and which can be easily removed. When these zincs are in place the soil is kept dark.

The idea of the cages is, that the space between the glasses being very narrow, a large part of the roots will ramify close to the surface of the glass, so that by removing the zinc slides the roots may be easily seen, and any root-inhabiting insects which it may be desirable to breed may thus be studied in their natural conditions without disturbing them. Prof. Comstock has used this cage very successfully in studying the habits of wire-worms, and its availability for many of the underground insects, such as the Cicadas, root-lice, larvæ, etc., is apparent. These frames may be made of various sizes, to accommodate particular insects. It will be of advantage in many cases, in order to secure the natural conditions as nearly as possible, to sink the cage in the soil, and for this purpose Prof. Comstock has had constructed a pit lined with brick for the reception of his cages, and employs a small portable crane to lift them out of the ground when it is desirable to examine them.

*Other Apparatus.*—Much of the breeding of insects can be done with the simplest apparatus, and for the rearing of Microlepidoptera, Gall-insects, and the keeping of cocoons and chrysalides of small species, nothing is more convenient than a medium sized test-tube, the end of which may be plugged with cotton. I have recently successfully carried over the winter the larva of *Sphecius speciosus*, which had been removed early in the fall from its earthen pod or cocoon, the larva transforming to a perfect pupa in the spring. In this case the test tube was plugged with cotton and inserted in a wooden mailing tube to exclude the light. Smaller jars with glass covers or with a covering of gauze may be employed for most insects, with the advantage of occupying comparatively little space and of isolating the species under study.

FIG. 125—Root cage: *a*, frame with slide removed; *b*, movable slide; *c*, top view (original).

Long glass tubes, open at both ends, are useful in many other ways, especially in the rearing and study of the smaller hypogean insects or those which bore and live in the stems of plants. An infested stem cut open on one side and placed in such a tube will generally carry any insect that has ceased feeding, or any species like the wood-boring bees which feed upon stored food, successfully through their transformations; while root-lice may be kept for a lengthy period upon the roots in such tube, providing a portion of the root extends outside of the tube and is kept in moistened ground or water. In all such cases these tubes, with their contents, should be kept in the dark, either in a drawer or else covered with some dark material which can be wound around or slipped over them, and the ends must be closed with cotton or cork.

The rearer of insects will frequently experience difficulty in carrying his pupæ through the winter, and, even though ordinary precautions are taken, the mortality will frequently amount to 50 per cent of the speci mens. Mr. H. Bakhaus, of Leipsic, thus describes a device which is sub stantially the base of the vivarium shown on page 114.

"The base consists of a round plate of strong zinc, with two vertical rims, an inch high, placed one within the other, an inch apart, and soldered to the basal plate so that the outer one is water-tight. The inner rim must be perforated with small holes as close to the bottom as possible. The space inside the inner rim must be filled with fine sand, on which the pupae should be laid. The space between the two rims is then filled with water, which, finding its way through the holes in the inner rim to the sand, causes the necessary moisture. Over the whole is put a bell-shaped cover of wire gauze, which must fit tightly over the outer rim. In this receptacle the pupae remain un touched, and receive fresh moisture, as above indicated, if required by the drying of the sand."

The hardy pupae of most Noctuids and Bombycids, as well as those of many Rophalocera, may be handled with little danger, but other species, if handled at all, or if the cocoons which they make for themselves are broken, can seldom be reared. Constant precautions also must be exercised in the care of the soil and the breeding cages. One of the great drawbacks is the presence of mites and thread worms (Entozoöns), etc., which affect dying or dead pupae and larvae in the soil. They also affect living specimens and are capable of doing very considerable damage. To free the soil of them it is necessary at times to allow the earth to become dry enough to be sifted, and then after removing the pupae submit it to heat sufficient to destroy any undesired life there may be in it.

*The Insectary.*—Up to the present time the work of rearing insects has been largely confined to the breeding cage and breeding jar, already de scribed, which have been kept in the rooms of the investigator. The advantages of having a special building for this purpose are at once apparent and need not be insisted upon. One of the best establish ments of this kind is that of the Cornell University Experiment Station, which was fully described in Bulletin No. 3, of that station, November, 1888. The Kansas Experiment Station has a similar building, and one has recently been built for the use of the Entomological Division of the United States Department of Agriculture. The insect-breeding house, or insectary, should comprise a building having workrooms, or labo ratories, for microscopic and general work in the study and preparation of specimens, and also a conservatory for the rearing of specimens and the growth of plants, and, where applied entomology is concerned, special rooms for the preparation and the test of insecticides. The building proper should also have a basement storage room for hiber nating insects. The laboratory should be fitted with all the apparatus used in the study of insects, including microscopes and accessories and a dark-room for photographic purposes.

## DIRECTIONS FOR TRANSMITTING INSECTS.

It is very desirable in transmitting insects from the field of exploration, or from one entomologist to another, for information, exchange, or
other purpose, that they be properly secured and packed. Pinned and
mounted specimens should be firmly fixed in a cigar box, or a special
box for mailing, and this should be carefully but not too tightly wrapped
with cotton or other loose packing material to a depth of perhaps an
inch, and the whole then inclosed in stiff wrapping paper. It is prefer
able, however, to inclose the box containing the specimens in a larger
box, filling the intervening space, not too firmly, with cotton or other
packing material. Where specimens are to be sent to a considerable

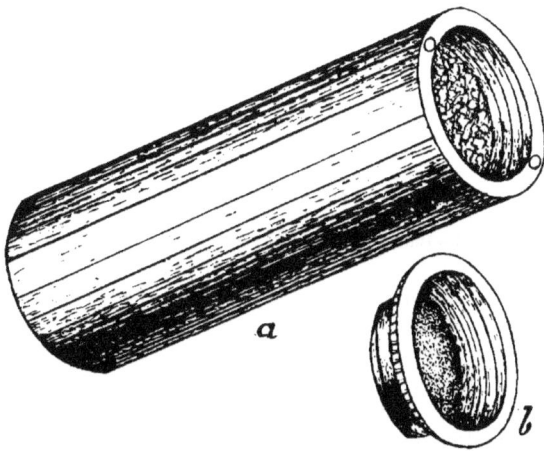

FIG. 126.—Wooden-tube mailing-box: *a*, tube; *b*, cover (original.)

distance it is advisable also to line the box in which they are placed
with cotton, which serves to catch and hold any specimens which may
become loose in transit. In the case of alcoholic specimens each vial
should be wrapped separately in cotton and placed in a strong wooden
or tin box. Special mailing boxes for alcoholic specimens have been
devised, and a very convenient form is herewith figured. It is an ordinary tube of wood, with a metal screw top, and the interior lined with
rough cork. These tubes are made in various sizes to accommodate
vials of different dimensions.

In mailing living specimens the essential thing is a strong box, preferably tin, made as nearly air-tight as possible. I have found it very
convenient on long trips to carry with me a number of tin boxes in the
flat (Fig. 127), combined in convenient packages, ready to be bent and
improvised in the field. For this purpose get any tinsmith to make out
of good tin a number of pieces cut of the requisite dimensions both for
the bottoms and the covers, carefully cutting the corners to permit
the proper bending of the sides. These improvised boxes will prove

useful for keeping living larvæ with their food-plants, especially if
tied up in stout brown paper to prevent any exit from the unsoldered
angles. They will also answer admirably for mailing or otherwise send-

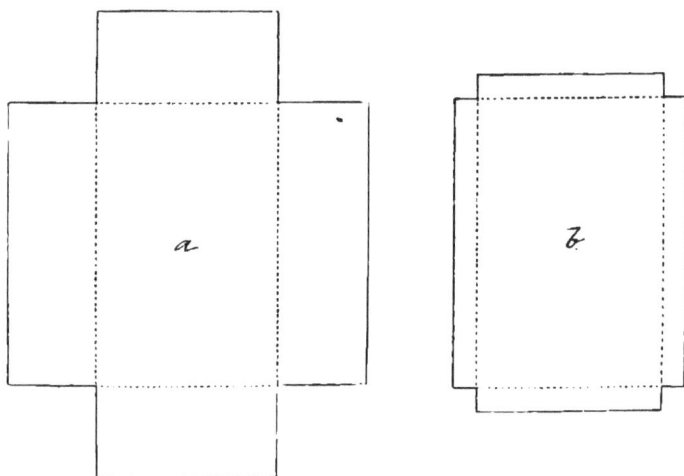

Fig. 127.—Tin mailing-box in the flat: *a*, box; *b*, cover (original).

ing specimens to their ultimate destination. In the case of larvæ a
quantity of the food-plant should always be inclosed in the box.

In transmitting insects for information the greatest care should be
taken to relieve the person of whom information is sought of as much
unnecessary work as possible. It is easy for any beginner to collect
more in a single day than an experienced entomologist can well mount,
study, and determine in a week, and as those who have the means and
information to give determinations or otherwise to assist beginners are
generally very much occupied, and their time is valuable, they are justified in ignoring miscellaneous collectings where the sender has made no
effort to either properly mount or
otherwise study and care for his
specimens.

Living specimens, especially larvæ,
should be packed in tin. with a supply of their appropriate food. The
tighter the box the fresher will the
food as well as the specimens keep. Insects do not easily suffocate,
and it is worse than useless, in the majority of cases, to punch air-holes
in such boxes. Dead specimens, when not pinned, may be sent in a
variety of ways. Small ones may be dropped into a quill and inclosed
in a letter, or a small vial fitted into a piece of bored wood. Those
which do not spoil by wetting may be sent in alcohol, provided the bot-

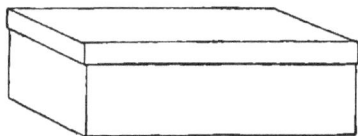

Fig. 128.—Tin mailing-box, bent into shape for use (original.)

tle is absolutely filled, or, what is better, in sawdust moistened with alcohol, or between layers of cotton saturated with alcohol.

The postal regulations permit the sending by mail of "dried insects * * * when properly put up, so as not to injure the persons of those handling the mails, nor soil the mail bags or their contents." Specimens in alcohol may also be sent by mail, provided that the containing vial be strong enough to resist the shock of handling in the mail, and that it be inclosed in a wooden or papier-maché tube not less than three-sixteenths of an inch thick in the thinnest part, lined with cork or other soft material, and with a screw top so adjusted as to prevent the leakage of the contents in case of breakage. Entomological specimens are of the fourth class of mail matter, the postage on which is 1 cent an ounce or fraction thereof, the limit of weight for a single package being 4 pounds, and the limit as to bulk 18 inches in any direction. Saleable matter is also non-mailable at fourth-class rates; so that the safer method, with small packages, is to send under letter postage. It is far better, however, for long journeys, and especially for transatlantic shipment, to send by express.

## NOTES AND MEMORANDA.

In the foregoing pages are given some of the more useful directions for those wishing to commence to collect and study insects. Experience will soon teach many other important facts not mentioned here, and the best closing advice I can give the novice is, to get acquainted, if possible, with some one who has already had large experience. He will be very apt to find such a person pleasant and instructive company whether in the field or in the closet. One important habit, however, I wish to strongly inculcate and emphasize: The collector should never be without his memorandum or note book. More profitless work can scarcely be imagined than collecting natural-history specimens without some specific aim or object. Every observation made should be carefully recorded, and the date of capture, locality, and food-plant should always be attached to the specimens when these are mounted. More extended notes may be made in a field memorandum book carried in the pocket or in larger record books at home. For field memoranda I advise the use of a stylographic pen, as pencil is apt to rub and efface in time by the motions of the body. The larger record book is especially necessary for biologic notes. Notes on adolescent states which it is intended to rear to the imago can not be too carefully made or in too much detail. The relative size, details of ornamentation and structure, dates of moulting or transformation from one state to another—indeed, everything that pertains to the biography of the species—should be noted down, and little or nothing trusted to mere memory where exact data are so essential. Many insects, particularly dragon-flies, have brilliant coloring when fresh from the pupa, which is largely lost afterward. The time of laying and hatching of eggs, the number from a single female, the character of the eggs, general habits, records of parasites and their mode of attack—all should be entered as observed. A great many species have the most curious life histories, which can not be ascertained except by continued and persevering observation, not only in the vivarium or insectary but in the field. It is almost impossible to follow, under artificial conditions, the full life cycle of many species like the Aphididæ, or the Gall-flies, etc., which involve alternation of generations, dimorphism, heteromorphism, migration from one plant to another, and various other curious departures from the normal mode of development, without careful field study and experiment. These studies are possible only to those who are able to frequent the same localities throughout the whole year, and can hardly be carried on by the traveling naturalist or collector.

## INSTRUCTIONS FOR COLLECTING AND PRESERVING ARACHNIDS AND MYRIAPODS.

The foregoing portions of this manual have dealt almost exclusively with the subject of the securing and preservation of Hexapods, but it is deemed advisable to include brief instructions for the collection and care of the near allies of the true insect, Spiders and Myriapods, the study of which will in most cases be associated with that of Hexapods.

### DIRECTIONS FOR COLLECTING SPIDERS.

*Apparatus.*—Many of the directions and methods given in the foregoing pages for the collection of Hexapods apply also to the animals named above. Little apparatus is necessary in the collection of spiders and other Arachnids. The essentials are vials containing alcohol, an insect net, a sieve, and forceps. Narrow vials without necks are best for collecting purposes, as the corks can be more quickly inserted. They should be of different sizes, from 1 dram to 4 or 6 drams, and the alcohol used should be at least 50 per cent strong and in some cases it is advisable to use it at a strength of 70 or 80 per cent. The net may be of the same construction as that used to collect insects and is used in the same way. Some arachnologists, however, use a net of a somewhat different make, which is much stronger. The iron ring is heavier and larger than in the case of the insect net, resembling in this respect the ring of the Deyrolle net. The bag is short and the handle is fastened to both sides of the ring. This net is used for beating the leaves of trees, bushes, and grass. Dr. Marx uses a net which is already described and figured under the name of the Umbrella Net (see p. 34, Fig. 52). The sieve is the same as that described on p. 35, Fig. 54, and is used to sift the spiders from leaves and rubbish, especially during winter. A mass of leaves and other material is thrown into the sieve and then shaken, the spiders falling through on a piece of white cloth, which is spread under the sieve on the ground. Many hibernating species can be readily secured in this manner. A forceps similar to that described for the collecting of hexapods should be used to capture or pick up specimens, for if handled with the fingers they are apt to be crushed, especially the smaller forms. As soon as

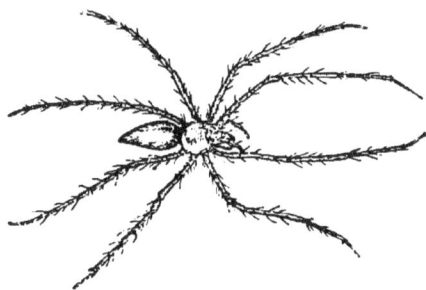

FIG. 129.—A ground Spider (*Oxyopes viridans*). (After Comstock.)

the collecting is finished or the vial is filled a label should be placed in this last indicating place and date of collection. Egg sacs and cocoons should be collected in pill boxes and properly labeled, and if possible the adults should be reared. Both sexes should be collected and descriptive notes or drawings made of the webs as found in nature.

*Time and Locality for Collecting.*—The best time to collect spiders is in the early fall, during the months of September and October. The great majority of the species are then mature. Many forms, however, occur in the adult state in late spring and early summer. Numerous species may also be collected during winter, some of these hibernating under stones, the bark of dead trees, etc., and others, more particularly the small forms, under dead leaves and rubbish on the ground in woods. Other species which have hibernated may be found about the earliest flowers in spring. No particular localities can be indicated for the collection of spiders, since they occur in all sorts of places, in wooded or open regions and also in and about dwellings. Many Lycosidæ are found in dry and rocky situations and quite a number in open fields. Thomisidæ may be found on flowers. The Therididæ affect shady places, and many Epeiridæ will be found in similar situations. The Attidæ love the sun and are found very actively engaged in hunting insects on plants and dead leaves. Many species of this family will be found in cases under

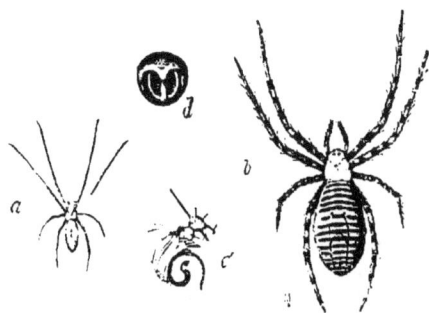

FIG. 130.—An orb-weaver (*Argiope argyraspides* Walck): *a*, male; *b*, female; *c* and *d*, enlarged parts.

loose bark in winter. Evergreen trees are also quite good collecting grounds for Attidæ. The Drassidæ are ground spiders and are mostly nocturnal, hiding during the day under leaves and stones; a few forms, however, disport in the hottest sunshine. Some genera are found most frequently near water or in damp places, as Dolomedes and Tetragnatha; others in sandy places, as Micaria, Targalia.

COLLECTING OTHER ARACHNIDS: MITES, TICKS, SCORPIONS, ETC.

Other Arachnids—as mites, ticks, scorpions, daddy longlegs or harvest-men—may be collected in the same way as spiders.

The Phalangidæ (Harvest-men) somewhat resemble spiders, and are at once recognized by their extremely long legs. They occur about houses, especially in shady places, under the eaves, etc., and in the woods and fields. They are carnivorous and feed on small insects, especially Aphides. They should be pressed a little when captured to extrude the genital apparatus, if possible, and are best collected in the early fall.

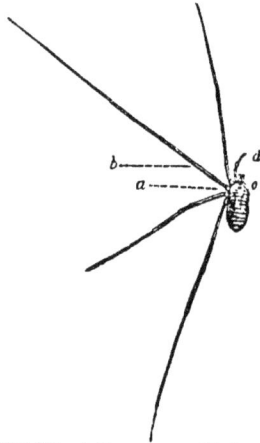

The Phrynidæ are very peculiar looking animals, the anterior legs being very long and slender and the maxillary palpi very large. The genus *Thelyphonus* is not uncommon in the South, and is known by its oblong body, ending usually with a long, slender, many-jointed filament, from which they are called Whip-tailed Scorpions. *T. giganteus* is the common species. They occur in moist situations, and are carnivorous, feeding on insects and small animals.

FIG. 131.—A Harvest-man (*Phalangium rentricosum*).—From Packard.

The false scorpions, Chernetidæ, may at once be recognized by their large maxillary palpi, resembling the maxillæ of the true scorpion. They are small insects, rarely exceeding a quarter of an inch in length, and are found in dark shady places and feed upon mites, Psoci, and other small insects. A common species is represented at figure 132.

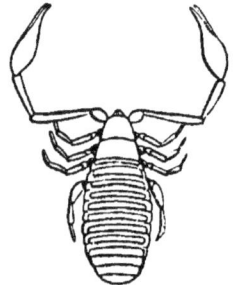

FIG. 132. False Scorpion (*Chelifer cancroides* L.). From Packard.

The true scorpions, Scorpionidæ, are well-known forms, and are easily recognized by their large, powerful, forceps-like maxillæ, and the long slender tail continuous with the thorax and ending with a sting, which is, in most cases, quite poisonous. They are found mostly in the Western and Southwestern States, and are dangerous in proportion to their size. The poisonous nature of the sting of these animals is, however, generally overrated, and the wounds, even of the larger species, are rarely fatal.

The Acarina or true mites are the lowest representatives of the Arachnida and include many genera and species differing very widely in habit and characters. Some of them are mere sacs, on which the mouth parts or other organs are scarcely discernible. In general they resemble spiders. The young, however, when they leave the egg, almost invariably have but three pairs of feet, resembling in this respect the Hexapods. The fourth pair is added in the later stages. They are parasitic on insects and other animals, and some of them are vegetable feeders or live in decaying vegetable and animal matter.

A very interesting group is comprised in the family Phytoptidæ or gall-making mites which occur on the leaves of various trees and shrubs and produce curious galls or abnormal growths. These mites are elongate in form, have rudimentary mouth-parts and but four legs. A common form. *Phytoptus quadripes*, produces a gall on the leaves of the soft maple. The galls of all species should be collected and pinned and also preserved in alcohol, and specimens of the mites should be mounted in balsam.

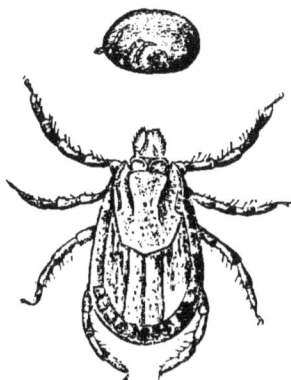

FIG. 134.—The Cattle-tick. (After Packard.)

The members of the genus Sarcoptes are very minute and are the active source of the itch in the lower animals and man. Another common genus is Tyroglyphus, which includes the common cheese mite, *T. siro*. Other species of this genus also sometimes occur in enormous numbers in grocers' supplies. Still others are parasitic on insects, and one species, *T. phylloxeræ* Riley, is very beneficial, since, as its name indicates, it feeds on the Phylloxera of the grapevine.

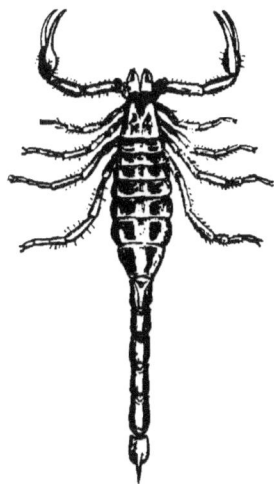

FIG. 133.—A true Scorpion (*Buthus carolinianus*).—From Packard.

The Ixodidæ comprise the ticks which attach themselves to cattle, hogs, and man, and are not at all uncommon objects. These insects can be found on the animals they infest, and distinct species will be found to occur on most wild mammals. The common Cattle tick *Boophilus bovis* Riley, is represented at Fig. 134.

The family Orobatidæ includes a number of small terrestrial mites, which occur on the moss on trees and stones. Some species are known to feed on the eggs of insects, and the one shown in the accompanying figure. *Nothrus orivorus* has been observed by Dr. Packard to eat the eggs of the Canker Worm.

The members of the family Gamasidæ are parasitic upon animals, but chiefly upon insects. The Hydrachnidæ are parasitic also upon the aquatic insects, and also affect fish or mussels or occur on fresh-water plants. .

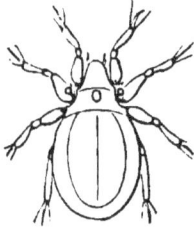

FIG. 135.—*Nothrus orivorus* Packard.

One of the most important families of mites is the Trombidiidæ which includes a large number of species, some of which occur in immense numbers. Most of them are vegetable feeders, but some species feed on the eggs of insects.

The genus Trombidium includes a number of the Red Mites which feed on insects in all their stages. The Locust Mite, *Trombidium locustarum* Riley, is one of the most interesting as well as one of the most important of our locust enemies, and will serve to illustrate the habits of the group. It differs so much in infancy and maturity that it has been referred to different genera and is known under different names. The mature form lives on the ground and feeds on all sorts of animal or decomposing vegetable matter, and wherever the ground is filled with locust eggs these afford an abundance of food and the mites flourish and multiply rapidly. In the spring the female lays 300 or 400

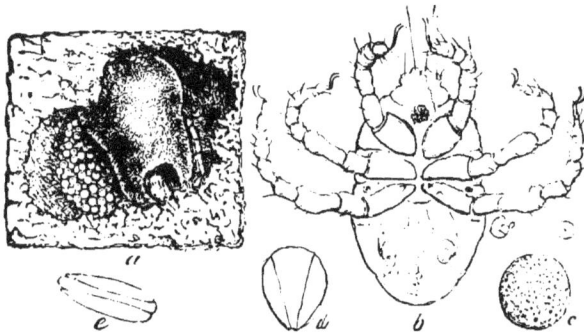

FIG. 136. *Trombidium locustarum*: *a*, female with her batch of eggs; *b*, newly hatched larva natural size indicated by the dot within the circle; *c*, egg; *d e*, vacated egg-shells.

minute spherical orange-red eggs in the ground (Fig. 136*a*). From these eggs, as shown enlarged at *c*, *d*, and *e* (the two latter being the vacated egg shells) emerge the six-legged larva shown at *b*. These are mere specks and crawl actively about, fastening themselves to the locusts mostly at the base of the wings or along the upper veins. They subsist on the juices of their host. They firmly attach themselves by the mouth and increase rapidly in size, the legs not growing and becoming mere rudiments. In this form they are shown at Fig. 137*a*. When fully developed they let go their hold, drop to the ground, and crawl under the shelter afforded by holes in the earth or under sticks. Here, in the course of two or three weeks, they transform within the

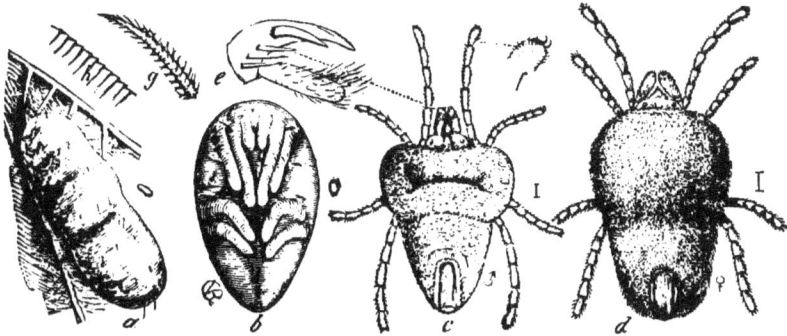

FIG. 137.—*Trombidium locustarum*. a, mature larva when about to leave the wing of a locust; b, pupa; c, male adult when just from the pupa; d, female—the natural sizes indicated to the right; e, palpal claw and thumb; f, pedal claw; g, one of the barbed hairs; h, the striations on the larval skin.

larval skin to the pupal stage shown at b, and eventually break through the old larval skin and escape in the form shown at c and d. This mature form passes the winter in the ground and is active whenever the temperature is a few degrees above the freezing point. A larger species *T. giganteum* Riley, also attacks locusts, while a third species attacks the common House-fly. This was formerly known in the larva state only and was referred to the genus Astoma, to which also the larval form of Trombidium was referred. I have described the adult together with the larva and pupa as *Trombidium muscarum*. An allied mite, *Hydrachna belostomæ*, attacks the large aquatic water bug, Belostoma, and has a mode of development precisely similar to that of Trombidium.

To this family also belong the common greenhouse mite, *Tetranychus telarius*, and also the Bryobia mite, *B. pratensis*, which of late years has attracted very considerable attention by its appearance in immense numbers about dwellings, coming from the adjoining fields of clover or grass. Generically allied to the greenhouse mite is the Six-spotted Mite

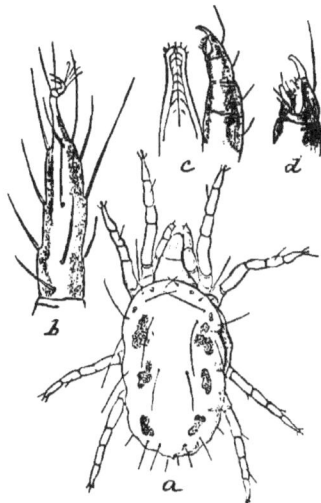

FIG. 138. — The Six-spotted Mite of the Orange (*Tetranychus 6-maculatus*): a, from above—enlarged; b, tarsus; c, rostrum and palpus—still more enlarged; d, tip of palpus—still more enlarged.

of the Orange (*T. 6-maculatus* Riley), which is shown in the accompanying figure.

Spiders and mites thus collected may be transferred to alcohol. Dr. Marx, who has had a very considerable experience in the preservation of spiders, recommends the use of the following mixture: Glycerin and Wickersheim's fluid, 1½ ounces of each, and distilled water 3 ounces, the whole to be shaken and thoroughly mixed and added to 30 ounces of 95 per cent alcohol. Alcohol which has previously been used for preserving spiders, and which has therefore dissolved some of the fatty matters from the specimens, he prefers to pure alcohol, using with this, however, somewhat less of the distilled water. The liquid thus composed answers all demands and keeps the specimens flexible and preserves their coloring. Should the stopper become loose and the liquid evaporate, there is always sufficient liquid, water or glycerine, left in the vial to keep the specimens from drying and thus save them from destruction. Dr. Marx also prefers to use cork stoppers rather than the rubber stoppers recommended for other alcoholic material. His objection to the rubber stopper is that, in a collection in which the specimens are often used and the stoppers are frequently removed, he finds that small particles of the rubber stopper come off and settle upon the specimens as a white dust, which it is difficult to remove. This objection applies only to a poor quality of rubber, and in all other respects the rubber is much to be preferred. The colors of spiders are apt to fade somewhat if exposed to light, and the collection should therefore be kept in closed boxes or in the dark.

### COLLECTING MYRIAPODA.

Centipedes and Millipedes are collected in the same manner as spiders. They live in damp places, under sticks and stones, and in decaying vegetation. They should be preserved in alcohol, and on account of their usually strong chitinous covering, precautions as to the strength of the alcohol are less necessary here than with softer-bodied specimens.

The members of this subclass comprise a number of well-marked groups. The Iulidæ are cylindrical insects and occur in moist places, as do most of the representatives of this subclass. A common form is represented in the accompanying figure. The Chiliopodæ comprise the flattened forms having many-jointed antennæ and but a single pair of limbs to each segment of the body, and are the forms to

FIG. 139.—A Milliped (Cambala annulata).

which the name centipede may properly be applied. They are predaceous in habit, live largely on living animal matter, and are very quick in their movements. Some forms are poisonous, having poison glands at the base of the first pair of legs, but the majority of the species are entirely harmless. A number of common species belong to the genus Geophilus and occur under stones and logs. The genus Scolopendra includes some of the larger species of the order. The largest known species, *S. gigantea*, occurs in the East Indies and attains a length of from 9 inches to more than a foot. Several species found within the limits of the United States attain a length of 5 inches or more. The family Cermatiidae includes the very common species *Cermatia forceps*, which, while abundant in the South and West, occurs somewhat more rarely in the North. It is commonly found in moist situations, in houses or conservatories, and on account of its long legs and agile movements frequently creates considerable consternation. It is, however, an entirely harmless and very beneficial species, since it feeds on various household pests, including flies, roaches, etc.

## TEXT BOOKS—ENTOMOLOGICAL WORKS.

Bulletin No. 19 of the Division of Entomology, U. S. Department of Agriculture, contains an enumeration of the published synopses, catalogues, and lists of North American insects, together with other information intended to assist the student of American entomology. This can be had upon application, and I would refer the student to it for specific information as to synopses, catalogues, and lists. I have deemed it advisable, however, to include here an enumeration of the more useful works of a general character; a list of the entomological periodicals, both home and foreign; and the entomological works published by the different departments of the Government, with some information as to how and of whom they can be obtained. Many of these publications are no longer to be had except as they may be picked up through bookdealers; but the titles even of those which are out of print will be useful to the student as a guide to what he should find in every good library. Requests for this kind of information are constantly received at the Department of Agriculture and at the National Museum. The most useful general works are given first, and, while a great many others in foreign languages might be cited, I would strongly advise the beginner in America to confine himself to these, and especially to read Harris's Insects Injurious to Vegetation, Kirby & Spence's Introduction, and Westwood's Introduction. This last, though published over half a century ago, is still one of the most useful entomological works in the English language. While these Introductions will be of great service in arranging and classifying material and in giving a knowledge of the relationships of species, there is no better text-book than the great book of nature, which is always ready to unfold its truths to every earnest inquirer. In field and wood alone can he become familiar with the insects in all their wondrous life habits, instincts, and intelligence. There alone will he receive the fullest inspiration and pleasure in his work or find the highest reward for his efforts.

COMPREHENSIVE WORKS MOST USEFUL FOR THE STUDY OF NORTH AMERICAN INSECTS.

H. C. C. BURMEISTER.—Handbuch der Entomologie. Berlin, 1832–1855. 5 vols.

MANUAL OF ENTOMOLOGY.—A translation of the above, by W. E. Shuckard. London, 1836.

J. O. WESTWOOD.—An introduction to the modern classification of insects, founded on the natural habits and corresponding organization of the different families. 2 vols. London, 1839–'40.

THOMAS SAY.—Complete writings on the Entomology of North America; edited by John L. Le Conte. New York, 1859.

H. A. HAGEN.—Bibliotheca Entomologica. Die Litteratur über das ganze Gebiet der Entomologie bis zum Jahre 1862. Leipzig, 1862.

A. S. PACKARD.—Guide to the Study of Insects. Henry Holt & Co., Philadelphia and New York. (First edition, Salem, 1869.)

——— Entomology for Beginners. Henry Holt & Co., New York, 1888.

THE STANDARD NATURAL HISTORY.—Edited by John Sterling Kingsley. S. E. Cassino & Co., Boston, 1884–'85.

> Volume II contains the insects, which are treated by the following authors: *Hymenoptera*, J. H. Comstock and L. O. Howard; *Coleoptera*, George Dimmock; *Lepidoptera*, Hy Edwards and C. H. Fernald; *Diptera*, S. W. Williston; *Orthoptera*, C. V. Riley; *Hemiptera*, P. R. Uhler; *Neuroptera*, A. S. Packard; *Arachnida*, J. H. Emerton.

J. H. COMSTOCK.—An Introduction to Entomology. Published by the author. Ithaca, N. Y. 2 parts. Part I, 1888.

ALPHEUS HYATT AND J. M. ARMS.—Guides for Science Teaching, No. III. Insecta. Bos. Soc. Nat. Hist. D. C. Heath & Co. Boston.1890.

GENERAL WORKS ON CLASSIFICATION.

HYMENOPTERA.

E. T. CRESSON.—Synopsis of the Families and Genera of the Hymenoptera of America, north of Mexico, together with a Catalogue of the described Species and Bibliography. Transactions Am. Entom. Society. Supplementary volume. 2 parts. Philadelphia, 1887.

COLEOPTERA.

JOHN L. LE CONTE AND GEORGE H. HORN.—Classification of the Coleoptera of North America. Prepared for the Smithsonian Institution. Washington, Smithsonian Institution, 1883.

> This is the most recent and the only complete classification of North American Coleoptera. It contains also Appendix II, a "list of bibliographical references to memoirs, in which more or less complete synopses of the families, genera, and species of the Coleoptera of the United States have been published."

J. T. LACORDAIRE.—Histoire naturelle des Insectes. Genera des Coléoptères, ou exposé méthodique et critique de tous les genres proposés jusqu'ici dans cet ordre d'insectes. [Completed by J. Chapuis.] Paris, France, 1854–1876. 12 vols. and 1 vol. plates.

*WILLIAM LE BARON.—Outlines of Entomology, published in connection with the author's Annual Reports upon injurious insects. Part first. Including the Order of Coleoptera. Fourth Annual Report on the Noxious and Beneficial Insects of the State of Illinois. Sep. Edit. Springfield, 1874.

## LEPIDOPTERA.

G. A. W. HERRICH-SCHAEFFER.—Sammlung neuer oder wenig bekannter aussereuropäischer Schmetterlinge. Vol. I. Regensburg, 1850–'58; Vol. II, Pt. 1, 1869.

> Contains a classification of the Lepidoptera, which forms the basis of our present arrangement.

JOHN G. MORRIS.—Synopsis of the described Lepidoptera of North America. Part I. Diurnal and Crepuscular Lepidoptera. Washington, Smithsonian Institution, 1862.

> Compiled descriptions of the North American Lepidoptera, from the Rhopalocera to the Bombycidæ.

H. STRECKER.—Lepidoptera, Rhopaloceres et Heteroceres, indigenous and exotic; with descriptions and colored illustrations. Reading, Pa., 1872–'77.

> Fifteen parts of this work have been published containing figures and descriptions of many North American species.

JOHN B. SMITH.—An Introduction to a Classification of the North American Lepidoptera. <Bull. Brookl. Ent. Soc., Vol. VII, 1884, pp. 70–74 and 81–83.

> A synopsis of the families of Lepidoptera based on Herrich-Schaeffer's classification.

——— Synopsis of the Genera of the North American Rhopalocera. <Bull. Brookl. Ent. Soc., Vol. VI, 1883, pp. 37–45.

E. DOUBLEDAY AND W. C. HEWITSON.—The genera of diurnal Lepidoptera, comprising their generic characters, a notice of their transformations, and a catalogue of the species of each genus; illustrated, with 86 colored plates from drawings by W. C. Hewitson. 2 vols., London, 1846–'52.

> This work was completed by Westwood after the death of Doubleday.

S. H. SCUDDER.—Butterflies: Their structures, changes, and life-histories, with special reference to American forms. Being an application of the "Doctrine of descent" to the study of Butterflies, with an appendix of practical instructions. 321 pp. and 201 text figs. New York, Henry Holt & Co., 1881.

——— The Butterflies of the Eastern United States and Canada with special reference to New England. 3 vols., Cambridge, Mass., 1889; pp. 1958, plates 59. (Published by the author. Cost about $75 for 3 vols.)

---

*Out of print.

G. H. FRENCH.—The Butterflies of the Eastern United States. For the use of classes in Zoölogy and private students. Philadelphia, Lippincott & Co., 1886.

Gives synopses of the genera and species, and description of the species.

W. H. EDWARDS.—Butterflies of North America. Boston, Houghton, Mifflin & Co.

Two volumes are completed and the third is in course of publication.

HEMIPTERA.

HERBERT OSBORN.—Classification of Hemiptera. <Entomologica Amer., Vol. I, 1885, pp. 21–27.

Short characterization of the whole order, with tables of suborders and families.

—— Pediculi and Mallophaga affecting Man and the Lower Animals. Constituting Bulletin No. 7 of the Division of Entomology, U. S. Department of Agriculture. Washington, 1891.

P. R. UHLER.—List of Hemiptera of the region west of the Mississippi River, including those collected during the Hayden explorations of 1873. <Bull. U. S. Geolog. and Geogr. Survey of the Terr., Vol. I, 1875, pp. 267–361, Pl. XIX–XXI.

—— Report upon the insects collected by P. R. Uhler during the exploration of 1875, including monographs of the families Cynidæ and Saldæ, and the Hemiptera collected by A. S. Packard, jr., M. D. <U. S. Geolog. and Geogr. Survey. Bulletin, Vol. III, No. 2, 1877, pp. 355–475.

TOWNEND GLOVER.—Report of the Entomologist. <Report of the Commissioner of Agriculture for the year 1877, pp. 17–46.

A popular treatise on the Homoptera, with illustrations.

A. H. HALIDAY.—An Epitome of the British genera in the Order Thysanoptera, with indications of a few of the species. <Entomol. Mag., Vol. III, 1836, pp. 439–451.

DIPTERA.

H. LOEW AND C. R. OSTEN-SACKEN.—Monographs of the Diptera of North America. (Smithsonian Miscellaneous Collections.) 4 parts. Washington, Smithsonian Institution, 1862–'72.

The several monographs will be found enumerated under the respective families.

H. LOEW.—Diptera Americæ septentrionalis indigena. 2 parts. Berlin, 1861–'72. (Originally published in 10 centuriæ in the Berliner Entomol. Zeitschrift.)

Descriptions of 1,000 North American Diptera, but without synoptic arrangement.

C. R. OSTEN-SACKEN.—Western Diptera: Descriptions of new genera and species of Diptera from the region west of the Mississippi and especially from California. <Bull. U. S. Geolog. and Geogr. Survey of the Territories, Vol. III, 1877, pp. 189–354.

F. BRAUER.—Die Zweiflügler des Kaiserlichen Museums zu Wien.
I–III. Wien, 1880–'83.
Important contributions to the classification of the Diptera.

ORTHOPTERA.

HENRI DE SAUSSURE —Orthoptera nova Americana (Diagnoses præ-
liminares). Series I–III. <Revue et Mag. de Zool., 1859–'61.
Contains synoptical tables of species, besides descriptions of numerous
North American Orthoptera.

SAMUEL H. SCUDDER.—Materials for a monograph of the North American Orthoptera. <Boston Journal of Nat. Hist., Vol. VII, 1862,
pp. 409–480.
Contains synoptical tables and a review of the system used for classification.

——Remarks upon the arrangement of the families of Orthoptera.
<Proc. Boston Soc. Nat. Hist., Vol. XII, 1868–'69; also separate
under the title: Entomological Notes, Vol. II, pp. 7–14.

——Synoptical tables for determining North American insects.
Orthoptera. <Psyche, Vol. I, 1876, pp. 169–171.
Synopsis of families; also list of useful works in the study of North American
Orthoptera.

NEUROPTERA.

HERMANN HAGEN.—Synopsis of the Neuroptera of North America, with
a list of the South American species. Smithsonian Miscellaneous
Collections, Washington, 1861.

——Synopsis of the Odonata of America. <Proc. Boston Soc. Nat.
Hist., Vol. XVIII, 1875, pp. 20–96.

SIR JOHN LUBBOCK.—Monograph of the Collembola and Thysanura.
London, Ray Society, 1873.
The introduction gives the full bibliography up to date.

MYRIAPODA.

THOMAS SAY.—Descriptions of the Myriapoda of the United States.
<Journ. Ac. Nat. Sc. Phil., Vol. II, 1821, pp. 102–114; Say's Entom.
Writings, ed. Le Conte, Vol. II, pp. 24–32.
This is the first paper of importance on the North American Myriapoda.

GEORGE NEWPORT.—Monograph of the class Myriapoda, Order Chilopoda. <Trans. Linnean Soc. of London, Vol. XIX, 1845, pp. 265–
302 and 349–439.

HORATIO C. WOOD, Jr.—On the Chilopoda of North America, with
Catalogue of all the specimens in the collection of the Smithsonian
Institution. <Journ. Ac. Nat. Sc. Phil., New Ser., Vol. V, 1863,
pp. 5–42.

——The Myriapoda of North America. <Trans. Amer. Philos Soc.,
Vol. XIII, 1865, pp. 137–248. 3 pl.
This is the first and only monograph of the Myriapoda published in this
country.

ROBERT LATZEL.—Die Myriapoden der Oesterreichisch-Ungarischen
Monarchie. Erste Hälfte: Die Chilopoden, Wien, 1880. Zweite
Hälfte: Die Symphylen, Pauropoden und Diplopoden, Wien, 1884.
The most recent comprehensive work on this order, and very important from
a classificatory standpoint.

LUCIEN M. UNDERWOOD.—The North American Myriapoda. <Ento-
mol. Amer., Vol. I, 1885, pp. 141-151.
A complete bibliographical review of the subject, with tables of families and
genera.

ARACHNIDA.

N. M. HENTZ.—Descriptions and figures of the Araneides of the United
States. <Journ. Boston Soc. Nat. Hist., Vols. IV-VI, 1842-'50.
These papers form the basis of the study of American arachnology. Numerous
species are described, but not in synoptic form.

T. THORELL.—On European Spiders. Part I. Review of the European
genera of Spiders. Upsala, 1869-'70.

N. M. HENTZ.—Araneae Americae septentrionalis. The Spiders of the
United States. Edited by J. H. Emerton and E. Burgess. <"Oc-
casional Papers" of the Boston Society of Natural History. 1875.
A reprint of Hentz's papers on North American spiders.

GRAF EUGEN KEYSERLING.—Amerikanische Spinnen aus den Fami-
lien Pholcoidae, Scytodoidae und Dysderoidae. <Verh. k. k. zool.-
bot. Ges. in Wien, Vol. XXVII, 1877, pp. 205-234.

———Neue Spinnen aus Amerika. (Six parts.) <Verh. k. k. Zool.-bot.
Ges. in Wien, Vols. XXIX-XXXIV, 1879-'84.

E. SIMON.—Les Arachnides de France. Paris, Vols. I-V, 1874-'84.
These two works represent the most recent systems of classification, and are
therefore of great general value, although they deal only with the European fauna.

LUCIEN M. UNDERWOOD.—The Progress of Arachnology in America.
<Amer. Natur., Vol. XXI, 1887, pp. 963-975.
A very useful review of the bibliography, with synoptic table of the families
of the Araneae.

AMERICAN PERIODICALS.

THE AMERICAN NATURALIST. A monthly journal devoted to the
natural sciences in their widest sense (24 volumes published up to
date. Now published at Philadelphia).

*ANNALS OF THE LYCEUM OF NATURAL HISTORY OF NEW YORK (8
volumes, 1824-'67. Continued since 1876 as Annals of the New
York Academy of Sciences).

*BULLETIN OF THE BROOKLYN ENTOMOLOGICAL SOCIETY (7 volumes,
1878-'85. Continued as Entomologica Americana).

BULLETIN OF THE BUFFALO SOCIETY OF NATURAL HISTORY (4 volumes completed; 1874 to 1883.

BULLETINS OF THE UNITED STATES GEOLOGICAL AND GEOGRAPH-
ICAL SURVEY OF THE TERRITORIES, F. V. Hayden in charge (Department of the Interior; 1875 to 1879.

———

* Publication discontinued.

BULLETINS OF THE UNITED STATES GEOLOGICAL SURVEY. J. M. Powell, director; beginning with 1883.
BULLETINS OF THE UNITED STATES NATIONAL MUSEUM (Department of the Interior: beginning with 1875).
THE CANADIAN ENTOMOLOGIST. (Published by the Entomological Society of Ontario; 22 volumes issued up to the end of 1890. Published at London, Ontario.)
*ENTOMOLOGICA AMERICANA. (Published by the Brooklyn Entomological Society at Brooklyn, N. Y. 1885 to 1890.)
ENTOMOLOGICAL NEWS [and Proceedings of the Entomological Section of the Academy of Natural Sciences] (Vol. I issued in 1890. Published at Philadelphia).
JOURNAL OF THE ACADEMY OF NATURAL SCIENCES OF PHILADELPHIA (commencing with 1817).
MEMOIRS OF THE BOSTON SOCIETY OF NATURAL HISTORY (commencing with 1866).
*NORTH AMERICAN ENTOMOLOGIST. (Published by the Buffalo Society of Natural Sciences, 1 volume. Buffalo, N. Y. 1879-'80.)
*PAPILIO. Devoted exclusively to Lepidoptera. Organ of the New York Entomological Club (4 volumes, 1881-'84).
PSYCHE. Organ of the Cambridge Entomological Club (5 volumes issued up to date. Published at Cambridge, Mass. Publication begun in 1874).
PROCEEDINGS OF THE ACADEMY OF NATURAL SCIENCES OF PHILADELPHIA (beginning with 1841).
PROCEEDINGS OF THE AMERICAN PHILOSOPHICAL SOCIETY OF PHILADELPHIA (beginning with 1860).
PROCEEDINGS OF THE BOSTON SOCIETY OF NATURAL HISTORY (commencing with 1841).
*PROCEEDINGS OF THE ENTOMOLOGICAL SOCIETY OF PHILADELPHIA (6 volumes, 1861-'67).
PROCEEDINGS OF THE ENTOMOLOGICAL SOCIETY OF WASHINGTON (2 volumes, beginning with 1884).
PROCEEDINGS OF THE UNITED STATES NATIONAL MUSEUM (Department of the Interior; beginning with 1878).
REPORTS OF THE UNITED STATES GEOLOGICAL AND GEOGRAPHICAL SURVEY OF THE TERRITORIES (Department of the Interior: beginning with 1867).
SMITHSONIAN MISCELLANEOUS COLLECTIONS (Smithsonian Institution, Washington, D. C.; beginning 1862).
TRANSACTIONS OF THE ACADEMY OF SCIENCE OF ST. LOUIS (4 volumes hitherto published).
TRANSACTIONS OF THE AMERICAN ENTOMOLOGICAL SOCIETY and Proceedings of the Entomological Section of the Academy of Natural Sciences (beginning with 1868; published at Philadelphia).

*Publication discontinued.

TRANSACTIONS OF THE AMERICAN PHILOSOPHICAL SOCIETY OF PHIL-
ADELPHIA (2d series beginning with 1818).

Papers on entomology are also published occasionally in other American periodicals, among which the following might be mentioned:

JOURNAL OF THE ELISHA MITCHELL SCIENTIFIC SOCIETY. Chapel
Hill, N. C.

JOURNAL OF THE NEW YORK MICROSCOPICAL SOCIETY.

NATURALISTE CANADIEN. Edited by Abbé Provancher, Cap Rouge,
Quebec.

PROCEEDINGS OF THE CALIFORNIA ACADEMY OF SCIENCES, San
Francisco, Cal.

FOREIGN PERIODICALS.

ANNALES DE LA SOCIÉTÉ ENTOMOLOGIQUE DE BELGIQUE. Publication begun in 1857. Brussels.

ANNALES DE LA SOCIÉTÉ ENTOMOLOGIQUE DE FRANCE. Publication
begun in 1832. Paris.

* BERLINER ENTOMOLOGISCHE ZEITSCHRIFT. 18 volumes, Berlin,
1857–1874.

Succeeded by the Deutsche Entomologische Zeitung.

BULLETIN DE LA SOCIÉTÉ ENTOMOLOGIQUE DE FRANCE.

BULLETIN DE LA SOCIÉTÉ ENTOMOLOGIQUE SUISSE. (See Mittheil d.
Schweiz. Entom. Gesell.)

BULLETINO DELLA SOCIETÀ ENTOMOLOGICA ITALIANA. Florence.
(Publication commenced in 1869.)

DEUTSCHE ENTOMOLOGISCHE ZEITSCHRIFT. Published by the Entomological Society of Berlin. (Publication begun in 1875.)

ENTOMOLOGISCHE NACHRICHTEN. (Now edited by Dr. F. Karsch, Berlin. Publication commenced in 1875.)

ENTOMOLOGISK TIDSKRIFT, PÅ FÖRANSTALTANDE AF ENTOMOLOGISKA
FÖRENINGEN I STOCKHOLM. (Commenced with 1880.)

* ENTOMOLOGISCHE ZEITUNG. HERAUSGEGEBEN VON DEM ENTOMOL-
OGISCHEN VEREIN ZU STETTIN. 36 volumes. Stettin. 1840–'75.

ENTOMOLOGISKE MEDDELELSER UDGIVNE OF ENTOMOLOGISK FORE-
NING. Edited by Fr. Meinert, Copenhagen (beginning with 1887).

THE ENTOMOLOGIST. A popular monthly journal of British entomology. Vol. I, 1840–'42. (Publication resumed in 1864, London.)

* THE ENTOMOLOGIST'S ANNUAL. Edited by H. T. Stainton. London.
(Publication begun in 1855; 22 vols. published up to 1876.)

ENTOMOLOGIST'S MONTHLY MAGAZINE. London (beginning with 1864).

Horae . . . Variis sermonibus rossiae usitatis. Societas Entomologica
Rossica. (Publication begun in 1861.)

* LINNÆA ENTOMOLOGICA. HERAUSGEGEBEN VOM ENTOMOLOGI-
SCHEN VEREINE ZU STETTIN (16 volumes, Berlin, 1846–'66).

* Discontinued.

MITTHEILUNGEN DER SCHWEIZERISCHEN ENTOMOLOGISCHEN GE-
SELLSCHAFT. Bulletin de la Société entomologique suisse. (Publication begun at Schaffhausen, Switz., in 1862. Afterward published at Geneva.)

REVUE D'ENTOMOLOGIE. (Published by the Société Française d'Entomologie, Caën, France. Publication begun in 1882.)

TIJDSCHRIFT VOOR ENTOMOLOGIE. NEDERLANDSCHE ENTOMOLO-
GISCHE VEREENIGING, Leiden, Holland (beginning with 1857.
Published by the Dutch Entomological Society).

TRANSACTIONS OF THE ENTOMOLOGICAL SOCIETY OF LONDON. (Begun
in 1834.)

*WIENER ENTOMOLOGISCHE MONATSSCHRIFT (8 volumes, Vienna,
1857–'64).

WIENER ENTOMOLOGISCHE ZEITUNG. Vienna. (Commenced 1882.)

*ZEITSCHRIFT FÜR DIE ENTOMOLOGIE. Edited by E. F. Germar (5
volumes. Leipzig, 1839–'44).

ZEITSCHRIFT FÜR ENTOMOLOGIE. VEREIN FÜR SCHLESISCHE IN-
SECKTEN-KUNDE ZU BRESLAU. (Publication begun at Breslau in
1847).

ZEITSCHRIFT FÜR WISSENSCHAFTLICHE ZOOLOGIE. Leipzig. (Begun
in 1848).

A large number of other periodicals devoted to entomology have been
issued, principally in Europe, but after continuing for a year or more
their publication has been abandoned, and they are not included here.
Important entomological papers have also been published in many
serials devoted to zoölogy or the natural sciences generally. Among
them may be mentioned the following:

ANNALS AND MAGAZINE OF NATURAL HISTORY. London (beginning
with 1838).

ARCHIV FÜR NATURGESCHICHTE. Berlin (beginning with 1835).

ÖFVERSIGT AF KONGL. SVENSKA VETENSKAPS ACADEMIENS FÖRHAND-
LINGAR (beginning with 1844. Published at Stockholm).
Proceedings of the Royal Swedish Academy of Sciences.

PROCEEDINGS OF THE ZOÖLOGICAL SOCIETY OF LONDON.

REVUE ET MAGASIN DE ZOOLOGIE PURE ET APPLIQUÉE. Paris (beginning with 1839).

SITZUNGSBERICHTE DER MATHEMATISCH-NATURWISSENSCHAFTLI-
CHEN CLASSE DER KAISERLICHEN ACADEMIE DER WISSEN-
SCHAFTEN ZU WIEN (beginning with 1848).

TRANSACTIONS OF THE LINNEAN SOCIETY OF LONDON (beginning with
1791).

TRANSACTIONS AND PROCEEDINGS OF THE NEW ZEALAND INSTITUTE.
Wellington, New Zealand.

VERHANDLUNGEN DER ZOOLOGISCH-BOTANISCHEN GESELLSCHAFT IN
WIEN (beginning with 1852).

---

* Publication discontinued.

LIST OF MORE USEFUL WORKS ON ECONOMIC ENTOMOLOGY.

T. W. HARRIS, Insects Injurious to Vegetation. (Flint edition.) New
York, Orange Judd Co. $4 or $6. (First edition, Cambridge, 1841.)

† ASA FITCH, Reports of the State Entomologist of New York. I–XIV,
Albany, 1855–'70. (For a full account of these, see First Annual
Report, by J. A. Lintner, State Entomologist of New York. pp.
294–297.)

* The Practical Entomologist. Vols. I and II. Published by the Entomological Society of Philadelphia, 1865–'67.

* The American Entomologist, edited by B. D. Walsh and C. V. Riley.
Vol. I. St. Louis, Mo., 1868. (Out of print.)

* The American Entomologist and Botanist, edited by C. V. Riley and
Dr. George Vasey. Vol. II. St. Louis, Mo., 1870.

* The American Entomologist, edited by C. V. Riley. Vol. III. Second series, Vol. I.] New York, Hub Publishing Co., 1880.

† B. D. WALSH, Annual Report on the Noxious Insects of the State of
Illinois. Chicago, Prairie Farmer Co., 1868.

† C. V. RILEY, Reports of the State Entomologist of Missouri. I–IX,
Jefferson City, 1869–'77.

† WILLIAM LE BARON, Reports of the State Entomologist of Illinois.
I–IV, Springfield, 1871–'74.

† CYRUS THOMAS, Reports of the State Entomologist of Illinois. I–VI,
Springfield, 1876–'81.

J. A. LINTNER, Reports of the State Entomologist of New York. Albany
(beginning with 1882).

S. A. FORBES, Reports of the State Entomologist of Illinois. Springfield (beginning with 1883).

——Miscellaneous Essays on Economic Entomology. Springfield,
Ill., 1886. (Published instead of Annual Report.)

MARY TREAT, Injurious Insects of the Farm and Garden. New York,
Orange Judd Co., 1882. (A small work compiled from Riley's
reports.)

WILLIAM SAUNDERS, Insects Injurious to Fruits. Philadelphia, J. B.
Lippincott & Co., 1883.

MATTHEW COOKE, Injurious Insects of the Orchard, Vineyard, etc.
Sacramento, 1883. (8vo., pp. 472.)

P. J. VAN BENEDEN, Animal Parasites and Messmates. New York,
D. Appleton & Co., 1876. International Scientific Series.

† Reports of the Entomologists of the U. S. Department of Agriculture,
T. Glover (1863–1878), J. H. Comstock (1879–1880), and C.V. Riley
(1878–1879, 1880 to date).‡

* Publication discontinued.        † Out of print.
‡The annual reports of the Entomologist are contained in the corresponding annual
reports of the Department of Agriculture. A limited author's edition, separately
bound, and with table of contents and index, is published each year.

Bulletins of the Division of Entomology of the U. S. Department of Agriculture. C. V. Riley, Entomologist (1883 to date).

Reports and Bulletins of the U. S. Entomological Commission.

JOHN CURTIS, Farm Insects. London, Blackie & Son, 1860.

ELEANOR A. ORMEROD. Manual of Injurious Insects, and Methods of Prevention, etc. London and Edinburgh, 1881. (A small work, costing about $1.50.)

————Reports of Observations of Injurious Insects and Common Farm Pests, with Methods of Prevention and Remedy. London. Simpkin, Marshall, Hamilton, Kent & Co., limited. (Fourteen reports issued up to 1891.)

J. H. KALTENBACH.—Die Pflanzenfeinde aus der Classe der Insekten. 8vo. Stuttgart, 1874. (A useful work for determining what insects infest plants in Europe.)

INSECT LIFE. Periodical Bulletin.—Devoted to the economy and the life-habits of insects, especially in their relations to agriculture. Edited by C. V. Riley, entomologist, and L. O. Howard, first assistant, with the assistance of other members of the divisional force (Publication begun in 1888.)

E. L. TASCHENBERG.—Praktische Insekten-Kunde. Parts I–V. Bremen, 1879.

FELICE FRANCESCHINI.—Gli Insetti Nocivi. Milan, 1891.

J. T. C. RATZEBURG.—Die Waldverderbniss, oder dauernder Schade, welcher durch Insektenfrass, Schälen, Schlagen, und Verbeissen an lebenden Waldbäumen entsteht. Two parts. Berlin, 1866-'68.

ENTOMOLOGICAL WORKS PUBLISHED BY THE UNITED STATES ENTOMO-
LOGICAL COMMISSION AND BY THE UNITED STATES DEPARTMENT
OF AGRICULTURE.

UNITED STATES ENTOMOLOGICAL COMMISSION.

(Members of the Commission: C. V. Riley, A. S. Packard, jr., and Cyrus Thomas.)

*BULLETIN NO. 1.—Destruction of the young or unfledged Locusts (*Caloptenus spretus*). (1877.) [pp. 15.]

BULLETIN NO. 2.—On the Natural History of the Rocky Mountain Locust and on the habits of the young or unfledged insects as they occur in the more fertile country in which they will hatch the present year. (1877.) [pp. 14, figs. 10.]

BULLETIN NO. 3.—The Cotton Worm. Summary of its Natural History, with an Account of its Enemies, and the best Means of controlling it; being a Report of Progress of the Work of the Commission. By Chas. V. Riley, M. A., Ph. D. (1880.) [pp. 144, figs. 84, plates 1.]

BULLETIN NO. 4.—The Hessian Fly. Its Ravages, Habits, Enemies, and Means of preventing its Increase. By A. S. Packard, jr.. M. D. (1880.) [pp. 43, figs. 1, plates 2., maps 1.]

*All of these bulletins and reports, with the exception of the fifth report, are out of print.

BULLETIN No. 5.—The Chinch Bug. Its History, Characters, and Habits, and the Means of destroying it or counteracting its Injuries. By Cyrus Thomas, Ph. D. (1879.) [pp. 44, figs. 10, maps 1.]

BULLETIN No. 6.—General Index and Supplement to the nine Reports on the Insects of Missouri. By Charles V. Riley, M. A., Ph. D. (1881.) [pp. 177.]

BULLETIN No. 7.—Insects injurious to Forest and Shade Trees. By A. S. Packard, jr., M. D. (1881.) [pp. 275, figs. 100.]

First Annual Report for the year 1877, relating to the Rocky Mountain Locust and the best Methods of preventing its Injuries and of guarding against its Invasions, in pursuance of an Appropriation made by Congress for this purpose. With maps and illustrations. (1878.) [pp. 477+294, figs. 111, plates 5, maps 1.]

Second Report for the years 1878 and 1879, relating to the Rocky Mountain Locust and the Western Cricket, and treating of the best Means of subduing the Locust in its permanent Breeding grounds, with a view of preventing its Migrations into the more fertile Portions of the trans-Mississippi country, in pursuance of Appropriations made by Congress for this purpose. With Maps and Illustrations. (1880.) [pp. XVIII+322+22, figs. 10, plates 17, maps 7.]

Third Report relating to the Rocky Mountain Locust, the Western Cricket, the Army Worm, Canker Worms, and the Hessian Fly; together with Descriptions of Larvæ of injurious Forest Insects. Studies on the embryological Development of the Locust and of other Insects, and on the systematic Position of the Orthoptera in Relation to other Orders of Insects. With Maps and Illustrations. (1883.) [pp. XVIII+347+91, figs. 14, plates 64, maps 3.]

Fourth Report, being a revised Edition of Bulletin No. 3, and the Final Report on the Cotton Worm and Bollworm. By Charles V. Riley, Ph. D. (1885.) [pp. XXXVIII+399+147, figs. 45, plates 64, maps 2.]

Fifth Report, being a revised and enlarged edition of Bulletin No. 7, on Insects Injurious to Forest and Shade Trees. By Alpheus S. Packard, M. D., Ph. D., with woodcuts and 40 plates. (1890 (1). Small edition; only a few for general distribution.

BULLETINS OF THE DIVISION OF ENTOMOLOGY, U. S. DEPARTMENT OF AGRICULTURE, UNDER DIRECTION OF C. V. RILEY, ENTOMOLOGIST.

*No. 1.—Reports of Experiments, chiefly with Kerosene, upon the Insects injuriously affecting the Orange Tree and the Cotton Plant, made under the Direction of the Entomologist. (1883.) [pp. 62.]

*No. 2.—Reports of Observations on the Rocky Mountain Locust and Chinch Bug, together with Extracts from the Correspondence of the Division on Miscellaneous Insects. (1883.) [pp. 36.]

* Out of print.

*No. 3.—Reports of Observations and Experiments in the practical Work of the Division, made under the Direction of the Entomologist. With plates. (1883.) [pp. 75, plates III.]

No. 4.—Reports of Observations and Experiments in the practical Work of the Division, made under the Direction of the Entomologist, together with Extracts from Correspondence on miscellaneous Insects. (1884.) [pp. 102, figs. 4.]

*No. 5.—Descriptions of North American Chalcididae from the Collections of the U. S. Department of Agriculture and of Dr. C. V. Riley, with biological Notes. [First paper.] Together with a list of the described North American species of the family. By L. O. Howard, M. Sc., Assistant, Bureau of Entomology. (1885.) [pp. 47.]

*No. 6.—The imported Elm-leaf Beetle. Its Habits and Natural History, and Means of counteracting its Injuries. (1885.) [pp. 18, figs. 1, plates I.]

No. 7.—The Pediculi and Mallophaga affecting Man and the lower Animals. By Prof. Herbert Osborn. (1891.) [pp. 51, figs. 42.]

*No. 8.—The Periodical Cicada. An account of *Cicada septendecim* and its tredicim race, with a chronology of all of the broods known. By Charles V. Riley, Ph. D. (1885.) [pp. 46, figs. 8.)

No. 9.—The Mulberry Silk-worm; being a Manual of Instructions in Silk culture. By Charles V. Riley, M. A., Ph. D. (1886.) [pp. 65, figs. 29, plates II.]

No. 10.—Our Shade Trees and their Insect Defoliators. Being a consideration of the four most injurious species which affect the trees of the capital, with means of destroying them. By Charles V. Riley, Entomologist. (1887.) [pp. 75, figs. 27.]

*No. 11.—Reports of Experiments with various Insecticide Substances, chiefly upon Insects affecting garden Crops, made under the Direction of the Entomologist. (1886.) [pp. 34.]

*No. 12.—Miscellaneous Notes on the work of the Division of Entomology for the Season of 1885; prepared by the Entomologist. (1886.) [pp. 45, plates I.]

*No. 13.—Reports of Observations and Experiments in the practical Work of the Division, made under the Direction of the Entomologist. (With illustrations.) (1887.) [pp. 78, figs. 4.]

No. 14.—Reports of Observations and Experiments in the practical Work of the Division, made under the Direction of the Entomologist. (1887.) [pp. 62, figs. 2, plates I.]

No. 15.—The Icerya, or Fluted Scale, otherwise known as the Cottony Cushion-scale. (Reprint of some recent Articles by the Entomologist and of a Report from the Agricultural Experiment Station, University of California.) (1887.) [pp. 40.]

No. 16.—The Entomological Writings of Dr. Alpheus Spring Packard. By Samuel Henshaw. (1887.) [pp. 49.]

* Out of print.

BULLETIN 39, UNITED STATES NATIONAL MUSEUM. [144]

*No. 17.—The Chinch Bug: A general Summary of its History, Habits, Enemies, and of the Remedies and Preventives to be used against it. By L. O. Howard M. S., Assistant Entomologist. (1888.) [pp. 48, figs. 10.]

*No. 18.—The Life and Entomological Work of the late Townend Glover, first Entomologist of the United States Department of Agriculture. Prepared under the Direction of the Entomologist, by C. R. Dodge. (1888.) [pp. 68, figs. 6, plates I.]

No. 19.—An enumeration of the published Synopses, Catalogues, and Lists of North American Insects; together with other information intended to assist the student of American Entomology. (1888.) [pp. 77.]

*No. 20.—The Root Knot Disease of the Peach, Orange, and other Plants in Florida, due to the Work of Anguillula. Prepared under the Direction of the Entomologist, by J. C. Neal, Ph. D., M. D. (1889.) [pp. 31, plates 21.]

*No. 21.—Report of a Trip to Australia, made under the Direction of the Entomologist to investigate the Natural Enemies of the Fluted Scale, by Albert Koebele. (1890.) [pp. 32, figs. 16.]

No. 22.—Reports of the Observations and Experiments in the practical Work of the Division, made under the Direction of the Entomologist. (1890.) [pp. 110.]

No. 23.—Reports of Observations and Experiments in the practical Work of the Division, made under the Direction of the Entomologist. (1891.) [pp. 83.]

No. 24.—The Boll Worm. Preliminary Report, made under the Direction of the Entomologist. By F. W. Mally. (1891.) [pp. 50.]

No. 25.—Destructive Locusts. A popular consideration of a few of the more injurious Locusts or "Grasshoppers" of the United States, together with the best means of destroying them. By C. V. Riley, Ph. D. (1891.) [pp. 62, figs. 11, plates 12.]

†No. 26.—Reports of Observations and Experiments in the practical Work of the Division, made under the Direction of the Entomologist. (1892.)

†No. 27.—Reports on the Damage by destructive Locusts during the season of 1891, made under the Direction of the Entomologist. (1892.) [pp. 64.]

†No. 28.—The more destructive Locusts of America, north of Mexico, by Lawrence Bruner, prepared under Direction of the Entomologist. (1892.)

SPECIAL REPORTS AND BULLETINS.

* REPORT ON COTTON INSECTS.—By J. Henry Comstock. (1879.) [pp. 511, figs. 77, plates III.]

* Out of print.
† Bulletins 26 and 27 are in press, and Bulletin 28 is in course of preparation.

†SPECIAL REPORT. No. 11.—The Silkworm; being a brief Manual of Instructions for the Production of Silk. Prepared, by direction of the Commissioner of Agriculture, by C. V. Riley, M. A., Ph. D., Entomologist. (First ed., 1879; fifth ed., 1885.) [pp. 37, figs. 8.]

* SPECIAL REPORT, No. 35.—Report on Insects injurious to Sugar Cane. Prepared, under Direction of the Commissioner of Agriculture, by J. Henry Comstock, Entomologist. (1881.) [pp. 11, figs. 3.]

* DIVISION OF ENTOMOLOGY.—INSECTS AFFECTING THE ORANGE.—Report on the Insects affecting the Culture of the Orange and other plants of the Citrus Family, with practical Suggestions for their Control or Extermination. By H. G. Hubbard. (1885.) [pp. x+227, figs. 95, plates XIV.]

* SPECIAL REPORT.—Catalogue of the Exhibit of Economic Entomology at the World's Industrial and Cotton Centennial Exposition, New Orleans, 1884–'85. (1888.) [pp. 95.]

SPECIAL BULLETIN.—The Horn Fly (Hæmatobia serrata), being an account of its Life-history and the means to be used against it. By C. V. Riley and L. O. Howard. (Reprinted from Insect Life. Vol. II, No. 4, October 1889.) (1889.) [pp. 11, figs. 5.]

BIBLIOGRAPHY OF THE MORE IMPORTANT CONTRIBUTIONS TO AMERICAN ECONOMIC ENTOMOLOGY. By Samuel Henshaw. Parts I, II, and III. The more important writings of Benjamin Dann Walsh and Charles Valentine Riley, Washington, 1890.

## HOW TO OBTAIN ENTOMOLOGICAL BOOKS AND PAMPHLETS.

Comparatively few of the works treating of the classification of North American insects have been published as separate books; but such as have been so published, if of comparatively recent date, can be obtained through the regular book trade. By far the greater number of the monographs and synopses mentioned in the preceding pages have been published in scientific periodicals and in the proceedings or transactions of scientific societies. These may be obtained either through the societies or through the publishers; but single volumes of transactions or proceedings, and more especially single papers, are seldom sold, and the older volumes are liable to be out of print. Moreover, the expense attending the purchase of all of the periodicals containing the publications on a given order of insects will be so great as to put them beyond the reach of most entomologists. The custom of placing at the disposal of authors a number of separate copies of their papers overcomes this difficulty to some extent and creates a small supply. Thus it often happens that a person interested can obtain a copy of a scientific paper by addressing the author personally. Many of

* Out of print.
† Bull. No. 9 of the Division of Entomology covers this subject.

these separate copies also fall into the possession of dealers in second-hand books, and may be purchased from them. The American Entomological Society of Philadelphia, and also a few other societies here and in Europe, offer for sale from their duplicates many of these authors' extras, and in some cases publish lists. There are, moreover, certain business establishments which make a specialty of the sale of works and pamphlets on natural history, including entomology, and it is chiefly through such establishments that the student is enabled to secure the larger portion of the works needed.

By subscribing to the entomological periodicals published in this country (a matter of but slight expense) the student may keep abreast of the current literature. Short book reviews or notes published therein call attention to the more important publications in other countries. Moreover, the Zoölogischer Anzeiger, edited by Prof. J. Victor Carus, in Leipzig, Germany, and published every fortnight, gives a tolerably complete bibliography of the current entomological literature at intervals of about six or eight weeks. The "Naturæ Novitates," published every fortnight by R. Friedlaender & Sohn, Carlstrasse, 11, Berlin, Germany, gives the titles of most recent works and pamphlets.

There are also three great annual publications, viz: "Die Fortschritte auf dem Gebiet der Entomologie," published in Wiegmann's "Archiv für Naturgeschichte;" "The Zoölogical Record," published by the Zoölogical Record Society, in London, England; and the "Zoölogische Jahresberichte," published by the Zoölogical Station at Naples, Italy, which give the full literature of the previous year, discussing the more important papers and giving a list of the new species, besides other information. These three publications are almost indispensable to the student in any branch of zoölogy, and some one of them at least ought to be found in every public library in the country. The volumes of the "Zoölogische Jahresberichte" since 1887 contain no titles upon systematic and classificatory zoölogy, but only such as refer to biology.

A not inconsiderable portion of the North American literature on the classification of insects has been published by the Government of the United States through various channels, foremost among which are the Smithsonian Institution, the U. S. Department of Agriculture, the U. S. National Museum, the U. S. Geological and Geographical Survey, and the various surveys of the Territories. Some of these publications are distributed free of cost; while others, like certain of the publications of the Smithsonian Institution and the Geological Survey, are sold at a moderate price to cover the cost of publication. Many of them are out of print, and can only be obtained through natural history book-dealers.

Of the more general works, some may be obtained direct from the publishers, and in such cases the publishers are mentioned in the general list. The older works are mostly out of print and can only be obtained from second-hand dealers. The current State reports of Lintner and Forbes may be obtained from the secretaries of the respective

State agricultural societies at Albany, N. Y., and Springfield, Ill., while the bulletins and reports of the entomologists of the various State experiment stations, of which a large number are being published, may be obtained from the directors of the respective stations. The older reports of the State entomologist of Missouri and the State entomologists of Illinois (Walsh, Le Baron, and Thomas) are all out of print and can only be obtained by purchase from second-hand dealers. The same may be said of the well-known and oft-quoted reports of Dr. Fitch, which were published with the old volumes of the Transactions of the New York State Agricultural Society.

www.ingramcontent.com/pod-product-compliance
Lightning Source LLC
Chambersburg PA
CBHW030554270326
41927CB00007B/912